Die b

A Novel of Ancient Rome

James Mace

Legionary Books
Meridian, Idaho 83642, USA
http://www.legionarybooks.net

First eBook Edition: 2017

Published in the United States of America
Legionary Books

Cover Image, *Pollice Verso*, by Jeon-Leon Gerome (1872), public domain as of January 2004

Sketches by Tracy Mace, copyright © 2017, Tracy Mace and Legionary Books

All other images are licensed through applicable copyright holders, or public domain

Thus, valour and skill have their reward...

- Martial

The Works of James Mace

Note: In each series or combination of series', all works are listed in chronological sequence

The Artorian Chronicles
Soldier of Rome: The Legionary
Soldier of Rome: The Sacrovir Revolt
Soldier of Rome: Heir to Rebellion
Soldier of Rome: The Centurion
*Empire Betrayed: The Fall of Sejanus
Soldier of Rome: Journey to Judea
Soldier of Rome: The Last Campaign

*Centurion Valens and the Empress of Death
*Slaves of Fear: A Land Unconquered

The Great Jewish Revolt and Year of the Four Emperors
Soldier of Rome: Rebellion in Judea
Soldier of Rome: Vespasian's Fury
Soldier of Rome: Reign of the Tyrants
Soldier of Rome: Rise of the Flavians
Soldier of Rome: The Fall of Jerusalem

*Die by the Blade

Napoleonic Era
Forlorn Hope: The Storming of Badajoz
I Stood with Wellington
Courage, Marshal Ney

The Anglo-Zulu War
Brutal Valour: The Tragedy of Isandlwana
Crucible of Honour: The Battle of Rorke's Drift

*=Stand-alone novel or novella

5

Table of Contents

Preface

The year is 77 A.D. On the frontier of the Roman Empire, a Dacian man named Verus is captured and enslaved during an imperial raid north of the Danube. He is sent to a rock quarry known as The Pit, as one among thousands of fresh slaves needed to mine marble for Emperor Vespasian's new amphitheatre. Funded by spoils taken during the Siege of Jerusalem, the Emperor promises it will be the largest gladiatorial arena ever; his personal gift to the people of Rome. Requiring years of herculean labour and millions of cubic feet in stone, Vespasian's son, Titus, worries whether his father will live to see its completion.

After months of back-breaking suffering and toil, Verus is taken from The Pit to become a gladiator. Whether by chance or fate, he knows that only by making a pact with death will he have a chance at life. In a savage world of blood, sweat, sand, and steel, his very soul is forged, until he no longer remembers the man he once was. As the Flavian Amphitheatre nears completion, with the possibility of fighting before the Emperor himself, Verus swears to either win his cherished freedom, or ignominiously die by the blade.

Cast of Characters:

Gladiators:
Verus – A young man from a tribal kingdom along the Danube, he was captured by the Romans and sold into slavery
Priscus – Slave from Britannia who made his name fighting in the arena at Isca
Marcus Antonius Drusus – Chief Magister (instructor) at an imperial gladiator school in Rome who won his freedom many years before
Aulus Vipsanius Narcissus – Lanista (owner) of the gladiator school
Severus – A fellow gladiator
Claudia – Wife of Severus

Noble Romans:
Flavius Vespasian – Emperor of Rome, who won the imperial civil war seven years prior
Titus – Eldest son of Vespasian, he finished the re-conquest of Judea and brought back the treasure from the destroyed temple at the end of the Great Jewish Revolt
Domitian – Youngest son of Vespasian
Julia Flavia – Daughter of Titus
Marcus Antonius Primus – Commanding Legate of Legio VII, Gemina, along the Danube, who won the civil war for Vespasian
Marcus Ulpius Trajan – Former consul and legate of Legio X, as well as one of Vespasian's closest friends
Marcus Ulpius Trajan (the younger) – Son of the elder Trajan, assigned as Laticlavian Tribune for Legio VII under Antonius Primus
Cornelius Fuscus – Prefect of the Praetorian Guard
Gaius Artorius Armiger – Former optio from Legio X, he was elevated into the equites during the civil war, following the death of his brother. He served as chief siege engineer under Titus during the Siege of Jerusalem
Aula Cursia Vale – Wife of Gaius and a close confidant of Vespasian

Chapter I: Verus

The tribal Kingdom of the Rhoxolani
Along the River Danube
August, 77 A.D.

Marcus Ulpius Trajan

For Verus, there was a certain tranquillity that came from forging iron. His hammer pounded the red-hot bar of metal, clasped between a pair of tongs. Sparks flew as the pounding echoed in his ears. Beads of sweat ran down his forehead and chest. What was once a formless chunk of raw iron was now slowly taking shape; a large curved blade. One not meant for fighting, but for the fields. Verus was a master of his craft, who could forge a sword as easily as a scythe blade. He had witnessed the horrors of war once before. With the incessant encroachment from the Roman Empire to the south, he feared it was only a matter of time before he would have to lay down his smithing hammer and take up the sword. Every night he prayed to the gods, *Spare my family from the unholy terrors*.

Nine years had passed since the last time he'd taken up arms. His people, the Rhoxolani, were magnificent horsemen whose lands lay north of the River Danube. They were a client state, under the protection of the Dacian king. Regrettably, there was always trouble with their Roman neighbours to the south. The Empire of the Caesars was like a plague of locusts devouring everything in its path. After decades of hostilities, King Duras of Dacia was determined to drive the Romans from their borders forever. His son and heir formed a large force of three thousand riders who crossed the Danube, intent on destroying any Roman settlements within fifty miles. Verus was part of this expedition.

To this day, the king swore it was the gods who defeated them, not the Romans. The invasion was met with torrential rainfall, churning the ground into an impassable quagmire. Verus would later learn that a treacherous warrior had betrayed their intents to the Romans, who were waiting for them. Blinded by the punishing downpour, their horses scarcely able to trudge through the muck, they stumbled into an entire army of imperial soldiers. It was just as the storm ceased that the Romans attacked, unleashing thousands of long throwing spears in a fearful deluge of destruction. Verus' horse, poor noble beast he'd named after the god, Safa, was killed during the initial barrage. The young warrior himself was pierced in the side by a javelin and thrown from his stricken mount.

Rendered unconscious by the fall, it was nothing short of miraculous that he did not drown in the sludge. By the time he awoke, he was all alone. The field was littered with the corpses of men and horses. His side was caked in coagulated blood, and he wondered why he had not bled to death. To this day, he still felt a nagging ache from his injury. Nothing short of divine intervention kept him from succumbing to injury or infection.

The raid was a disaster. Over a thousand men were killed and several hundred more taken prisoners. These hapless souls were sold into slavery, to spend the rest of their miserable lives toiling in the mines and quarries or sentenced to die in the various arenas around the Empire, where men killed each other for sport. With his prize force of horsemen shattered, and no standing army to prevent the Romans from crossing the Danube, King Duras was compelled to seek immediate terms. The Rhoxolani surrendered much in the way of treasure and hostages, as was demanded by the imperial governor.

This came during a traumatic time for the Empire. Emperor Nero was deposed and committed suicide before receiving word of the raid. A succession of usurpers followed. For the next year and-a-half, Rome was wracked by the blight of civil war. This proved fortuitous for Duras and the Rhoxolani, as the legions were forced to withdraw from the Danube, and the region enjoyed a period of peace and prosperity. Eventually, a general named Vespasian emerged victorious and now sat upon the imperial throne. What his intentions were for the disputed territory along the River Danube was unknown.

Losing his horse had been a crippling blow to Verus' lifestyle and manhood. The following year saw many changes to his life. His father passed on to the afterlife, leaving him the blacksmith forge where Verus apprenticed as a boy. It was also a time of joy. Verus' son, Fillon, was born just a few months later. The lad had since grown much, and Verus looked forward to teaching him the skills of his chosen trade.

On this morning, he was crafting a new scythe blade for an old farmer named Goson. Goson was a childhood friend of Verus' father; despite his advanced age, he still laboured with the strength of youth from sunrise to sunset every day. It seemed his work was all he lived for these days, for his son was among those killed during the raid against the Romans. His two daughters were both married and living many miles from the village. The farm was all Goson had left. He told Verus on several occasions, since his daughters had yet to give him any grandchildren, he would leave the farm to him. Such an expanse of land, coupled with his blacksmith forge, would make Verus a man of great prominence and wealth in the community. The slaves who did most of the actual work were relatively young and had been treated well by Goson. While the thought of men owning other men as property always felt perverse to him, Verus usually supressed such feelings. Slavery was simply part of the world they lived in.

With a continuous pounding of the hammer, sparks flew from the red-hot iron that was slowly taking shape. The echoing of the hammer strikes was like a song to Verus; a song of fire and steel.

It was warm and extremely humid during the hour before sunrise. The young Roman officer's eyes darted back and forth as he

11

tried to see through the clinging mist along the riverbank. It was maddening. He struggled to discern anything past the head of his horse. He quietly reminded himself, if they were blind, then so too was their enemy. The blade of his spatha cavalry sword lay across his lap, lest it get soaked in the gentle flow of the fording point across the River Danube. Ahead of him, a cohort of imperial soldiers from Legio VII, Gemina, slogged through the water. Their shields were balanced atop their helmets, convex side up, to carry their javelins and gladii. As for the mounted officer, he cringed at the amount of noise his horse made as it sloshed along, stumbling occasionally. His own feet and ankles drug through the water. It was brisk and jolted him fully awake.

"Just a little further," he said quietly to his horse, hoping the beast would not slip on the smooth rocks of the riverbed and dump him into the drink. Such embarrassment in full view of several hundred legionaries would not do for an officer of his status!

His name was Marcus Ulpius Trajan. Just a month shy of his twenty-fourth birthday, he arrived at the Seventh Legion's camp along the Danube three months prior. His father, of the same name, was a famous Roman general and statesman who commanded the venerable Tenth Legion during the recent war in Judea. Furthermore, the elder Trajan was a close friend and confidant of Emperor Vespasian. He, therefore, had little difficulty in securing a posting for his son with the legions. The laticlavian, or *chief* tribune, was always a young man of the senatorial class. Second-in-command of the legion, he answered only to the commanding legate; however, his primary task was learning how to lead, and to see if he might one day be deemed worthy of becoming a legate. With only twenty-five legions in the whole of the Empire and each tour lasting three years, competition for any vacancies was fierce among the near-thousand families in Rome's senatorial class.

Much to the chagrin of numerous senators still seeking this auspicious posting for their sons, it was in fact the younger Trajan's second tour as a laticlavian tribune. His first appointment came just after his eighteenth birthday, when he was dispatched to his native Hispania. It was a relatively safe and uneventful tour. After his three-year term was over, with a strong recommendation from his legate, Vespasian decided to give the young man a chance to prove his worth along a more 'active' frontier of the Empire. And on this day, his commanding legate was practically giving him independent command for the coming raid.

Trajan let out a sigh of relief as his horse clambered up the muddy riverbank on the far side, clumps of clay and trampled grass sticking to its hooves. He could just barely make out the shapes of legionaries to his front, who were wordlessly forming into battle lines.

"Eighth Cohort has secured the crossing, sir," a centurion said, walking up to the chief tribune. "No sign of the enemy."

"Let us hope they don't know we're here," Trajan said with a relieved sigh. "What of our scouts?"

"Nothing yet. Do you want us to hold or to press on?"

Trajan sensed the seasoned professional was testing him. While the legates and laticlavian tribunes came from the senatorial class, and staff tribunes from the lesser-noble equites, centurions were battle-hardened veterans promoted from the ranks. Well-educated, tactically sound, and utterly fearless in battle, they were truly the men who ran the legion. This particular soldier was a *centurion pilus prior*; an elite officer who commanded a cohort of six eighty-man centuries. The marks of age and weathering upon his face told Trajan this man had first donned his armour before the chief tribune was even born.

"Send out picquets to cover the flanks," he ordered. "But keep them close, as we can't see a bloody thing in this shit. If our scouts have not returned by the time the rest of the legion crosses, we'll have to advance without them."

"Very good, sir."

Without another word, the centurion returned to his assembled officers to give them their orders. Trajan took a deep breath and let it out with a ragged sigh; nervous yet confident he'd made the correct decision. Had he not...well, centurions had ways of keeping young tribunes from committing terrible blunders. Even an experienced legate, such as his father or even Emperor Vespasian, would often defer to the judgment of their centurions.

The next element to cross the river was a lone regiment of around five hundred mounted auxilia troopers. Known as the *Siliana Regiment of Horse*, they mostly came from the nearby provinces of Illyricum and Moesia, making them familiar with the region.

"Commander Liberius," Trajan said, addressing the unit's senior officer as he led his men across. "I'm afraid our scouts have not turned up yet."

The auxilia officer—a former centurion given command of his regiment by the Emperor himself—gazed upward for a few moments. It was still very dark, despite being midmorning.

"There's still time," he said, though his eyes betrayed his concern for his men.

The two scouts were Rhoxolani by birth and knew the area well. However, there was always the risk of capture, especially when bumbling around in the hours before dawn with a clinging fog encompassing all.

"Shall we continue with the same plan as before?" Liberius asked.

Trajan nodded. "Yes. The legion's indigenous cavalry will cover the flanks, while your regiment pushes through the woods beyond the village. Get behind the enemy and close the trap."

"Provided the woods are still there," the commander noted. "What intelligence my lads had is several years old. For all we know, the entire area could be deforested."

"I suppose we'll know soon enough," Trajan stated, a touch of resigned finality in his voice. It was not ideal. But, if he had learned anything during his time with the legions, it was that the best-laid plans rarely went as expected.

Meanwhile, cohorts from the Seventh Gemina Legion continued to cross. Occasionally, a legionary would lose his footing and fall into the drink, spilling his shield and weapons into the river. Thankfully, the current was relatively slow at this fording point, allowing them to recover with little more than a few bruises, embarrassed egos, and berating curses from their officers.

It took over an hour-and-a-half for the entire legion to reach the Rhoxolani side. Only a single cohort could cross at a time, and this took roughly ten minutes each. Last to splash their way onto the riverbank was the legion's indigenous cavalry of three hundred troopers, along with the staff tribunes and their commanding legate, Marcus Antonius Primus.

"General, sir," Trajan said, riding up to his superior and snapping off a salute.

"Save the formalities," Primus replied with a dismissive wave.

14

Trajan then briefed him on the state of the legion and auxilia cavalry. All cohorts were in position, forming a large battle front with five cohorts in the lead and the remainder in reserve. Commander Liberius' cavalry occupied the extreme left, ready to advance on what they hoped was still a thick wooded grove.

"Unfortunately, we've had no word from our scouts," the chief tribune confessed.

Primus appeared unconcerned. "Probably just got lost is all. Would not be surprising in this shit." He looked to his chief tribune. "Carry on. Let's give these barbarians a damn good thrashing. The men know the orders?"

Trajan nodded. "I personally briefed all cohort commanders. We are here for prisoners and spoils, not slaughter."

With a wicked grin, Primus added, "The Emperor needs an astounding amount of labour for the mines, and to build his new amphitheatre. We'll send him a few fresh slaves, with our compliments."

The young chief tribune scrunched his brow in thought before asking a question that had troubled him since Primus first ordered the army to assemble, the week prior. "Does Vespasian even know we're here?"

"Of course he doesn't," the legate answered curtly. "It takes at least a week for imperial couriers to reach Rome. And besides, one does not need permission from the Emperor to launch a raid against some unruly frontier barbarians. Now, let's get this lot sorted."

Trajan nodded and rode back to the centre of the large formation, occupied by the venerable First Cohort. The legion's centurion primus pilus, a fifty-two-year-old veteran named Vitruvius, rested his hands on his shield and stared into the mist. The aquilifer stood close by, wearing the lion's hide over his helmet and shoulders, hands clutched around the legion's magnificent eagle standard. Also with the primus pilus were several cornicens, carrying their large, circular horns.

"Make ready to sound the advance," Trajan said to these men.

"I advise we not do that, sir," Vitruvius spoke up.

"Well, we cannot exactly use visual signals in this fog," Trajan observed.

"True," the master centurion concurred. "But if my cohort simply starts its advance, the others will get the idea soon enough.

It's not perfect, and it will make for a bit of an awkward start. But it is still preferable to announcing our presence to all within ten miles of this place."

The chief tribune nodded and started to ride away to inform all cohort commanders.

Vitruvius stopped him. "Use your staff officers, sir."

"What?" Trajan looked around, confused. For the first time, he noticed four of the tribunes who had crossed with Primus. The legate kept two with him, while dispatching the rest to follow his chief tribune. Trajan gave a quick nod of understanding, recalling the one lesson that both Primus and Vitruvius had first instilled in him; the art of delegation.

He addressed a pair of staff officers. "Ride the length of the front line. Inform all cohort commanders to refrain from using trumpets or audible commands until the enemy is in sight." Pointing to the others, he added, "You two, inform the reserves."

Even in close formation, their frontage stretched nearly a half-mile in width, and it took several minutes for the tribunes to seek out each of the centurions pilus prior, relay the instructions, and return to Trajan. Once they were reassembled, the chief tribune looked to Vitruvius, who gave a simple nod. The corner of his mouth turned up in a grin, Trajan drew his spatha and raised it high. The aquilifer hefted the eagle standard. As the chief tribune waved his long sword forward, the aquilifer titled the standard likewise.

Vitruvius drew his gladius and signalled for his men to follow him. "Come on, lads," he said in a low voice.

Though it lacked in grandeur and spectacle, and was a bit awkward as the cohorts on either flank began to advance, Trajan was satisfied he'd performed his duties well, so far.

"Now let us hope we don't walk right past them," General Primus said from over his shoulder, startling his young second-in-command. Though he was giving Trajan control over the legion for this raid, he was keeping a close eye on his young protégé.

Marcus Antonius Primus

The red-hot scythe blade hissed as Verus plunged it into the water trough. His face felt the burn of steam as the water bubbled in protest. Quickly withdrawing the blade, he placed it on the anvil and began hammering once more. He hefted it, appreciating its weight and balance. No doubt Goson would be pleased. A few more minutes of pounding, and soon he would begin sharpening the instrument. All the while Fillon watched, his eyes wide as his father perfected his craft.

"Any man can pound iron," Verus said. He showed the blade to his son, who ran his hand over it. "But we, my son, are craftsmen. Once sharpened, this will slice through stalks of grain with ease."

"Can it cut through men?" the boy asked with morbid curiosity.

"I suppose it could," his father replied, taken aback by the question. "But we make swords and spears for fighting men, not scythes."

"Will you teach me to make a sword some day?"

"Perhaps." Verus smiled. "Serve as an apprentice, prove your mettle with the forge, and once you've come of age, I will teach you to make a fine sword. But for now, let us go to the grinding wheel, and you can help me sharpen this blade for Goson."

A chill went up Verus' spine as feelings of dread came over him. He gazed over his shoulder to where the mist was finally starting to dissipate. A long line of shadows appeared to be advancing, like phantoms straight from the abyss. He heard the faint sound of thousands of feet marching in step.

"Go to your mother," he said. "Tell her I need you both to head for the grove of Safa...quickly!"

The boy was startled by the distress in his father's voice, but he immediately complied. He ran towards the small barn where his mother would be milking the goats.

Verus' heart pounded in his chest, and he picked up the scythe blade. "Not a sword, but it will have to do."

He fears were confirmed when a voice shouted, *'Romans!'*

There was no mistaking the sounds of soldiers marching now. The phantoms of the mist took on the shapes of men wearing armour, carrying large rectangular shields and long spears.

Verus closed his eyes and let out a sigh of resignation. He raised his eyes skyward and said a silent prayer. "Safa, God of the hearth, protect my family. Keep them safe, and I will suffer an eternity of torment in their place."

He rushed from the blacksmith forge and saw scores of men converging from their huts and rushing in from the fields. Many of the women were gathering up their children and fleeing into the woods east of the town, though plenty grabbed whatever implements they could find and stood defiantly by their men.

Few of the people had actual weapons, mostly just hand axes, pitchforks, and other farming implements. Some of the men, who had once served as cavalrymen in the king's service, were rushing to their stables, intent on facing this unholy threat from horseback. Yet for most, there simply wasn't time. The early morning fog had completely masked the Romans' approach, and by the time they were spotted, the front ranks of legionaries were shouldering their javelins.

"Get back! Get back!" Verus screamed.

It was too late. A shower of heavy javelins rained down upon them, killing several of his friends outright. At least a dozen more were badly injured; pierced through the arms, legs, and bodies. They fell to the ground, crying out in anguish. What surprised Verus, however, was the lack of subsequent waves of the enemy's flying

18

spears. Inexplicably, only the imperial soldiers in the front rank had unleashed.

Orders were shouted by their centurions, and with a loud *'Rah!'*, the wall of armoured soldiers unsheathed their blades.

His eyes wet with tears of sorrow, his face red with rage, Verus gave a loud cry and charged the wall of pending death. His surviving companions did likewise; with every last measure of courage, they attacked.

It was the first time Verus had seen Roman soldiers up close, as he had been knocked unconscious so early during his last battle. Every legionary wore a Gallic-style helmet, complete with cheek guards and a wide brim in the back. Their armour consisted of banded plates wrapped around the torso with additional strips covering the shoulders. Such armour, called *lorica segmentata*, was magnificent; worthy of the king. And every soldier on the imperial battle line wore it! Swords and spears were useless against it, let alone a half-forged scythe blade. The weak point on a legionary was the unprotected lower abdomen and legs; however, these were covered by the large, curved rectangular shields the soldiers carried. These were painted blue with a sun encircling the metal boss in the centre. A brass strip ran along the entire edge. It was here, on the closest soldier, that Verus' scythe blade smashed as he aimed for the legionary's head.

He rammed his shoulder into the shield, yet the man would not be moved. His adversary's mates on either side of him kept close, forming a wall of shields which neither the blacksmith nor his friends could hope to break through. And even if one managed to do so, there were numerous ranks of legionaries behind these men, ready to skewer any poor fools who breached the line.

The soldier smashed Verus in the face with the boss of his shield, sending him reeling. He placed a hand over his forehead, which was now bleeding. Looking around in despair, he briefly gained a small measure of hope as hundreds of men and a handful of women from the surrounding villages swarmed into the fray. Some of these were mounted, wielding their long lances and oblong shields. Sadly, their numbers were few, and they were unable to mass their strength against the impenetrable shield wall. Men and horses alike shrieked in agony, as legionaries in the rear ranks loosed their javelins upon them.

19

Despite the surrounding carnage, Verus was struck by the notion that the Romans were not trying to kill them all. It seemed as if they were holding back; content to simply continue the advance, pushing back their assailants with their shields. Only periodically did one plunge his gladius into the guts of a hapless warrior who'd come too close to breaching the line. The mist was slowly burning off, and the blacksmith could now see how large the Roman force was. This was not a mere raiding band, but an entire legion of over 5,000 fighting men; greater than the entire population of scattered villages in the valley. Their line was starting to curve on the flanks, slowly encompassing the desperate band of fighters who continued to hammer away against the shield wall in vain. A few imperial soldiers were injured, stabbed either in the legs or arms. They were quickly pulled from the line, only to be quickly replaced by one of the soldiers behind them.

Verus, who spoke passable Latin, heard an officer shout, *'Set for passage-of-lines!'*

This was echoed by the men in the first and second rank. He blew his whistle and with alarming speed and precision, the men in the front clutched their shields against their bodies, turned sideways, and lunged back between the files of the soldiers behind them, who then surged forward into the battle. Fighting had been minimal, and surely the Romans were not tired yet. Perhaps this was simply a matter of grandstanding to intimidate their opponents?

"Horsemen!" a voice shouted behind them, drawing Verus out of his stupor. He grinned and turned, hoping to see one of the king's mounted regiments coming to their rescue. His feelings of hope immediately vanished, as he noted the tall metal standard carried by one of the troopers, bearing a bronze hand encircled with a wreath. The horsemen wore not Dacian leather with bronze scales, but Roman chain mail. Their helmets were similar to the legionaries, and their officers' helms were adorned with feather crests.

The Rhoxolani fighters looked around in desperation. They were now surrounded on three sides by the Roman infantry and on the fourth by a force of several hundred cavalry. Just then, a lone imperial officer rode between two of the infantry cohorts. He wore a polished metal cuirass and an ornate helmet with a magnificent plume. He looked rather young, likely a couple years younger than Verus. His sword was drawn, yet hanging loosely by his side.

"Lay down your weapons," the young man said, speaking to the villagers in their own tongue.

Verus and his companions knew they were choice-less. As he glanced at the terrified mob on either side of him, his feelings were of both fear and cautious relief at not seeing his wife or son amongst the throng. Many other families were not so fortunate. Wives and young children were prodded towards them by the lances of imperial horsemen. Men cried out as they embraced their loved ones; glad to see them alive, yet sorrowful that they had not escaped. Despondent and defeated, Verus closed his eyes, bowed his head, and dropped the scythe blade.

An hour had passed since the barbarians surrendered. Trajan removed his helmet, handing it to a servant, before slowly riding his horse down the line of imperial soldiers who guarded the Sarmatian prisoners. Their faces bore a mix of fear, despondency, and even traces of defiance. The legion and auxilia cavalry had been thorough, and he conjectured that only a small handful had managed to escape.

"Over a thousand prisoners," Legate Primus said with a grin of satisfaction, as he rode up next to his chief tribune.

"We counted fifty dead," Trajan observed. "And about a hundred more that were so badly injured, we put them out of their misery. Our own losses were two dead troopers, fifteen wounded, along with another dozen injured legionaries."

"A splendidly successful venture," Primus said triumphantly He turned to face his second. "Now tell me, young Trajan, what's to be done with the prisoners?"

"Well, sir, they should be sorted. Women and young children in one group; men and boys close to maturity in the other."

"And what of those that do not fit either category?" the legate asked. "What do you propose we do with the old and infirm?"

Trajan thought for a moment, choosing his words carefully. "That would depend on your intentions, sir. If this was simply a raid to capture some slaves, then we could simply let them go, as they are no threat to us. But, if the objective is to punish the Rhoxolani and teach them a harsh lesson for past incursions into Roman territory…" His voice trailed off and he looked to his commanding legate, whose expression was passive, yet with a sinister edge.

"And what do *you* think our intentions were?" Primus' voice was calm, but had an icy tone that the young chief tribune had never heard before.

He gave a nod of understanding. "We should at least address them first, sir."

"And why is that?"

"Because it would be best if we let a few of them go, so that they might spread the word about what fate awaits those who violate our borders and attempt to pillage Roman lands."

"Agreed," Primus concurred after a few moments. "Mind you, I had no intention of doing so…but I figure, why not? I'll indulge you. Let's have a bit of fun with this lot, before we sort them and drag their sorry backsides across the river to the slave traders. Those filthy cunts are, no doubt, slobbering in anticipation."

Every man, woman, and child had their hands bound in front of them as they were tied together in groups of ten. Numerous tears were shed as wives and children were torn from the men's clutches. These were followed by many a fist to the face as the merciless imperial soldiers beat any who protested too loudly. What happened next would consume the Rhoxolani survivors with absolute horror for the remainder of their lives.

Ten young men, all in their late teens to early twenties, were untied and taken away. The Roman officers and many of their soldiers had formed a large rectangular perimeter. As the sun was falling, the entire area was lit with torches, adding an eerie feel to the spectacle. Verus had managed to find a tree stump to stand on and was able to see over the heads of their guards. His eyes grew wide as the young men were each handed a gladius and paired up. He then lowered his head and sighed. He could just overhear what an interpreter was telling the hapless lads.

"What's happening?" one of the prisoners nearest him asked. The man was especially nervous. One of those taken away was his son.

"They're being told to fight to the death," Verus explained. "They've promised freedom to the victors."

"Bastards!" the man snarled. "And they dare to call *us* barbarians!"

"No!" another man shouted. "They can't do this."

Numerous cries of protest arose from the assembled men, coupled with profane insults towards their captors at their brutality. Legionaries drew their gladii and proceeded to smash the pommels across the faces and heads of those who screamed the loudest. Two men tried to attack the Romans, despite their hands being bound, and were stabbed through the guts for their efforts. The soldiers did not even bother to finish them, instead letting them slowly die writhing in pain, still bound to their companions.

As for the poor souls who'd been ordered to fight to the death, there was much hesitation. Two men outright refused. One even tried attacking the Romans with his borrowed gladius. He and his friend were roundly beaten and dragged away. While most of the others continued to hesitate, one young man seized the initiative and plunged his blade into the throat of his opponent. His eyes were filled with tears, and he pleaded for his friend to forgive him.

The Romans let loose a cheer, and with an exaggerated gesture, the imperial general signalled to the killer that he was free to go. Fighting back his sobs of sorrow and shame, the young man threw down the gladius and shoved his way past the wall of legionaries, before stumbling away into the engulfing night. This spurred the remaining three pairs to fight; fear of death against the faint hope of salvation overwhelming them.

Verus watched the horrifying spectacle. Consumed by shame, he privately wished he'd been among those selected to fight. He was quite skilled with a blade, and knew he could easily best any one of the six men who now fought for their freedom and survival. It filled him with revulsion to admit this. But in his desperate state, he would kill if it meant seeing his wife and son again.

The entire spectacle was over in a matter of minutes. Once the last fallen combatant was slain and the survivors set loose, General Primus dismissed his soldiers and retired to his principia tent.

"Well, that's nearly the end of that," the legate said. Servants helped him out of his armour, and he threw himself onto his dining couch. "Not the best display of prisoners fighting each other to the death, but not bad."

"That one fellow showed quite the initiative, killing his mate before he had a chance to defend himself," Trajan remarked appreciatively.

The legate was then handed a long scroll by a scribe, and he began to review the final figures from the raid. "Two hundred and forty-four women, three hundred and twelve children, three hundred and ninety-seven men, and one hundred and sixty-five boys near their full measure. Not a bad day's work."

"Less the four who were killed in our little gladiatorial display," Trajan remarked. "Oh, and the two we had crucified for their impertinence."

"Yes, well, perhaps they were the bravest of them all," the legate conjectured. "So willing to die a long, agonising death upon the cross rather than kill their friends in exchange for freedom. One has to respect that."

"Indeed."

Primus then ordered one of his tribunes, "Have their throats cut. The least we can do to show our appreciation is grant them a quick passage into the next life." He clapped his hands and servants brought trays of wine for him and his senior officers.

In addition to Primus, Trajan, and the six staff tribunes, were the master centurion and the four centurions primus ordo from the First Cohort. These men were the pinnacle of the centurionate, outranking even the cohort commanders, and answering only to the legate and primus pilus.

"We've sent word to Viminacium and Montana," a tribune said, referring to the Moesian cities to the west and to the south. "I imagine the first of the slave traders will arrive within the next few days."

"King Duras will not take this incursion well," Trajan spoke up, thoughtfully turning his cup around in his hands.

"Our thrashing of his raiders gave him pause," Primus conjectured. "But those damned barbarians had not been properly chastised for their incursions nine years ago. The Empire was a little 'busy' at the time, what with a string of pretenders and a pair of civil wars. As for King Duras, he can get stuffed. I doubt that he'll risk an all-out war with Rome over a single village and a handful of peasants sold into slavery. He now understands what will happen if he so much as glances south of the Danube."

"One question, sir," the chief tribune said, his brow scrunched in contemplation. "Did Governor Saturnius approve of the raid?"

This caused Primus to almost spit out his wine and break into a fit of laughter. "I don't answer to that pompous twat," he scoffed. "The Emperor himself sent me here to keep order along the Danube. If Saturnius does not care for my methods, he can take it up with Vespasian."

This drew a derisive snicker from one of the centurions, which briefly made Trajan uncomfortable. Despite the intense political rivalries which existed within Rome's ruling class, it was a serious breach of decorum to speak ill of one's peers in front of subordinates. However, Marcus Antonius Primus was anything but a typical nobleman. He was notorious for his personal corruption and financial irregularities, to say nothing of attempts at helping a friend forge a kinsman's will, which led to his banishment from Rome for five years. Even Emperor Vespasian, to whom the legate was fiercely loyal, once said, *'I would trust Primus with my life on the battlefield, but not with a single sestertius, nor with my daughter!'*

By his own admission, the only thing he seemed to excel at, besides coaxing the gullible to part with their coin, was leading men into battle. His harrowing defeat of the Vitellians, both at Bedriacum as well as Rome, ensured his immortality in the history of the Empire. He'd also rather curtly declined the senate's offer to name *him* Emperor in the immediate aftermath. Yet, while Vespasian was most certainly grateful for the legate's fealty and tenacity on the battlefield, he knew he could not trust Primus with any sort of magisterial posting or governorship. And so, he was left on the less-than-glamourous Danube frontier in command of a single legion, with the rather vague directive of 'maintaining order'. This suited Primus just fine. He was left to his own devices, could conduct the occasional raid in order to fatten his purse and, while he was officially subordinate to the provincial governor, it was abundantly clear that he answered only to Emperor Vespasian.

25

Despite the rather austere conditions of life on campaign, General Primus still managed to have enough wine and delicacies added to his baggage to properly celebrate the successful raid. He was also the only one with an actual dining couch. The rest sat on camp stools. The sparse décor within the large tent consisted of several ornate bronze oil lamps, hanging from chains, and a lone five-foot tall marble pillar adorned with a bust of the Emperor. The wine flowed freely, as did the traditional toasts to Emperor, Senate, and People of Rome, along with whichever deities the assembled officers decided to credit with their victory. The men feasted well into the night, only deciding to retire back to their tents as the sentry change was taking place around midnight.

As the others departed, Primus asked Trajan to remain. "Well, my boy, this is where it ends for us."

"What do you mean, sir?" Trajan asked, his brow furrowed in confusion.

Primus handed him a scroll. "It would seem the legion is being transferred to Hispania. The Thirteenth Gemina will replace us. And as you know, Vespasian has ordered Twelfth Fulminata to eastern Moesia, where the Danube meets the Black Sea."

"And to think I was just getting used to the Danube frontier," the chief tribune said with a mocking grin.

"Well, you may get your chance to return. As you probably noticed, the lands north of the Danube are rich and fertile. So who knows? Perhaps Vespasian will want to claim such rich ground for Rome. But for us, our time is over. I shall accompany the legion as far as Rome, and then you will take them the rest of the way to Tarraco. I'm sure you know the way."

"Indeed, sir. I was born and raised in Hispania Baetica. Tarraco was like a second home to me." He paused for a moment. "If I may ask, why are you leaving us?"

"It is but a happy coincidence that my current tour as legate is set to end within the next three months. Did you know this is my fifth term in command of a legion?"

Trajan shook his head.

"Vespasian doesn't know what else to do with me, so he's kept me posted on the frontiers. But now I'm tired. I'm forty-six years old, and I've commanded Seventh Gemina damn-near since its inception. Time for me to step aside and leave someone else in

26

command. Oh, and don't think that it's going to be you. Sorry, young Trajan; though you show promise, I don't think any man is ready to command a legion of five thousand fighting men at the age of twenty-four. But not to worry, I will send a favourable report in my next despatch to the Emperor, regarding your conduct during the raid. Granted, they were nothing more than a handful of farmers without the means to actually fight back, but you performed well."

"Thank you, sir."

"I'll even send a personal note to your father, who I understand is Governor of Syria."

"Actually, he returned to Rome six months ago," Trajan corrected.

"Ah, well, I won't send my despatch to Syria then. Still, no doubt he will be pleased."

"Will you stay in Rome?" the chief tribune asked. "I thought you hated it there."

"Not as much as my colleagues despise seeing my face." Primus chuckled. "If any man was ever more hated by his peers in the senate, I'd like to meet him. Besides fearing reprisal for banishing me from Rome all those years ago, they hate being reminded that I led Vespasian's armies to victory against Vitellius. And it was I who was Master of Rome for a time. I think the greatest pleasure of my life was watching the lot of them grovel at my feet."

"Those were...*interesting* times, to be certain," Trajan remarked. He was just sixteen during the civil war between Vespasian and Vitellius and recalled many a sleepless night, as he feared for both he and his mother. His father was a close confidant of Vespasian, and there was concern that the young Trajan and his mother might be taken as hostages by Vitellius.

Their fears had come to naught, as Vitellius' forces suffered a string of defeats at the hands of Primus' army. The triumphant general, once banished from Rome following convictions for fraud and corruption, became Regent of the Empire for a brief time. Despite the implied promise of a governorship, Vespasian knew Marcus Antonius Primus was the worst possible candidate to lord over any of the imperial provinces. So, he essentially dismissed him by sending him back to the Danube with his legion. And while a legate's posting was much sought after by members of the senate,

27

few complained about Primus being given multiple tours with the Seventh Gemina. At least it kept him away from Rome.

For Trajan, it seemed like a chapter was closing in his life. However, for reasons he could not explain, he was certain the Danube was not finished with him yet. In the fullness of time, he would return.

All around Verus, prisoners tossed and turned, with some snoring loudly. They hoped to wake and find themselves free of this nightmare. Exhaustion left him numb. His thoughts consumed by Tamura and Fillon. Were they alive? Did they make it to the Grove of Safa? Had they avoided the imperial soldiers? He did not see their faces when the Romans were sorting the prisoners, so that gave him hope.

His mind was further clouded with images of horror; friends murderously butchered by the savage demons in steel armour. Afterwards, poor Goson, the elderly farmer whom he'd forged the scythe blade for only that morning, was dragged away, hobbling from the wound to his leg. No doubt the barbarous bastards had slit his throat, knowing he'd be useless as a slave.

And now, what would happen to him? Slavery was certainly not unheard of in Dacia, though usually only the nobility could afford them. That Goson had had a handful of slaves on his farm was most unusual. Verus' greatest fear was that he would be sent into one of the mines. Far beneath the surface, once you went in, you never saw the sun again. Yet whatever terrible fate lay waiting for him, he gladly accepted it.

"And so begins my torment," he said quietly, before gazing up into the starlit sky and addressing whatever gods may be listening. "I've kept my promise. You had best keep yours."

Chapter II: Priscus

Isca Augusta, near the River Usk
Western Britannia
August, 77 A.D.

The Roman Amphitheatre at Isca Augusta

It was a sunny, cloudless day. Yet, this did little to brighten the Priscus' demeanour as he was fitted into his armour. He glowered at a slave, whose hands were trembling, fumbling with the leather ties. The poor wretches who strapped his bronze breastplate to his chest were utterly terrified of this fearsome beast. Standing a half-head taller than either of them, his frame was wrought with powerful muscle. He was said to be a fearsome barbarian from the far north. Indeed, he had a beastly demeanour about him. That his hair was cropped short and his face shaved smooth added to his fearsome visage, far more than a wild-haired barbarian with a long beard.

If only that damned horse hadn't been lame, he thought to himself, as a pair of greaves were fitted to his shins.

Priscus was thirty years of age and born in the northernmost reaches of Britannia, far beyond the reach of the Romans. In fact, he'd scarcely even heard of the Empire that now occupied the lower

29

regions of the isle, until his recent venture south to the Kingdom of Brigantes.

Orphaned as a boy, all he'd ever been good at was fighting. It was the only way he knew to survive. As he slowly reached manhood, his reputation grew right along with his impressive size. Chieftains in the high country would pay handsomely to watch him test his skills against their best warriors. However, he was not welcomed in all territories. On one occasion when a rather ignoble warrior was killed by his blade, the fallen man's friends came calling for Priscus' blood.

And it wasn't just fighting that got him into trouble. Around the beginning of the year, when the snows still clung to the ground, he found warmth in the home of the sister of a powerful warlord. When his lover's brother got wind of this, he and a dozen warriors chased Priscus into the forest, threatening him with castration, among other unpleasantries. It was soon after that he ventured further south and offered his services to Venutius, the new King of Brigantes. Venutius was the former consort of Queen Cartimandua, an ally and lapdog of the Romans. Eight years before, while the imperial occupiers were engaged in their own petty squabbles, Venutius overthrew his estranged wife and seized the throne. It was during his consolidation of power that Priscus arrived. A skilled and proven warrior, he offered his services in whatever capacity the king saw fit. After leading numerous raids against imperial outposts, marvelling at his prowess in one-on-one combat, Venutius tasked him with stealing horses from an auxilia outpost. It was then that misfortune struck.

The horse had been ridden lame the day before and could barely move at a trot. While his companions fled, Priscus was run down and captured by a Roman patrol. Despite being only lightly armed, he attacked his assailants, breaking the nose of one and ripping the helm off another, before he was overwhelmed. The troopers beat him mercilessly and he fully expected to die. Their decurion then stated, 'I've got plans for this one'.

It took him and his captors six days to reach the fortress-city near the southern coast of Britannia. Priscus had never ventured lower than Groat Haugh and did not realise just how large the isle was, or that it was but a small province within a vast empire. Dragged before the Roman governor-general in chains, he was surprised when an interpreter told him the imperial governor was impressed by his tenacity, and that he would not be executed or sent to the mines. Instead, he would make his living by fighting in the arena. Priscus was pleased with his good fortune.

During his first actual contest, when the martial was explaining to him the 'rules' of the arena, he became disgusted with his lot. The Romans were more interested in sport and spectacle than martial skill. Still, if they wanted him to put on a performance, he would make it memorable.

It was a great day for Sextus Julius Frontinus, the current Governor of Britannia. Not only did he have a new prized gladiator, courtesy of a quick-thinking cavalry decurion, he had a far more important reason to celebrate. The decades-long struggle against the rebellious, and extremely violent, Silures tribe to the far west was coming to an end. Possessing a darker complexion and naturally curly hair, which stood in stark contrast to most of the various peoples in western Britannia, it was rumoured that they had mass-migrated from the Iberian Peninsula about five hundred years earlier. Extremely aggressive and warlike, they had established themselves as the most powerful tribal nation in the mountainous regions west of the River Sabrina.

Ever tenacious, the Silures caused the Romans much grief since the initial conquest more than thirty years before. Preferring to hide in the dense woods and rocky hills, even the defeat of High King Caratacus failed to break their fighting spirit.

For their part, the Romans proved to be utterly relentless; burning Silures settlements, selling their women and children into slavery, and forcing the various tribes to live in constant fear. Though the indigenous resistance was initially successful with their ambush tactics, the imperial army quickly adapted, utilising local auxiliaries and light skirmishers in addition to their heavy infantry. The conflict soon devolved into a brutal test of wills, with most battles ending in stalemate. That it would take more than three decades to finally subdue the Silures was a testament to their prowess and bravery.

It was only during the previous spring that Frontinus succeeded in luring his elusive foe unwittingly into an open battle against two of his legions. Using a defector as a spy, he planted information about a massive convoy of wagons making its way from the gold mines at Dolaucothi. It was all a ruse. When informed of the proposed ambush, the Roman governor attacked their would-be assailants with a force of cavalry, drawing the Silures out and into the waiting arms of the legions. The slaughter was horrific, though the tribal warriors proved steadfast, many refusing to flee or surrender. Much blood was shed by the imperial army, and in the aftermath, the wagons bearing the wounded stretched for miles.

A week after their return to the fortress at Isca Augusta, a deputation from the Silures king arrived to discuss the terms of surrender. While the battle had been crushing, it was the Roman 'scorched earth' tactics of destroying villages and devastating their crops that finally defeated the Silures' pride.

"Death in battle is a fitting end for a warrior," the emissary had said. "But death by starvation is an abominable fate for our children."

In a move that greatly surprised the Silures, the Romans proved amiable. While subjected to total surrender, with an imperial magistrate assigned to lord over them while they were slowly 'Romanised' throughout the coming decades, there were no calls for hostages or retribution. The king was forced to abdicate, yet he was allowed to keep his lands and even given an advisory role to the Roman magistrate.

Frontinus was relieved that the incessant fighting along this troublesome frontier was at last at an end, for he knew it would win him much favour with both the senate and Emperor Vespasian. To commemorate this great victory, he levied a one-time tax on the regional magistrates to sponsor a series of games. Despite the grumblings from noble and commoner alike, the necessary coinage had made its way to Londinium. While the provincial capital was initially established at Camulodunum, following the suppression of the Iceni Revolt under Queen Boudicca, Londinium became the hub for both commerce and government.

With the Silures now subdued, Frontinus wished to celebrate his victory in the most 'Roman' way possible.

32

"What I need is gladiators," he explained to his assembled guests, as they walked along the grassy plain leading from the fortress to the large amphitheatre. "Britannia is still a very young province, currently devoid of any gladiatorial schools. I intend to change that."

The fortress of Isca Augusta was recently established by Legio II, Augusta; the very legion once commanded by Emperor Vespasian during the Conquest. Due to the Silures hostility, Governor Frontinus had posted the fortress not far from where the River Usk flowed into the sea. And just like most fortresses, a growing city soon emerged in its wake. Even the lowliest of legionaries made a considerable wage compared to the poor farmers and tradesmen in the provinces; so there was much opportunity for sutlers, tavern owners, and brothels to relieve them of excess coin.

Of their own initiative, the soldiers of the Second Legion constructed the amphitheatre just outside the fortress walls, along a large grassy plain. Larger than most of the smaller venues in towns and cities throughout the Empire, it doubled as a drill field for both the legion and attached auxilia cohorts. It was here the governor intended to hold a series of showcase matches, in the hopes of finding suitable fighters for the celebratory games in Londinium.

The late August day was warm and sunny. Of course, the weather could change at a moment's notice in this region of the isle. The climate west of the River Sabrina was notoriously cool and damp even in summer. Yet on this day the sun shone brightly, blinding the governor and his guests.

"It's as if the gods themselves are smiling upon you," said a former soldier-turned magistrate named Gaius Artorius Armiger.

Born into a great military family and raised in Britanni, Gaius spent most of his career in the east, battling Armenians and the rebellious Jews in Judea. A serious injury during the civil war against Vitellius, coupled with the death of his elder brother, led him to being discharged from the legions and elevated into the equites. His prowess in battle earned him a place on Titus' staff during the Siege of Jerusalem. Now a civilian magistrate, and at just thirty-five years of age, he had seen and experienced more than most would in a dozen lifetimes. His unique and varied knowledge made him an asset to the Britannic governor.

"Indeed, it is a great day for Rome, my friend," Frontinus said triumphantly. He handed a stack of scrolls to his guest. "As a military man, I thought you might be curious to read through some of the despatches from the campaign."

They sat in a large pavilion tent just outside the arena, where the governor intended to entertain his guests, as soon as the rest arrived from around the province.

As Gaius read through the first scroll, Frontinus said, "We've finally put down the Silures. It was a promise I made to the Emperor upon my assuming the governorship. And I thank the gods that I was able to keep it."

"Forget the gods, thank your legionaries who won the battle," Gaius said. "I thought for certain they would fight to the death. You're not the first governor to attempt to subdue those blood-drinking heathens."

"As you will see from reading the reports from my legates, many did fight to the death," Frontinus conceded. "And some of the more fanatical may still require extermination. But ever since Caratacus was defeated, they have not been the same. Mind you, it's been twenty-six years since Governor Scapula crushed that vile upstart. However, we've had a litany of problems to deal with in the province during that time, not least of which was sorting out that bitch, Boudicca."

"Yes, she was a bit troublesome, wasn't she?" Gaius remarked.

"If sacking Londinium and Camulodunum while killing over 80,000 people is *a bit troublesome*, then yes. And only last year, right after I assumed the governorship, I had to deal with our former allies, the Brigantes. Thankfully, the Fourteenth and the Ninth Legions gave them a right thrashing. With Vespasian contemplating taking the Ninth away from me, it's good that the Second and Twentieth Legions have sorted out the Silures. Honestly, I think I think it was simply a matter of them running out of warriors to send to the slaughter. I mean, how many people do we really think live in those mountains in such a small portion of the province?"

Gaius did not reply, but continued to read.

The governor then apprised the former army officer, trying to recall what he knew about him. "You were with the Twentieth Legion, were you not?"

34

"No," Gaius replied, shaking his head. "That was my father and grandfather; both of whom took part in Plautius' initial conquest of this land. I was with the Tenth Fretensis in Judea."

"Ah, yes," the governor recalled. "The fellows who destroyed Jerusalem and later built that giant ramp out of a mountain to destroy the last bastion of Jewish resistance."

"Masada," Gaius recalled. "I had left the legion, as well as the east, long before then. That was quite the marvel of engineering, and I sometimes wish I'd stayed long enough to see it. I do recall the destruction of Jerusalem well enough, though." He gave an involuntary shudder as images of the horrific slaughter and pestilence came back to him.

The Great Jewish Revolt, not to mention the civil war that won Vespasian the imperial throne, were filled with traumatic and terrible memories for him. His older brother, Lucius was killed fighting for the Vitellians; a bitter irony being that allowed Gaius to attain his position within the equites. He left the legions immediately after, receiving an appointment as tribune in command of the army's siege works during the Siege of Jerusalem.

Following the war, he returned to Britannia, the home of his youth. Now the governor-mayor of Magnus Portus, the great port city along the southern coast, he was among the select few invited by Frontinus to observe the gladiatorial exhibition at Isca Augusta.

"And now, dear Artorius, I have a special treat for you," Frontinus said.

"As I've told you before, I have my wife to manage that for me," Gaius said with a grin.

"Not *that*, you twat," the governor said, shaking his head. "It's a shame Lady Vale could not accompany you, given her condition. This will be, what, your second child?"

"Third," Gaius corrected. "And our last. Since we already have a daughter and son, I am fine with whichever this one will be."

"To the Artorian Legacy," Frontinus said, raising his cup in salute. Both men took a long pull off their wine chalices before the governor stood. "But come, I have something to show you."

"Oh?" Gaius raised his brow.

"As a fellow brother-in-arms, I think you deserve a private exhibition of some of the fighters I'm bringing in for the games. We also have a *lanista* from Rome who is searching for fresh talent

35

along the Empire's frontiers. I told him, while I do intend to eventually see a gladiatorial school here, I would make him an offer on any gladiators who appeal to him."

Gaius frowned in contemplation. A lanista was the owner of a gladiatorial school, known as a *ludus*. Despite the ravenous desire of nearly every citizen in the known world for the type of blood-sport they provided, lanistae were at the very bottom in terms of respectability within Roman society. It was a striking paradox that the same nobles who decried lanistae as low-life scum, would pay them fortunes in gold and silver for putting on a display of violence and martial virtue, for the amusement of the mob.

They were soon joined by a pair of men, one of whom Gaius surmised was the lanista. This man, who'd come all the way from Rome to Isca Augusta, was named Narcissus. Fortunate enough to own an imperial ludus within the capital city, he was extremely wealthy. He dressed modestly for the occasion, however, in a simple tunic, belted around the middle. In addition to a pair of bodyguards, he was accompanied by a man named Drusus, who served as the ludus' chief instructor.

"Narcissus, Drusus," Frontinus said by way of introduction. "May I present Tribune Gaius Artorius, formerly of the Judean legions. He helped quash the Jewish rebellion; not to mention acquiring the vast spoils which are now funding the Emperor's favourite civic project."

The two men bowed slightly, and Gaius simply nodded in return. Like just almost every citizen in the Empire, he was aware of Vespasian's plan for some of the treasure taken from Jerusalem. A merchant captain who'd recently docked at Portus Magnus spoke of the massive amphitheatre, stating it was larger than any in the world.

"A magnificent structure of absolute splendour," Narcissus said. He then added with a cocked smile, "Provided they ever finish it, of course."

"Oh, they will," Frontinus stressed. "I've actually seen the treasure taken from Jerusalem, as I know you have, too, Tribune Artorius. The work may take a decade, but it will last for eternity, I promise you that."

"Any great work takes time," Gaius noted. He then recalled a rather sombre memory. "When I saw the Temple of Jerusalem burning, I could feel the intense heat even from half-a-mile away.

36

The stone walls and towers collapsed upon themselves, as a greater column of flame than any I have ever witnessed shot up into the heavens. And at the time, I could not help but wonder just how many years it took the Jews to build such a magnificent monument to their god."

"And now their temple's legacy will live on in the Flavian Amphitheatre," Frontinus surmised. "But come, my friends. I believe the fighters in the first pairing are almost ready. Wait until you see the colossus who was brought down from the far reaches of Caledonia!"

Priscus sneered as he listened to the martial give his instructions. He was told repeatedly that this was only an exhibition. He was to refrain from attempting to kill his opponent outright.

Then you should not have given me sharpened weapons, Priscus thought to himself.

He stood, clasping the bars of the gate which looked out onto the arena. The stands were mostly empty. Just a Roman noble and a few others seated in a box near the bottom row. A large canopy shielded them from the sun or inclement weather, which seemed to change from day-to-day.

Priscus' attention was drawn to the first pair of combatants striding towards the centre of the arena. Like him, they were young men who'd been captured by the Romans and were now slaves. But unlike Priscus, neither appeared to know the first thing about handling a sword and shield. Their balance was fine, but their technique was awful. Neither seemed to understand that the short Roman gladius was primarily a stabbing weapon. They continued to smash their blades in vain against each other's metal bucklers. Priscus counted a score of times where one left himself drastically exposed and could have easily been stabbed beneath the armpit. He shook his head and glanced down at the scars on his forearms. There were more along his torso and legs; painful lessons of past battles, that he was fortunate to have lived long enough to profit from.

After a tedious number of minutes, the fight finally ended. Both men were now exhausted, and one managed to trip his opponent, who fell onto his back, his weapon flying from his grasp. The victor

37

did not even bother to place the point of his gladius over his fallen opponent. He simply collapsed onto his knees as fatigue overcame him.

"Pathetic," Priscus grumbled.

"That was rather pathetic," Gaius said, resting his chin in his hand.

Narcissus and Drusus were equally unimpressed.

"Well, that is why I'm holding a series of exhibitions," Frontinus replied. "Back to the Dolaucothi mines for those two sorry cunts!"

"Governor, I hope you have something worth our time," the lanista remarked. "We've spent two weeks at sea just to get here. And it'll be another month before your scheduled games; provided you can find anyone worthy of fighting in them." He then looked to the tribune. "A pity you did not bring some of the prisoners from Jerusalem. From what I heard, those Jews knew how to fight."

"That they did," Gaius concurred. "But I was not exactly in a place to purchase large numbers of men to be disposed of in the arena. Besides, that was seven years ago. What prisoners we did make use of were mostly slaughtered during the various triumphal games General Titus hosted immediately after the war."

"Yes, I heard he has quite the taste for blood."

"Perhaps. Though when dealing with enemy prisoners of war, one does not have to concern themselves with the cost of replacing slain combatants."

"Not to worry, Narcissus," Frontinus spoke up. "I have one potential gladiator who I think might make a fine addition to your ludus...after my games, of course. He's a bit raw, like all of them, but he knows how to fight."

Drusus was the only man in the box who had remained silent thus far. He watched each match with intense interest, even those like the previous pair, who acted as if they'd never handled a weapon in their lives. Even in the weakest of men, he could find the smallest measure of potential with which to make a star of the arena. For this very reason, Narcissus insisted his senior trainer accompany him on this two-month trip to Rome's most northern province. The next six pairings showed greater promise than the first. Drusus gave a subtle nod to Narcissus each time he saw a fighter with potential.

"And now, my friends," Frontinus said, standing and waving his hand towards the near entrance gate, "the moment we've been waiting for."

The gate opened and two men walked towards the centre of the arena. One was of average height, well-muscled, and appeared nimble on his feet. The other was a titan, standing half-a-head taller than his opponent. His muscles were large and strong, yet not obscenely sized as to be impractical. He had a smooth face and hard, chiselled jaw that looked carved out of granite. Because none of these men had been formally trained in the various gladiatorial arts, all were given a metal buckler and battered gladius for weapons. Their armour consisted of a simple leather cuirass and skull cap helmet with a brim off the back.

A martial stood between the men, his staff held across his body, keeping the combatants apart. He looked to Frontinus, who gestured for the match to begin. The two men turned to face each other, and it looked as if the larger man was snickering under his breath. His eyes clouded with rage, and he settled into his fighting stance; right foot staggered back, crouched slightly, shield arm partially extended, and weapon held near the chest, point forward. His opponent attempted to do likewise, though he seemed less natural and sure of himself. With a wave of the martial's staff, the match commenced.

"The big man is a Pict from the northernmost reaches of Caledonia," Frontinus explained to his guests. "He answers to the name *Priscus*. Was captured by an auxilia patrol, after he stole a horse from an officer at one of the northern forts. Bastard put up one hell of a fight. We could have just crucified him, but what a waste of talent that would have been."

"Indeed," Narcissus said appreciatively.

They watched Priscus repeatedly smash his shield against his adversary's. He was deceptively quick for his size which baffled his opponent, who had hoped to use speed to best him. The lanista looked to Drusus, who gave a nod of approval.

"He's raw and undisciplined, but there's a dearth of aptitude there. Give me a year with him, and he'll become the fiercest gladiator Rome has ever seen."

39

Priscus sniggered with amusement, knowing he could finish his opponent at any time. It wasn't that the man was a bad fighter, he was simply inexperienced. And Priscus was too strong for him to handle. Once it became apparent that their speed and agility was about equal, the monstrous Caledonian could sense his foe breaking mentally. Priscus knew from a lifetime of fighting, once a man's spirit was broken, his body would follow. Many a time did he face adversaries who were bigger, stronger, quicker, or just better than he was; still he triumphed by breaking their will to fight. This man, whose counter-strikes were becoming less frequent and diminishing in power, was equal to him in speed, but was neither stronger nor a better fighter. And though Priscus was told repeatedly that this was a simple exhibition, he was determined to make as loud a statement as he could in front of this small group of noble Romans.

With a short grunt, he lunged forward, smashing his shield against his opponent's. His blade stabbed with rapid precision, causing the man to stumble backwards lest he end up impaled. By the time the martial sought to break the men up, it was too late. Priscus hooked his shield inside his foe's, wrenched him off-balance, then smashed him in the face with a short backswing. In the very next motion, he thrust his weapon beneath his adversary's cuirass into his guts. The man howled in pain, falling to his knees, then onto his back. The martial's staff then smacked Priscus in the chest, as he forced his way between them.

"Damn it, man, what the fuck do you think you're doing?" the martial shouted at him.

"Winning my match," Priscus said, expressionless.

"You stupid cunt, this is supposed to be an exhibition!"

"So you said, yet you gave me a sharpened blade." He held up the blood-soaked gladius, which he ceremoniously dropped onto the arena floor before turning and walking away.

"Brilliant!" Narcissus said with a laugh and clap of his hands.

Drusus, who rarely showed emotion, frowned slightly and nodded. "He lacks discipline, but there's no doubt he can fight."

"The discipline, I will leave to you," Narcissus stressed. He then looked to the Roman nobles.

Governor Frontinus was aghast, and Tribune Gaius Artorius was chuckling softly to himself.

"Apologies, gentlemen," the governor said. "I had intended this to simply be a showcase, not a death-match." He heard the sobs from the gravely stricken man still on the arena floor. Frontinus shouted to the martial, "Someone put that man out of his misery!"

"He will need some work," Narcissus confessed. "If a gladiator gains a reputation for deliberately killing without permission, no one will want to book him for a match. Replacing slain combatants is extremely expensive for the sponsor."

"Yes," the governor concurred. "Well, I can't exactly use him for my upcoming games now."

"Then you won't mind if I take him off your hands for, let's say, one thousand denarii."

"One thousand?" Frontinus asked in astonishment. "He's worth five times that!"

"If he was trained and disciplined, perhaps. Understand, governor, I am taking a great risk with him." As Frontinus rose from his seat, Narcissus held up his hands in resignation. "To be fair, I'll give you twelve-hundred. You'll not get a better offer. And like you said, you cannot use him in your upcoming games in his present state. The ludi in the provinces are a poor fit for one of his raw skill and barbarism. And no magistrate will want him once they hear he's completely unhinged in the arena."

"Fifteen hundred. Give the coins to my clerk, then piss off." Frontinus stormed away, furious at Narcissus' impudence.

As all lanistae were *infames*—the lowest and most despised within imperial society—Narcissus was used to being treated far less cordially by members of Rome's stuffy aristocracy. The former tribune, Gaius Artorius, looked to the men and simply shrugged before walking after the governor.

"Well, that didn't quite go as planned," Gaius said, as he caught up to Frontinus. "Still, better it happened here than during the games."

41

"I'm starting to think these games were a bad idea," the governor confessed. "Even a modest number of gladiatorial matches will cost me a fortune. And as the Silures surrendered willingly, it's not as if I have a slew of prisoners I can sacrifice in the arena."

"Expensive or not, and even with the occasional cock-up like we just witnessed, don't allow it to tarnish your victory. You accomplished what governors and generals have tried for more than thirty years. To not host celebratory games would be viewed as miserly by the public."

"This is true," Frontinus conceded. "And though I think that vulgar heathen, Priscus, should have netted me far more coin, I'm relieved to be rid of him before he caused me any embarrassment. I'll be glad to see the back of that lanista, too."

"They are quite the paradox," Gaius remarked, as they reached Frontinus' tent where servants quickly brought them wine, along with some bowls of nuts and various cheeses. "Scum of the earth, who cannot vote, provide testimony in the courts, be buried in imperial cemeteries, and who are viewed as the lowest form of life within the Empire. And yet, they mingle within society's elites, because they are needed to provide that most base form of entertainment, which keeps the masses from murdering the elites. And since there is potential to become quite wealthy, few give a damn about giving up the benefits of being 'accepted' as members of civil society."

Frontinus allowed himself a brief chuckle at this analogy. "You've always been one to speak openly and bluntly," he observed. "I suppose that is one aspect of being a soldier that's never left you."

"It's served me well at times, and cost me during others," Gaius admitted.

"Does it ever bore you?" the governor asked, changing the subject. "Being the mayor of a port city, when not long ago you marched with the legions."

"If I'm being honest, I think of it as a reprieve. My family has a proud military history. But between all the campaigns I fought in the east from Armenia to Judea, along with our own hateful civil war, only to be sent back to Judea to take part in the destruction of Jerusalem, I can honestly say I've done my part. It's been seven years since we sacked the Jewish Holy City, and I can still smell the

42

stench of pestilence and rotting death. Nothing in all my campaigns could have prepared me for that. I thought launching the severed head of an enemy general from an onager during the Siege of Tigranocerta—back when I was a young decanus—was morbid enough. That was but a trifle compared to what I saw and did in Jerusalem." Gaius shuddered at the horrific memories.

Though Frontinus was no stranger to war, he'd heard horror stories about what the army witnessed within the Jewish holy city. Most of the approximately one million who perished died not from legionary blades, but from starvation and any number of ungodly diseases. "And yet, from the ashes of Jerusalem rises an even greater monument in Rome," the governor observed.

Gaius nodded slowly, though his gaze was fixed elsewhere. "It is the way of things, I suppose," he said, at last. "Life is a cycle; one often accented by abject suffering and horrific brutality. I will be haunted forever by the memories of Jerusalem, even if I live to be a senile old man. I suppose it is fitting, that the Emperor's monumental amphitheatre be the legacy of that ghastly rebellion. Strange as this may sound, I actually look forward to seeing it once it's completed."

"If I am still Governor of Britannia, I'll make certain you are one of my honoured guests," Frontinus said with a grin.

Narcissus rarely dealt with the gladiators directly. Even as an infamis, he felt it was beneath his station. That was what Drusus and his subordinate trainers were for. Drusus was fifty-two years old and a former *auctoratus*; a free man who sold himself to the gladiator school for a fixed period, usually four or five years. Drusus had sold himself to the arena to pay off a substantial debt. After his term of service was over, his arrears paid, and a sizeable sum of gold and silver coin to his name, he elected to remain with the ludus as an instructor.

He had been quite the celebrity during his time in the arena, with many victories to his credit. The echoes of the crowd's cheers and the relentless chanting of his name still echoed in his mind. Yet fame was fickle, especially in the arena. Fifteen years had passed since his last match, and few among the mobs who ravenously came to the arena to watch blood spill could recall his name.

He found Priscus seated on a long bench, his hands resting in his lap, a contented smile on his face. His wrists were shackled, though he appeared not to notice. Aside from the gaoler, he was the only man in the room.

"Priscus," Drusus said.

The man looked up, as if noticing him for the first time. When the instructor signalled for him to rise, the hulking fighter leapt to his feet, lunging at him. He stopped just short and glared down at him. The gaoler began to shouting in a panic.

Drusus raised his hand, silencing him. "Do not try to intimidate me, boy." His expression was calm, yet his eyes bore into the man. "I've bested men who were larger, stronger, and better than you."

He was not certain if Priscus could understand a word he was saying, nor did he care. The fact that he had not so much as budged when the big man lunged at him was enough. Priscus snorted and grinned. He then bowed slightly and held his hands up in what Drusus decided was a sign of respect. The instructor grabbed the chain that bound his wrists together and snapped his fingers. The gaoler quickly walked over to them. With his eyes nervously fixed on Priscus' face, he produced a key and undid the shackles. Still clutching the chain, Drusus handed them to him and dismissed the man.

Priscus then spoke to him in his native tongue and bowed again. Though Drusus could not understand him, the meaning was clear. He gave a short nod in return and signalled for the ludus' newest prize gladiator to follow him.

Chapter III: A Troubled Dynasty

The Imperial Palace, Rome
October, 77 A.D.

Julia Flavia

It was just before dawn when Titus Flavius Vespasian, Emperor of Rome, decided to take his weekly stroll down to the large chamber that served as a vault for the treasures taken during the war in Judea, which had ended seven years prior. A squad of praetorian guardsmen remained on constant vigil outside its large double doors, and at least twice a week the two prefects were required to personally inventory and account for the contents within. On this morning, the Emperor was accompanied by his eldest son, Titus. Walking beside the prince imperial was his teenage daughter, Julia.

"A fine morning," the Emperor said, taking a deep breath through his nostrils. "By Juno, but I do love the autumn air!"

"What little manages to reach past the stench of the city," his granddaughter said quietly. She caught the reproving gaze from her father and quickly said, "Apologies, Caesar."

"Please, no formalities from my own kin," Vespasian said with a dismissive wave. "And you are correct, my dear. The air is much fresher once one gets beyond the Seven Hills and into the country. Still, if one knows where to look, or smell for that matter, you can find a trace of autumn's pleasantries even in the heart of the world's largest and most congested city. And I am glad to see you this day, dear Julia. I remember when you were just a baby, and now look at you. Almost a fully-grown woman!"

Julia smiled and blushed slightly. As one of the Emperor's few grandchildren, he had doted on her since the time she was born. She was just a girl of six when Vespasian won the imperial throne. Julia could still recall the splendid parades that had honoured him, as well as her father, when he returned from Judea.

"She's been asking to see the treasure, before it's all gone," Titus said by way of explanation.

"Yes, well I'm surprised you have not brought her sooner," the Emperor remarked.

The three walked along the stone path in one of the many gardens within the palace grounds. "What remains is still quite the display of grandeur, though it is but half of what your father brought back from Jerusalem."

"Thankfully, Neptune and Triton granted us calm seas during the journey," Titus remarked. "Even they wished for the treasure to reach Rome."

They were soon joined by Praetorian Prefect Tiberius Alexander. He carried one of only two keys to the vault. Titus possessed the other. In addition to being prince imperial and Vespasian's heir, he served as the other Prefect of the Guard.

"A fine morning, Caesar," Alexander said, before acknowledging the Emperor's granddaughter. "Lady Julia."

"Prefect Alexander," she replied with a warm smile.

Tiberius gave a friendly nod to Titus. Despite his status, they shared a close and rather informal relationship. Alexander had served as Titus' chief-of-staff during the Siege of Jerusalem; his superior organisational and logistical skills directly responsible for keeping the vast army fed and well-supplied. His appointment to this position raised a few eyebrows, as Alexander was also an Egyptian Jew. Following the revolt in Judea, many felt he would better serve the Empire in Rome. To say nothing of the imperial capital being much safer for him! Possibly the only man more hated by the Jewish people in the east was the turncoat, Josephus ben Matthias. A former rebel general, who'd fought against Vespasian at the Siege of Jotapata, he later changed his allegiance and now lived in Rome at the imperial palace.

The small group walked in silence down to the large stone building. The section of guardsmen quickly snapped to attention.

Their decanus saluted. "Hail Caesar."

Vespasian returned the salute before allowing Alexander to receive his briefing from the night watch. It had been uneventful like most nights. The prefect produced his key and opened the heavy lock, which held the thick iron bar across the door in place.

As the early morning light cast its glow upon the interior of the vault, Julia gasped at what she saw. From floor to ceiling were rows upon rows of crates and chests bearing gold and silver coins, candelabras, piles of tapestries, vestments, and various other valuables. What was missing, however, were any forms of statuary.

"The Jews view statues of people as a form of idolatry," Alexander explained. "During the reign of Tiberius, Pontius Pilate insisted on parading the images of the Emperor through Jerusalem. He nearly caused a riot."

Giddy with excitement, the young woman reached into one of the open chests, pulling out a handful of dusty gold coins. "These must be very old," she gasped.

"From what I can tell," the prefect said, taking one of the coins from her and turning it over in his hand, "these are from the First Temple of Solomon, over a thousand years ago. Their value extends infinitely beyond mere gold or silver."

"And each will fetch a handsome price at auction," Titus said, taking the coin from his former chief-of-staff.

"Jewish bankers and merchants living in Rome are notorious misers when it comes to opening their purse strings," Alexander added. "Yet once they saw we had the treasure from the temple, they flung open their vaults to purchase even the smallest pieces of our people's history."

It felt strange to everyone in the room, most of all Alexander himself, to hear him refer to the Jews as 'our people'. An Alexandrian Jew by birth, his father had been a member of the Roman equites and raised his son as a Roman. Alexander knew much about Jewish history and customs, though he was never an

47

active participant in the faith. For him, the study of Judaism was strictly academic.

"Josephus came here once," Titus remarked. It was soon after his capture that Josephus claimed to receive a vision from God, that Vespasian would become Emperor. Two years later, his prophecy came true. Following his eventual changing of sides, he served as an advisor to the imperial army during the Siege of Jerusalem. Though the most hated man in Judea, the patronage of the Flavians allowed him to live rather comfortably. He spent most of his days working on a detailed account of the Great Jewish Revolt, as well as a definitive history of the Jewish people.

"It wasn't easy for him," the Emperor recalled. "Though he blamed the zealots for the destruction of both the city and temple, it must feel like blasphemy seeing the greatest treasures of his people now property of Rome."

"Perhaps I'll make a gift of this for him," Titus said, holding up a small golden vessel. While there was no end to riches in the vault, the largest treasures taken from the temple, including the golden trumpets and enormous menorah, were left on display at the recently erected Temple of Peace near Velian Hill. Everything else was gradually being sold off at auction in order to pay for many of the Emperor's public works. Most notable among these was the gigantic amphitheatre, slowly taking shape just a few blocks north of the imperial palace.

After an hour of admiring the vast hoard of wealth and valuables, they left the vault. Alexander locked the iron bolt in place. The first shift of the morning guard had relieved the night watch, with the decanus saluting and giving a 'Hail Caesar' to the Emperor as they departed. Tiberius Alexander then took his leave, as did Julia. Though Vespasian cherished the time spent with his granddaughter and was fond of his Praetorian Prefect, he needed to speak with his son alone. Titus grew uncomfortable as his father led him towards a remote corner of the gardens, rightly suspecting what he wished to discuss.

"Still giving no thought to remarrying?" Vespasian asked, steeling himself for the coming argument. One he'd had on several occasions with his son.

"You know the answer to that, Father," Titus replied, his voice showing the strains of tension. "Queen Julia has been one of our

48

closest allies, during the Judean war as well as our campaign to seize the Empire from that pretender, Vitellius. You say I need to find a worthy bride, and I tell you I have found one. Why do you hate her so?"

"Your words are unfair, son, for I do not hate Julia Berenice at all. I am very fond of the woman, and I always have been. Much of the assistance her brother rendered to us was due to her influence. She even deployed Judean loyalist troops to keep the peace after we sacked Jerusalem. And...I know you love her." There was an uncomfortable pause. The Emperor stood tall, his next words hard. "We, as the imperial family, do not have the luxury of marrying for love, and those who do marry for love are fools."

"Is that why you never married Caenis?" The question caught Vespasian off-guard. Antonia Caenis was a former slave and in her younger years the secretary to Antonia, the mother of Emperor Claudius. Though his brother, Domitian, resented their father for consorting with such a lowly-born woman, Titus was very fond of her. He mourned with Vespasian when she passed away two years before and immediately regretted his present retort.

"Caenis and I were lovers many years before you were born," the Emperor said, keeping his voice calm. "We always knew that we could never be husband and wife, regardless of our feelings for each other. When the time came, we did the right thing, breaking off our affair so that I could marry your mother. And after your mother's passing we waited two years, out of respect, before continuing our relationship. Yet, not once did I ever consider trying to make her Empress Consort."

Vespasian shook his head, more frustrated than angry. "We must think about the stability of the Flavian Dynasty. You are my heir, but who will be yours? Your brother? Gods help us if we turn to him to continue our legacy! Who then? One of Julia Berenice's *Jewish* sons from her first husband? She is twelve years older than you and well beyond the age of bearing you a son. And besides..." The Emperor's voice trailed off.

Titus glowered at him. "Besides *what*, Father?"

"Queen Julia was raised amongst Romans, as was her brother. Their father was practically a member of the imperial family, having been raised in the court of Emperor Tiberius. But the people do not see it that way. We know Julia as an ally, who is more of a true

49

Roman than most of the populace. The plebeians see a foreign queen; a modern-day Cleopatra."

"Are we, then, to stake our marriages on the whims of the mob?"

"Yes," the Emperor replied bluntly. "It is an empress consort's duty to win the love of the people. If they love her, they are more likely to forgive her husband's shortcomings. We've seen what happens when an empress is loved or loathed by the public. Their love of Livia kept them from seeing Augustus' many short-comings. Tiberius was ill-served by never remarrying after he became emperor; and if I'm being brutally honest, the same could be said for me. The people loved Emperor Claudius, and they mourned with him after Messalina's betrayal. But they reviled his later marriage to his own niece, Agrippina. The people were so repelled by her, they celebrated when Nero later had her killed."

It was no secret that Vespasian was among those who celebrated Agrippina's downfall. The two utterly despised each other. An ill-timed profane diatribe against the Empress-Mother had even led to Vespasian's expulsion from the imperial court for a time.

"All of this takes us back to the matter of an heir," he continued. "No one will dispute the claims of a biological son; which Queen Julia simply cannot give you."

Titus countered, "In the hundred years since the downfall of the Republic and rise of the Empire, no biological son has ever followed his father onto the imperial throne. Barring any unforeseen disaster, I will be the first."

It was indeed strange, in the hereditary monarchy which Rome now was, a son had yet to succeed his own father. The first emperor, Augustus, had only one daughter and went through a slew of potential heirs before finally settling on his stepson, Tiberius. Tiberius' only son, Drusus, was murdered in his mid-thirties. Tiberius then named his great-nephew, Gaius Caligula, as his heir. The young Gaius was a mentally incompetent despot; murdered just four years into his reign. His lone child, an infant daughter, was also slain. Caligula's uncle, Claudius, was then proclaimed 'Caesar' by the Praetorian Guard. He was already in his fifties, with a son, Britannicus, who was underage. Claudius later named his stepson, Lucius Domitius, who took the name 'Nero', as his heir. Nero had Britannicus killed soon after Claudius' passing. At the time of his own death, he had no sons or designated heirs. The man whose

50

rebellion saw him deposed, the aged and tyrannical Galba, lost both his sons decades before and had no grandchildren. His murderer and successor, Otho, was unmarried and childless. Vitellius, who overthrew Otho following the first Roman civil war in over a century, had a son. However, he was only six years old when he and his father were killed by Vespasian's soldiers. Thankfully, there were no further potential usurpers or claimants to the throne. This was, in part, because the new Flavian emperor had two healthy, adult sons.

Titus was clearly upset. He loved his father deeply and hated the spiteful dispute that threatened to drive a wedge between them. But he also loved Julia Berenice, who he had sworn would sit beside him once he came to the imperial throne.

"With respect, *Caesar*, I will discuss this no more," he said with finality. The prince imperial bowed and quickly left the gardens.

This left his father feeling distressed and heartbroken. Like his son, Vespasian hated it when they argued. However, the issue of succession was too grave for him not to make his feelings clear. The promise of the Flavian Dynasty was one of peace and stability. He feared that his son's love for a foreign queen could undo everything. And there would be no heirs coming from the womb of a woman who was already nearly fifty! And yet, if Titus was determined to have Julia Berenice sit beside him on the imperial throne, there was little Vespasian could do about it after he was gone.

"Augustus managed with far less to work with than us," he said quietly to himself as he sat pondering on the edge of a fountain. He had done all he could to secure the dynastic legacy of his family. He could only hope that Titus came to his senses before Vespasian departed for his place among the gods.

It was another two months before Narcissus and Drusus returned to Rome. Though they had travelled to Britannia by ship, they made their way home through Germania and Cisalpine Gaul in search of other fresh talent. They had first travelled to Londinium, to watch the series of matches Frontinus put on for the public, allowing them to acquire three more potential gladiators in addition to Priscus. He was the real prize, and Narcissus was convinced they would find no other to compare with him.

As well as being a superior fighter, the Caledonian was quickly proving his intelligence and ability to learn. Though he always remained silent around his masters, Drusus speculated that he understood them far more than he let on.

"Let us hope you can teach him discipline and hone his skills," Narcissus said one night, as they sat at an inn near Augusta Raurica.

"He won't be any trouble, trust me," Drusus reassured him. "I may be a much older shell of what I was in the arena, who he could break with his bare hands. However, he knew I was not afraid of him. Men like him respect strength above all else. Within a year he'll be more valuable to us than the rest of the lot we procured combined."

"I hope so," Narcissus replied. "I spent a damn fortune taking us all the way to Britannia. The only reason I even took Frontinus up on his offer for the other three was because they were so cheap. And, I confess, I did not wish to leave with only one gladiator to show for it."

"The others have potential, albeit very little," Drusus remarked. "Most likely they'll end up in the gregarii."

"Fit for mass slaughter, the next time the Emperor or some senator demands a blood-bath," Narcissus added. "But we are an imperial ludus, not some backwards shithole school from the provinces. I don't mind producing the occasional gregarii brawl, but I want our fighters to be the best in the Empire. I want Vespasian himself asking…no, *demanding* that our gladiators highlight the games of his new arena."

"We have time," Drusus assured him. "We have a strong core of gladiators, though a shame we are losing thirty within the next two months."

"Yes, it was quite the boon when they all came to me at once to sell their bodies and souls to the arena," Narcissus recalled. "Fifty came to us then, and we were fortunate enough to only lose twenty over the next five years."

"And half of those we lost in the first few months, mostly from accidents or sickness. It was after that you let me institute a standard of fitness before we allow prospective candidates to remain at our school. Sadly, there seems to be a shortage of men willing to sell their bodies and souls to the amusement of the mob."

"If we can't find volunteers, we'll continue to acquire them by other means," Narcissus noted. "Though to be honest, I hate dealing with slaves. And those condemned to the arena by the judges are fucking worthless. But that is why I have you, my friend."

"Not to worry, I'll weed out the chaff."

Troubled by the quarrel he'd had with his son, Vespasian decided to let the matter be. His attention was now focused on the largest of the many public projects being funded by the vast treasure taken from the Jerusalem temple. Accompanied by his personal bodyguard, Octavianus, and a handful of praetorians, he departed the palace and made his way towards the home of a man named Silvanus, one of Rome's greatest architects. Unlike his predecessors, who rode in a covered litter or chair, Vespasian preferred to travel on horseback. He did not fear the people, as some emperors before him, but he did keep enough guardsmen with him to clear the road and keep onlookers at bay.

Though he wore a modest tunic rather than his purple and gold imperial robes, there were many shouts of *'Hail Caesar!'* as he made his way through the city. It was all rather perplexing. His name was well-known long before his rise to the throne, particularly after the Conquest of Britannia and his numerous victories during the Judean Revolt. Yet while the people knew the name Flavius Vespasian prior to his becoming Emperor, few had had any idea what he looked like.

"And now your image adorns all the public buildings," Octavianus said with a grin. "Perhaps you should not have been so insistent to the sculptor on accuracy."

"It was misplaced modesty." The Emperor smiled and gave a friendly wave towards a group of onlookers who hailed him from a nearby market square. "I thought it was needlessly vain to have all my blemishes removed from my statues. During public spectacles and games, only a few are ever close enough to see my face. And yet, I cannot go anywhere without being recognised by the mob. You praetorians don't help the matter any."

"Even if we travelled in plain clothes, Caesar, the people would still recognise and flock to you. Any chance of anonymity in public vanished with the defeat of Vitellius."

"A lesson I've been trying to learn for the past eight years," Vespasian concurred with a chuckle.

It was late afternoon when they reached the home of Silvanus. Guardsmen opened the outer gate, and Octavianus banged on the large wooden doors leading into the main house. It was quickly answered by a servant who led them into a large room the architect normally used for entertaining guests. Instead of dining couches and tables, a single large table now occupied the centre of the room. Atop was a detailed model of an amphitheatre. The size and scale were beyond any the world had ever seen.

"A pleasant afternoon, Caesar," Silvanus said, briskly walking into the chamber.

"And to you," the Emperor replied. "I have not been to the build site in a few weeks and thought it best to simply ask you about the progress."

"It goes well, albeit methodically," the architect replied. "As you know, excavating the ground was tedious and time-consuming. While it was simple enough to tear down Nero's gaudy *Domus Aurea*, the private lake left a large quagmire once it was drained. We left a lot of the piping and canal networks in place, should one ever wish to stage naval battles within the new arena."

"And the construction itself? All one can see is the surrounding scaffolds and large piles of stone and timber."

"The floor and staging areas are finished, as are the lower two levels," Silvanus explained. "The concept is the same as any other amphitheatre, just on a colossal scale. And because we're anticipating much larger crowds than ever, entrances, exits, walkways, and especially latrines must be incorporated. The Circus Maximus is an oblong course designed for chariot racing, but we incorporated many of the same concepts to accommodate the anticipated crowds."

"And each level can support twenty-thousand spectators," the Emperor recalled as he ran his fingers over the carved sandstone of the lowest two levels of the model.

"Yes, so even in its current state, forty-thousand could attend the games. Once complete, we'll be able to host nearly eighty.

54

Although, sixty-five thousand would be far more manageable, not to mention comfortable."

Vespasian grinned. Gladiatorial matches were an emperor's most effective way of winning favour with the common rabble. Though chariot racing was enormously popular, it was the visceral manliness of watching men engage in mortal combat that appealed to the Roman sense of martial virtue. It was also far more versatile than the races. There were many classes of gladiator who could fight, not just each other, but men against beasts, or even beasts against beasts. For those with more obscure tastes, there was even the occasional battle between women or dwarves.

"How long?" the Emperor asked, his gaze still fixed on the model. He envisioned the completed splendour in his mind, and it was beautiful.

"Keeping to the standards we agreed," Silvanus said, "three years. The quarries are setting a blistering pace trying to keep us supplied with stone and marble. This naturally destroys slaves rather quickly."

"The raids across the Rhine and Danube should help refresh their numbers," Vespasian remarked. He then gave an affirmative nod. "Three years, then."

"It will make for two great anniversaries," Silvanus observed. "Ten years since Titus triumphed in Judea and eleven since the rise of the Flavians."

Chapter IV: The Pit

Cottanello Quarry, Italia
Forty-five Miles North of Rome
October, 77 A.D.

Marble Quarry, north of Rome

The slave auction was a humiliating affair for Verus. Herded onto a stage like livestock, prospective buyers poked, prodded, and checked their health and suitability for whatever the potential master needed. Many times, they were ordered to strip. Any man found with numerous scars on his back was considered rebellious and irredeemable. Something Verus learned was that most slaves in Roman cities were women. Scholarly men were sometimes purchased to act as scribes for nobles and magistrates, or tutors for their children. Most imperial noblemen did not otherwise want slave men, particularly those of muscular build with robust health, occupying their homes. That is, unless they had a taste for that kind of carnal flesh. And because slaves were the absolute property of their owners, who could do with them as they pleased, it came as little surprise that sexual lust often played a role in a slave's marketability, not to mention the price an auctioneer could demand.

A fertile and fetching young woman could fetch nearly three times the coin as a robust man.

While Verus was physically strong and reasonably attractive, he was illiterate and only spoke passable Latin. His body was the only thing for sale. Unless the prospective buyer was a woman or a man with homosexual tendencies, his chances of finding himself within a household staff were minimal. He knew there was likely only one thing his body was good for in the eyes of Roman slave buyers, and his suspicions were confirmed two weeks after he was captured.

The sun hid behind black clouds this morning, and the ominous roll of thunder could be heard in the distance. All the women and children were long since sold, and none of the buyers were looking for fit young men. While he wished to leave the fetid slave market as soon as possible, Verus hoped he would not be purchased.

The omens are poor, he thought to himself. It was a strange feeling, for Verus was not overly superstitious. And yet, a chill ran up his spine as lightening flashed in the distance. The boom of thunder that followed a few moments later felt as if the gods themselves were mocking him.

At a battered tent belonging to the slave drivers, a modestly-dressed man and a pair of overseers met with the auctioneer. They came as soon as they received word of Antonius Primus' expedition across the Danube. Slaves rarely remained on the market for long, as disease and malnutrition would soon render them unmarketable. These men, however, did not need the best and most fit; only men who were healthy enough to wield a pickaxe and carry heavy loads until their broken bodies expired.

"Half this lot won't even make it to Italia," the buyer argued. "I'll give you a thousand denarii for the lot and not a sestertius more!"

The auctioneer was clearly unhappy. He still had fifty men remaining, which meant he was only getting twenty denarii apiece. He'd fetched a thousand denarii for a woman and her daughter just a week prior. However, he knew these were the last of the lot, to be disposed of in the rock quarries. It was either take the money or wait for them to rot away to the point that no one wanted them.

"Piss on it," he swore, shaking his head in frustration. The overseer grinned.

It was an hour later when the crack of a whip against the post of their pen roused the remnants of the slave market. "On your feet, scum!" a harsh voice shouted.

Verus let out a sigh of resignation as they were herded out into the now empty courtyard. A flash of lightning lit the ground, followed by a crash of thunder in the distance. Though it was late morning, it was nearly as dark as night, and the collection of slaves knew it was going to be a long, miserable day. They were quickly chained together, and with another crack of the whip, hurried out of the courtyard and onto the main road that led out of the town. As they passed a nearby field of broken husks from the recent harvest, the skies opened and the heavens unleashed a deluge upon them. They did not see their new owner, for he and his overseers rode in the back of a wooden carriage. Only the guards and slave drivers walked beside them, scowling and occasionally cracking their whips for dramatic effect.

The days passed. The road seemed never ending. Each morning they were roused before sunup, plodding along under the drivers' whips until sundown. Whenever possible, the caravan stopped in towns so the slavers could sleep under a roof. Most nights, however, they simply halted as soon as it was dark and slept under the stars. For Verus and the other slaves, there were no beds. By the end of each day, they were ready to collapse from exhaustion. The only time they got fed was in the morning, just prior to beginning the long trek. Each night they laid down, beyond tired, with sore feet, and stomachs rumbling. It was now late October. The days were warm and pleasant, and the nights cool. About every fourth or fifth day the rains would come, soaking the miserable slaves. This also placed their drivers in a foul temper. They would lash at them with their whips, simply out of spite.

Besides the ill-fated raid from nine years before, Verus had never ventured south of the Danube. In fact, he had never wandered more than fifty miles from his home. He had no way of knowing just how large the world was, and he marvelled that the Romans Empire could extend so far. Most days, he had no idea where they were, let alone when they reached Italia. All he knew was that the road they spent endless days stumbling along, eventually veered towards the south. The sun no longer rose to their backs, but instead off to their left. It was decidedly warmer, though the rains became more frequent the further south they ventured. However, on the day they reached their destination, the skies were clear and the sun warm.

"Fifty days," he said, as the massive quarry came into view. These were the first words he had spoken in weeks and his voice was raspy. He no longer cared where they were going, he was simply glad the journey was finally over. His feelings would change in the coming days.

The owner of the quarry did not stand on ceremony. It was midmorning, and the workers were already toiling with hammer and pickaxe. With a few grunts and shouted profanities from the drivers, the newest batch of slaves were herded into a large pen. The ropes that bound their hands for the last two months were removed. Verus rubbed his raw, sore wrists. They were then shoved down a long, narrow path that led into the bottom of the large pit. The white stone glared in the bright sun, blinding them as they stumbled along. A group of men awaited them. Forceful shoves sent each man either to the left, where a large pile of pickaxes, hammers, and chisels lay, or to the stack of baskets to the right. Verus was sent left.

Few verbal commands were used by their masters, as many of the slaves came from outside of Italia and could not understand Latin. Besides, words were not needed. Verus was roughly guided over to a large platform and handed a hammer and chisel, the driver pointing to a raised platform butting against the side of the quarry. Taking the tools, he climbed a half-rotted rope ladder to where three other men stood chiselling away at a large slab.

"Fresh meat to feed *The Pit*," one of the men said with a maniacal chuckle.

Verus said nothing, but took the chisel and placed it in a long seam that had already been worked into the rock. He took a few swings with the hammer, suddenly missing his forge. The man who'd spoken grabbed him by the shoulder, causing Verus to spin and raise the hammer, eyes filled with rage.

"Easy, friend," the man said. "Though I should just let you strike and end it all."

"What do you want?" Verus asked, pushing the man's hand away.

"Ah, so you speak Latin. Good. I wish to save you, and all of us, from the overseers' whips. Our task is to cut slabs of marble out of this section of the quarry. You can see where they've been marked. Should anyone become careless and crack the slab, it's the lash for the lot of us." His gaze darkened. "I must warn you, *friend,* accidents tend to happen, especially to those who earn us the lash."

Verus did not even acknowledge his companion's words and simply went back to chiselling. He spent the remainder of the day with his eyes fixed on the growing seam in the rock. The pounding of his hammer soon became a background noise he scarcely noticed. His mind returned to his village, his forge, and his family. Not a moment went by since his capture that he did not see Tamura's face, and he prayed that she and their son were safe. Worst of all were the feelings of utter helplessness, that he was not there to provide for and protect them. He could only trust in the gods, that they would honour his pact with them. But then, how could he trust in deities who so easily allowed his people to be slaughtered or enslaved?

After several hours, the sky became red, and an overseer shouted for them to cease in their labour for the day. Without even looking at the other men on the platform, Verus dropped his tools and climbed down the rope ladder. He followed the other workers to a long, rickety vendor stall, where several men waited to serve them from large iron pots. Verus was famished and eagerly took a wooden bowl of what he assumed was barley gruel. It was runny and utterly tasteless. He did not care and ravenously finished every bite. The others were equally famished and greedily downed their humble portions.

There were no shacks or huts for them to sleep in, only long pens like those used for cattle. They stood in long lines, as overseers clasped metal irons around their ankles before shoving them into the pen. Lined with rotting straw, the stench was terrible, and Verus wished he could sleep on his work platform. Finding a spot along the inside wall, he sat with his knees curled up to his chest, lowered his head and closed his eyes.

"Quite the first day, wasn't it?" It was the man who'd spoken to him on the platform. Verus remained silent and lowered his head once more.

"Not one to make friends, eh? Probably wise. After all, what don't you notice here? Besides no women, I mean."

Verus raised his head and gazed around at the faces of the other workers. Many had thick, unkempt hair, and none had shaved in months. And then there were those whose youthful faces simply could not grow beards.

"They're all young," he replied at last.

In the growing darkness, he looked at the other man, who appeared to be in his late twenties. He had a mane of matted hair and only traces of scruff growing on his face.

"Exactly. One does not grow old in The Pit. The strong may last a year, but most only survive a few months."

"How long have you been here?" Verus asked.

"Six months," the man replied. "I was not always a slave, mind you. Was once a highway robber, which earned me a fair living. Then one day, I attempted to rob a rather charming young lady riding alone on the Via Appia. Like a fool, I did not even notice she was armed; and she could fight. Could have killed me right then. Instead, she hamstrung me, drug me to the nearest town, and turned me over to the local vigiles. They, in turn, sold me to The Pit for a few denarii." He looked at his swollen, blistered hands and sun-burnt forearms. "I'm wasting away here. I was nearly twice the man then that I am now."

Only then did Verus notice just how emaciated the man was. His face was gaunt and leathery, making him appear much older. Despicable thief he may be, yet Verus found that he pitied the poor wretch. Would this place destroy him just as quickly?

With the demand for greater quantities of marble, slaves were dying from exhaustion and the terrible conditions in The Pit faster than they could be replaced. Within the first week, nearly a quarter of those who arrived with Verus were broken corpses, carried away to the burn pit. He wondered if perhaps they were the fortunate ones. From atop his work platform, he watched as the latest victim was carted off; his head exploded from a falling boulder. Verus knew that suicide would be easy enough. He could simply leap from the high platform headfirst or impale himself with pickaxe or chisel. Some slaves did take their own lives on occasion, and Verus had already witnessed two men fall from high scaffolds in the first few days. While their deaths were ruled accidental, many speculated it was murder or self-slaughter.

"Either way, their suffering is over," his companion, whose he learned was March, said.

61

"Never thought about ending it yourself?" Verus asked.

"Every day since I came here," Marcus replied. "Death is the only reprieve for those condemned to The Pit. But truth be told, I'm a coward. Simple as that. Besides, if the gods are making me atone for my crimes now, perhaps they will show me a touch of mercy in the afterlife. And what about you? If you're going to murder yourself, do it quickly. That way you don't suffer as much."

"Unfortunately, I also owe a debt to the gods," Verus remarked. "Not for any crimes, but in payment for the protection of my family."

Marcus was curious to know more, but did not press the matter when Verus remained silent. They continued to work in silence. The slab they were cutting was almost ready to be extracted, and overseers came to supervise the attaching of a large rope sling, hung from a tall wooden crane. It took twenty men to hold the immeasurably heavy slab in place as Verus, Marcus, and a pair of others finished cutting it free from the quarry wall. It was then slowly lowered onto a waiting cart and immediately taken up the long path and off towards wherever it was being sold.

"Most likely for the Emperor's latest project," Marcus speculated.

"Latest project?" Verus asked.

"Something I heard about before I was captured. I've never been to Rome. It's too crowded, and too easy for one to get into trouble. But apparently, Vespasian ordered the construction of a huge amphitheatre. His way of suckling the masses, who are too easily distracted to see just how shitty their pathetic lives are. There must be a rush for more stone and marble, which is why they are working us to death quicker than usual."

While the work hours had grown longer, with a sense of urgency coming from their masters, there was something else that was completely unexpected for the poor souls condemned to The Pit. Normally, they were fed at sunrise and sunset, and even then, just enough barley gruel to keep them alive. But as they watched the large slab being carried away by the bouncing donkey cart, Verus and Marcus were surprised when the overseer blew his whistle and shouted for them to halt their work. The ration shacks were flung open, and the cooking pots stirred up. But rather than just barley and water, there were strips of pork tossed into each bowl.

"I guess they figure it's cheaper to keep us fed and alive than replace us every few months," Marcus remarked as they ate hungrily.

They were given a few minutes to fill their bellies, and then with shouts and cracks of the whips, they went back to toiling in the sun once more.

For Verus, the timing of his arrival was fortuitous. It had been only a week, and now they were being given ample food to at least keep them from wasting away. For Marcus, however, it was far too late. His condition had deteriorated greatly, and two weeks after receiving their first additional rations, he slumped into the straw of the pen one night, never to wake again. For Verus, it was another reminder why he should never make friends in The Pit.

Chapter V: A Chance for Life
Cottanello Quarry
August, 78 A.D.

The Via Flaminia

Ten months had passed since Verus came to The Pit. Since the death of Marcus, who was the closest thing he'd had to a 'friend', he never spoke to anyone. Despite the additional food rations, over half the men brought with him from Dacia had perished. The work was both backbreaking and extremely hazardous. Injuries were common, yet only a few died outright. Most were left badly crippled and taken away, never to be seen again. Disease was also commonplace, for no attempts had been made to improve their sleeping conditions. Rains in the winter and spring came every three to four days. This created additional slipping hazards where they worked, while making the nights utterly miserable. To compound it all, many pissed or shit where they lay each night, attracting swarms of flies and other parasites, creating a pestilence that could destroy even the most stalwart constitution.

Verus was still quite strong, a relentless desire to survive sustaining him far beyond the breaking point of most men. But after ten months, he could feel his fortitude starting to crack. Though he was fed just enough to prevent starvation, he had lost a considerable amount of weight. His usually close-shaven face was now covered in a thick beard, and his hair had grown long. He was perpetually filthy. After the first month, Verus did not even notice his own stench anymore. If anything, the grime helped shield his skin from the blistering sun, which intensified as it glared off the quarry walls. Even the strongest of men eventually broke in The Pit, and Verus worried that his own time would come sooner, rather than later.

During mid-August, his fortunes changed.

Like every other morning, the slaves were herded out of the pen to the shack where their breakfast of gruel and fatty lamb or pork awaited them. But instead of sending them off to work, one of their handlers shoved them towards the long, rocky path that led out of the quarry. Verus had not been out of The Pit since his arrival, and he was puzzled. Atop the plateau overlooking the quarry, the quarry master stood waiting with two men he had never seen before. Guards roughly grabbed each man, pushing him to the right or left. As he watched from his place in line, it became apparent to they were sorting the fit and healthy from the weak and broken. Perhaps one in every ten men was sorted into the left group. These were mostly young men who'd been in The Pit for a few weeks or less. When they got to Verus, one of the guards attempted to shove him into the right group. He refused to budge.

"Move your filthy ass, slave!"

The guard raised his whip, but before the guard could react, Verus landed a fierce punch to his jaw. It sent the guard flying onto his back, his eyes rolling into the back of his head.

"By Hades' cock!" the lead overseer roared, rushing towards Verus with a long spear in his hands.

The slave met his gaze for the briefest of moments and walked over to the group on the left. The quarry master gave a grin of appreciation.

One of the other two men nodded. "Well, at least we know that one still has some fight in him."

The unconscious guard was dragged away, and his mates sorted the remainder of the prisoners. All the while, the man who had spoken kept his gaze fixed on Verus. He was more humbly dressed than his companion, though his tunic was still clean and well-made. He had several visible scars on his right forearm, as well as another running along his cheek.

65

The other man was dressed in a more resplendent green tunic with gold trim. His belt was lined with bronze fittings, and it was clear he was a man of some wealth and status. "Find us some good stock, Drusus," he said to the scarred man. He and the quarry master continued to converse amongst themselves.

Drusus walked along the front row. He spent the better part of a minute checking over each man; their hands and feet, their bodies, arms, and even their teeth. Teeth were a good indicator of overall health. If they were rotted, it usually meant the slave had far greater problems than his general appearance denoted. Verus was thankful he still had his, and that they were both straight and white. Aside from a quick glance at his teeth, Drusus scarcely gave him a second glance. Of the fifty or so men in the group, six were singled out. They were escorted away, not by the quarry guards, but by those Drusus and his companion brought with them.

After about an hour of inspecting the other slaves, Drusus came back around to Verus.

"So, you have some fight in you." He looked the slave over. He noted the blistered hands and shabby appearance. "You've been here for some time, I see."

"Ten months," Verus remarked, drawing a smile from Drusus.

"Ah, you speak Latin."

"Well enough. My people live north of the Danube, near the edge of your empire. I thought it wise to learn the speech of our southern neighbours, though I never thought you would raid our lands to murder and enslave our people."

"And yet I sense no bitterness or hate in your voice."

"It is there," Verus emphasised. "More than you will ever know."

"At least you have some control over your emotions," Drusus surmised. "Good. We need men who are not only fighters, but can also learn discipline."

"Who is 'we'?"

Drusus chuckled softly. "My boy, you are about to make a pact with death."

He then waved to one of his guards, who took Verus by the arm and led him away from the mob. There were shouts from the overseers, cracks of their whips, and whimpers from the unfortunate slaves they led back into The Pit. Verus never looked back.

Around the far side of the quarry master's house awaited a large, open cart, drawn by a pair of mules. A guard approached them with a rusted iron key in his hands. He loosed their shackles, and the slaves let out a sigh of relief, rubbing at their raw ankles.

"You won't be needing those anymore," a well-dressed man explained, as he joined them. "And if you ever give us a reason to put them back on you...well, let's just say there are worse fates for slaves than The Pit."

This man, Verus learned, was named Narcissus. He was well-dressed in a green tunic with gold trim and rode a magnificent brown and white horse. Drusus and one of their guards drove the cart. The remaining six guards walked on either side. Verus sat near the back of the cart, bowing his head and shutting his eyes as it lurched up the dirt path leading to the main highway about a mile away. He wanted to burst into tears of relief but forced himself to maintain calm. He was not entirely certain where they were headed or what Narcissus wanted with them. He had his suspicions, though. He knew the Romans had a passion for watching men fight in the numerous arenas around their empire. Such was not unheard of in Dacia, though these were normally bouts between warriors, either to settle personal scores or to prove their manhood. Was Verus now being taken to a place where he would be compelled to fight for his very survival? And what was this 'pact with death' Drusus spoke of? He no longer cared. He was out of The Pit, and that was all that mattered.

For the first time in almost a year, Verus closed his eyes and turned his face up towards the blazing sun. It felt good. He breathed in the fresh air as the cart ambled past a grove of lilacs and tall trees.

The road meandered through the rolling hills of central Italia, the occasional stand of trees, vineyard, or farm field on either side. About an hour after they departed, he finally looked to his companions who sat mostly in silence. Only a couple had any sort of scruff on their faces, and not one appeared to be any older than twenty. Their ethnicities varied somewhat between blonde hair and fair-skinned Germans and Dacians and the olive complexions of those who lived closer to the Mediterranean. Verus could only imagine how frightful he must have appeared to them!

Late in the afternoon, his mouth parched and stomach grumbling, he saw the glint of sunlight dancing off a river in the distance. Trees lined either bank, and one could see a fisherman's boat out on the water.

"It's beautiful," a Germanic man said, his voice heavily accented.

"Everything is beautiful, coming from The Pit," a darker complexioned man replied. With a nod he added, "That is the Tiber; the most famous river in the world. We're probably only a day or two from Rome herself."

The rest of their companions said nothing, and Verus wondered if they could even understand what was being said. Speaking for the first time, he asked, "Have you ever been to Rome?"

"All my life," the man replied. "I ended up with you lot after getting caught stealing from the wrong nobleman, who happened to be prefect of the sodding Praetorian Guard. Worst damned luck ever. The judge sentenced me to death in The Pit. Though I suppose Fortuna has not completely abandoned me. After just a week, it would seem I've been commuted to death in the arena."

"That is where we're going, the arena?" Verus asked.

"If only you knew what *the* arena was," the man said with a short laugh. "There are plenty of sandy floors where gladiators can spill their blood. But I've seen what the Emperor is building in the heart of the Eternal City. If we're lucky, we may get one day a chance to fight there ourselves." He noticed Verus' puzzled expression. "You mean you didn't know why they came looking for healthy young slaves? There are only two fates that await men taken as slaves, particularly those convicted of capital crimes. Either we die under the pickaxe in those cursed mines, or we die in the arena for the amusement of the mob."

The Dacian shook his head. "Honestly, I did not care where they were taking us. I was just glad to be away from The Pit."

"Oh, you'll care soon enough. However, it is still preferable to rotting away in one of those fucking rock quarries. If I thought they might grant me a quick death, I would have attacked the guards on my first day and been done with it. However, scourging and crucifixion just did not sit well with me." He extended his hand. "The name's Severus."

"Verus."

The two men clasped hands and Verus allowed himself to smile for the first time in many months.

Severus was a jovial fellow who seemed eager to have someone to talk to. He began to tell Verus his life story. How he was raised in one of the poorest districts in Rome and had been only fifteen when he married his wife, Claudia. As far as he knew, she was still in Rome. He'd worked in a bakery until losing his livelihood when the entire structure burned down in a fire.

"I didn't know what else to do," he explained. "My wife was great with child. We were destitute, and I couldn't find work anywhere. So, I grew desperate and…well, you can guess the rest. I have not seen my wife in over a month. I can only hope she and our child are well. It's not likely I will ever see them."

Verus gave a sad smile, thinking back to his own family. Every morning and every night he prayed to Safa to protect Tamura and Fillon. It was maddening that he had no way of knowing whether they'd survived the raid. Had they been captured later and sold into slavery? Like every other day, he forced such terrible thoughts from his mind. Tamura was strong and clever, and it was likely she'd abandoned their village, moving further inland away from the threat of Rome. Surprisingly, he found himself pitying young Severus, who was returning to his home city and would be so close to his wife, yet never able to see her. Claudia and Tamura were separated by thousands of miles and infinitely different cultures, yet they shared the same feeling of loss regarding their husbands. Something else Verus often wondered was if Tamura had remarried. The thought troubled him greatly, though it was reasonable for her to assume that after all this time he was dead. She would take the time to properly mourn, but then needed to look to her own future and that of Fillon. Verus loathed the thought of his beloved lying with another man, yet it was preferable to her and their son either killed or in bondage.

The cart suddenly lurched to a halt, bringing Verus out of his stupor. A large meadow lay to their right with the River Tiber less than two hundred paces away.

"Feel free to stretch your legs and empty your bladders," Drusus said. He slipped down from the bench seat and rubbed his backside.

Only then did Verus notice that Narcissus was no longer with them. He'd likely ridden ahead. His horse could travel much faster than the mule cart.

A pair of guards carried wooden buckets down to the river, filled them, and brought them back to the group. Drusus filled a cup from one of the buckets, drinking thirstily before refilling and quaffing it again in a single gulp. He then handed the cup to Severus. The slaves took turns quenching their thirst. After gulping down a cupful so fast it made his throat hurt, Verus refilled the vessel and splashed it onto his face, letting out a sigh before rubbing his fingers through his thick mop of matted hair and unkempt beard.

"We'll have all that off you soon enough," Drusus chuckled. He produced a canvas sack filled with crusts of bread and chunks of goat cheese and passed it around.

While the bread was hard and the cheese pungent, to the Dacian they tasted like a feast fit for a king. Soon they were ordered back into the cart. It rattled along the cobblestone road for another couple of hours, passing numerous towns and villages. Severus explained that the road was known as the *Via Flaminia*. Connecting Rome to the Adriatic Sea, it stretched for 210 miles and would take them all the way into the imperial capital. Around nightfall, they halted at a city near the crossroads called Narnia. It was built atop a steep mountain, highly fortified, and looked like an impregnable fortress.

Verus said as much to his new friend.

"And yet, during the civil war, the pretender's armies surrendered without so much as striking a blow against Vespasian's forces." Severus went on to explain the war that wreaked havoc upon the whole of the Roman Empire when rival emperors Vitellius and Vespasian fought for control of the known world.

"As I understand it, Vitellius' men were badly outnumbered, but they maintained control of the city as well as the surrounding heights. And as you can see, there is no way to take an army southward without first capturing Narnia. Inexplicably, the garrison quickly surrendered. Whether they lost the stomach to fight or actively plotted to betray Vitellius, we'll never know."

Something else Verus would never know was that the Roman general who captured Narnia, and later Rome herself, was the same man whose legion destroyed his village and sent him into slavery.

There would be no going into Narnia for the small collection of slaves. While Drusus and the senior guard found a room at a local inn, the rest kept watch over their charges who spent the night sleeping in a grassy field just off the road. The guards made a small campfire and took turns staying awake to make certain no one wandered off. It surprised Verus that they were not shackled, yet it seemed as if no one in their group had any inclination to run away. As he curled up, using one of the wooden wheels as a rough pillow, he wondered how easy it would be to make a run for it. Where would he go? He was thousands of miles from home, with no food, and only the scabby clothing of a slave from the mines. And besides, he did not think that Safa had saved him from The Pit just so he could flee like a coward. No, he would face his fate with his head high and defiant.

Let us make this Pact with Death, he thought as he drifted off.

Chapter VI: A Pact with Death

The Gladiator Ludus of Vipsanius Narcissus
Rome
August, 78 A.D.
***

It was often said that Rome was the greatest city in the world; the very heart of civilisation. Severus asserted that over one million souls inhabited *The Eternal City*. Verus thought his new friend was putting them on, or in the very least exaggerating. He had seen numerous towns and cities while being taken from Dacia to The Pit, as well as along the central mountains of Italia. Yet nothing came close to holding such a vast multitude of people.

"That is because Rome is larger than all the other cities of Italia combined," Severus explained.

On the third day of their journey, they reached the capital. It surprised Verus to know how close to Rome he'd been this entire time. As the Via Flaminia continued its way south, they crested a large hill that overlooked the city in the distance. When they reached the summit, he and most of the others let out a gasp.

The view was breath-taking! The Eternal City stretched over a series of hills, and Verus could not even see where it ended. The multitude of buildings was incomprehensible, from temples and palatial homes of the nobility, to the endless blocks of cramped flats where the poorer citizens dwelled. Adorning the highest hill was a massive temple complex. Its large stone pillars and roof were adorned with carvings of eagles and the gods of Rome.

"The Temple of Jupiter," Severus stated. "Destroyed during the civil war, and only recently rebuilt."

The cart slowly descended the hill. Verus noted the numerous vineyards and farms covering the landscape away from the city. Various inns and market stalls lined the road with many side lanes leading up to farm houses or palatial homes. The number of people on the road increased substantially the closer they came to the city proper. Wealthy businessmen and nobles rode on horses, while merchants came with carts laden with goods. The road followed a tall aqueduct far larger than any Verus had seen since coming to

Italia. Unexpectedly, the cart veered off the road and came to a halt not far from the city gates.

"From here, we walk," Drusus said, as he slid off the bench seat.

Verus shot Severus a puzzled look.

"Wheeled traffic is prohibited within the city during the daytime," his friend explained. "Trust me, you'll understand why soon enough."

A section of four guardsmen from the city's vigiles stood near the gate. One of them waved to Drusus. "Got some fresh meat to quench the sand's thirst for blood, I see." The man let out a boisterous laugh.

Drusus smiled and nodded as he handed some papers to the men. Verus reckoned he must be relatively well-known for a random guardsman to recognise him. Passing into the city, he felt as if he might choke. The streets were crammed with people, in what appeared to be a cacophony of chaos and disorder. And yet, every man and woman seemed to know exactly where they were going. Venders hawked their wares, while wafts of various smells came from the food stalls where men worked feverishly over heated stoves and ovens. The stench of burning incense came from another covered stall, where an eastern man in flowing robes sat upon a multi-coloured carpet. Others sold various oils and scents. Still more peddled textiles and fabrics. The mass of humanity stretched on endlessly, and Verus thought he might get lost in the mob.

One of his guards prodded him along with the butt of his spear when he lingered for too long to watch the selling of slaves from atop a large raised dais. As expected, they were mostly women.

"Move your ass," the guard grumbled impatiently.

They were then led down a side street a bit less congested and hectic, yet still full of people. At the end of the lane was a walled complex well away from the cluster of flats and shops. Two heavily armed guards stood outside the gate, which consisted of cracked wooden slabs held together by hastily hammered bands of iron. Verus' blacksmithing mind cringed at the terrible workmanship, and he shook his head.

The gate was opened, and Drusus led them through. The complex was even larger than it appeared on the outside. Fences of metal bars separated various sections of an otherwise vast open space. All the buildings lined the edges of the outer wall. Most of these were multi-story dormitories with a few larger houses detached from the rest.

Waiting for them was Narcissus and a handful of men standing on either side of him. They consisted of instructors, scribes, and other workers. There was a cluster of other men gathered nearby, and he wondered if they were prospective gladiators as well. Their manner of dress was humble, mostly simple tunics, but all were clean and well-groomed.

"Auctorati," Drusus said, when he saw his charges staring at them. He explained that they were, "Volunteers who've come to sell their bodies to a life of brutality in the sand."

"There are men who actually become gladiators by choice?" a man asked in disbelief.

"More than you realise. Mostly, they are poor wretches who've fallen in debt, or young fools who are willing to damn themselves to infamy on the chance of winning fame and fortune in the arena."

Drusus abruptly ceased when he saw Narcissus staring at him. He quickly walked over and took his place with the other members of the staff. The slaves and auctorati were lined up together, twenty men in all.

"Welcome, to the ludus!" Narcissus' voice boomed. "Look around you, for you will know this place well. Here is where home and family dwell; your *familia gladiatoria*. I am your *lanista*-both father and master. My word is law; your bodies and souls mine to dispose of as I see fit." He then directly addressed the auctorati. "Those who came here as volunteers, I've already spoken with individually. Each of you comes to the ludus of his own free will, having sold his body for a period of five years, unless death takes you first. Know that within the ludus, whether you were born slave or free, you are all my property."

Verus looked to the faces of the freemen. Some had their heads bowed, their expressions ones of doubt or hopelessness at whatever circumstances led them to volunteer for the arena. Others looked eager and excited.

"Train hard, fight well, and you will find me a loving father," Narcissus continued. "Embarrass me in the arena, or otherwise offend me, and you will be taught a lesson that you will not live long enough to profit from."

Narcissus then clasped his hands behind his back, and paced in front of the prospects for a few moments. He nodded to Drusus and the other staff members.

"Most of you have met Drusus, our chief *doctor*. Do not confuse his title with that of the medics. Here, the doctor is your instructor— a master of the fighting arts. Drusus was once an auctoratus whose name was well-known in the arenas of Italia. In addition to being chief instructor, he serves as *magister* of the ludus. It is he you will deal with most during your first few months of training. And it is he you must prove your worth to, before we allow you to fight in the arena. The other roles of our staff, you will learn in due course. And now for the oath. Auctorati, this is your final chance to leave through the gates behind you as free men. For those of you that are slaves, your choice is simple; take the oath, or be sent back to the mines or other shit-holes where I found you...that is if you survive the savage flogging that awaits you for wasting my time."

None of the men budged. Given the brutal conditions that existed in the ludus, Verus could only assume the lives of the freemen were indeed dire if they were willing to sell their bodies so readily.

The men were ordered to stand tall, their right fist clenched over their heart. They came forward five at a time, echoing the words of Narcissus, as they swore their lives to the ludus.

"I will endure to be burned, to be bound, to be beaten, and to be killed by the sword, with my very life bound to the will of the lanista."

With the oath complete, and their lives now property of Vipsanius Narcissus, a trainer escorted them to a large building near the centre of the western wall of the complex. Smoke escaped from stone chimneys along one end. Verus, at first, thought this might be a cookhouse. He was soon proved wrong.

A Roman bathhouse was a completely foreign concept to him. One of the large rooms contained a heated pool, which explained the source of the smoke from fires beneath the floor. Another pool was filled with frigid water, and still one more was a warm plunge.

There was a room for changing one's clothes, plus another with numerous tables where slaves massaged and rubbed oil into the tired muscles of various gladiators.

"First thing, we need to get this off you," their guide said, grabbing a handful of Verus' mane.

He was shown to a pair of slaves who washed his hair and beard in a large basin. Mats of hair were chopped from his head, while an impossibly sharp razor sheered away his beard while scraping away the ingrained grime. A bucket of icy water was splashed over his face and remaining hair. Verus let out a gasp of shock and relief. There was a mirror of polished metal on a nearby bench, and he apprised his face for the first time in months. Tiny hairs clung to his neck and shoulders, causing him to itch. His face felt completely raw. It was a rather quirky sight, as his forehead, ears, and upper cheeks were dark from the months in the sun. Whereas his chin and the rest of his face was pale white, streaked with red from the scraping of the razor.

Verus was ordered to strip out of his ratty tunic. The newest members of the ludus were shown into the *caldarium*, or hot bath. This would be followed by a plunge in the *frigidarium*, or cold bath. In between, or sometimes after the cold plunge, one could rest in the *tepidarium*, which was either a warm pool or a heated steam room.

For Verus, who in his previous life had only been able to wash in the brisk tributary from the River Danube, this was an entirely new experience. He stepped gingerly into the steaming hot waters of the caldarium, letting loose a sigh as he sank up to his chest and sat upon a submerged stone bench against the side of the large pool. He took a deep breath and plunged beneath the waters, letting them rinse away the stray hairs and filth. As he slicked what remained of his hair back, he closed his eyes for a few moments and tried to wrap his mind around this profound turn his life had taken. He shuddered to think, had he not assaulted the guard at the quarry, he would still be labouring within the confines of The Pit. He may have just made a pact with death, yet for the first time in nearly a year, he felt a spark of life within himself.

He jolted when a slave touched him by the shoulder. He was puzzled as the man handed him an open bottle of oil and a curved metal strigil. He wordlessly pointed to some of the other bathers pouring oil onto their skin, then running the tool over it to scrape away any dirt or grime.

Having cleaned his skin to the point it felt raw and rinsing the remaining clipped hairs from his head, Verus stepped from the heated pool and made his way through the tepidarium and into the cold room where men were quickly splashing in, letting out yelps of shock as the frigid waters bit into them. Verus, no stranger to bathing in cold water, snorted derisively before jumping in. He, too, let loose a yowl as the freezing waters clenched shut the pores of his skin. Taking a deep breath, he completely submerged himself, relishing the biting cold on his face, neck, and head. He managed to remain in the freezing bath longer than most, though trembling afterwards and deciding to spend a few minutes in the warm pool before retiring to another foyer where he was laid down on a large table. A masseuse vigorously worked the soreness out of his arms and legs, rubbing a pleasantly scented oil into the skin. Afterwards, he found a slave waiting for him with a fresh tunic and new caligae sandals. His threadbare rags and broken shoes from his time in the quarries had been tossed into the rubbish.

"From the rock mines to a place where they bathe and massage you," Verus said, letting loose a short laugh at the perplexity of it all.

His head was stooped as he rubbed the back of his raw neck, which was also shaved during his haircut. Not watching where he was going, he almost ran into quite possibly the largest and most terrifying man he'd ever seen. He stood about half-a-head over Verus, with thick muscles that looked as if they were carved from granite. The man's square jaw appeared to be made of stone that could break the hand of anyone foolish enough to strike him. The colossal figure grinned at Verus and shook his head as he walked around him.

"Who is that?" he whispered to a nearby gladiator, also donning a fresh tunic and sandals.

"Ah, you must be new to the ludus," the man said. "That is Priscus. Quite possibly the most feared man to ever set foot within these walls. He came to us last year, said he was from the furthest reaches of northern Britannia beyond the Empire."

"How many times has he fought in the arena?"

"Just once. But he made such short work of his opponent, Narcissus worries he'll be difficult to book for future matches. And don't let his size fool you; he's as quick as a cat, that one."

The newest members of the ludus were left to their own devices for the remainder of the afternoon. Their guides assured them that their days would be full, and they should make the most of this brief reprieve. It was also made clear to these newest recruits that they were not full-fledged gladiators until they proved themselves worthy of the ludus family. It would be several months of intense training before they were formally tested. If they passed, they would become *tirones*; gladiators who had proven their mettle but had yet to fight in the arena.

"I feel like a new man," Severus said excitedly, as they were shown to their dormitory. He cocked his head before adding, "Bugger me, I almost didn't recognise you! You look completely different without the unkempt mane and beard. Almost...*civilised*."

The men shared a laugh. A slave escorted them to a large section of flats built against the outer stone wall of the complex. The interior walls and stairs were made of stone with wooden floors on the upper levels.

Verus found an unoccupied room on the second floor. The door was dry-rotted and rickety and hung loosely on rusted hinges. Inside, the room was tiny. Yet, it was worlds away from lying exposed in the open with nothing but rotting straw to sleep on. Here, he had an actual bed with a mattress and blankets. There were no other furnishings, just a small alcove cut into the wall across from his bed where sat a tiny oil lamp covered in dust. The entire room was, perhaps, eight feet by eight feet, with just enough height to clear his head. It felt more like a prison cell. However, the door was left unbarred. He could come and go as he pleased. There was also a window across from the door with a single clapboard for a shudder. Verus peered out and saw that it overlooked an open square lined with tall poles, each about six feet in height. He watched for a moment as a score of gladiators attacked these with wooden swords, following the shouted commands of their instructors.

He saw that he was well away from the latrine house. That long, narrow building where gladiators went to relieve themselves was closer to the main gate. A constantly flowing sewer ran beneath the latrine, to wash away the copious amounts of human waist deposited each day, and lessen the stench. It still smelled awful and was constantly attracting flies. Yet it was still a far cry from The Pit, where one practically slept in their own filth.

While his new quarters were very austere, they were by no means the humblest in the establishment. He would have to earn his keep to maintain this measure of freedom and privacy. Gladiators who were *damnatio*—convicted criminals condemned to die in the arena—were confined to actual cells at night with bolted doors and iron bars over their windows.

"I should have been locked in the cells with the rest of the damned," Severus noted, when apprising his friend's quarters. He had found a room on the ground floor.

"Well, don't say anything," Verus remarked.

"Believe me, I don't plan to. If the lanista has forgotten that I was sentenced to death in quarries, or simply doesn't care, then I have a real chance to earn my freedom. I was certain that I was being taken from The Pit, simply to die in the arena."

Something they had overhead Drusus say to one of the condemned new arrivals was that even the damnatio had it better than the gregarii. They were fighters who were deemed useless, as they possessed little to no talent or aptitude for the arena. Their sole purpose was to fight in large brawls with other worthless scum, often-times to the death. They were kept in large, open dormitories, with bunks stacked several high and crammed next to each other. If Verus wished to avoid the fate of the gregarii, he knew he needed to learn his craft well and prove his worth to the instructors. He said as much to Severus, though his friend seemed not to hear him. Instead, his face broke into a broad grin as he grabbed Verus by the shoulders.

"By Jupiter, I can see my family again!"

When Verus gave him a puzzled look, he quickly explained,

"Gladiators who are not condemned can leave the ludus on occasion. If I earn my keep and become a productive member of the gladiatorial familia, I'm certain they will let me go see my wife. I'll finally know if I have a son or daughter!"

Severus was beside himself with joy, and Verus was happy for him. As his friend bounded down the stone steps, practically laughing, Verus let out a sigh. It felt like an added cruelty, knowing that he would not always be confined behind the walls of the ludus. His chances of seeing Tamura and Fillon again were no better now than they were when he was sent to The Pit.

Chapter VII: Forged in Blood

The Gladiator Ludus
Late August, 78 A.D.
***

Verus slept more soundly than he had in months. The mattress on the bed was old and hard, the blanket moth-eaten and threadbare, and used his rolled-up tunic for a pillow. And yet, after nearly a year of sleeping on rotting straw next to scores of equally-decaying souls, exposed to the elements, the crude bunk at the ludus was a bed fit for the gods. So deep and dreamless was his slumber that when a horn sounded at the break of dawn, he forgot where he was. The Dacian bolted upright, eyes wide in confusion.

"Let's go, fresh meat!" a voice shouted from outside their dormitory.

Verus let out a sigh of relief. His memories of his journey from The Pit suddenly flooded back into his conscious. He threw on his tunic and laced up his sandals before rushing down the steps and out into the small, fenced courtyard nearest their billets where Drusus and his team waited impatiently. He spotted Severus, who greeted him with a tired smile.

The twenty prospects assembled in front of several hard-faced instructors. At their feet lay various logs, stones, and all manner of heavy instruments. As the chief *doctor* at the ludus, Drusus personally oversaw the training of their newest prospects. He stood atop a raised platform, a long wooden staff in his hands.

"Before you can wield the sword, your bodies and minds must first be forged. Look to those who have earned their place within the *gladiatorial familia.* You will not find a weak or feeble body among them. To be a gladiator, you must become strong. Now take up the stocks!"

The stocks were large wooden poles with a curve cut out near the centre. This rested on the neck, while the hands went through a pair of holes on either side. The apparatus was both heavy and uncomfortable. It more resembled a means for torturing criminals than for building strength. Several instructors walked the lines wielding staffs like Drusus'. They shouted profanities and gave a sharp rap to the skinnier prospects who struggled just to get the stocks onto their shoulders. There were no whips, however. While physical chastisement was commonplace at the ludus, neither Narcissus nor his instructors wished to break their charges beyond repair. The stinging slap of their vine sticks across the back or legs usually sufficed. While leaving angry welts in their wake, they would not cause any lasting injuries. Those deemed lazy or untrainable would be sentenced to the gregarii.

"The foundation of your bodies begins with the legs," Drusus said. "Upon a strong base will you build a powerful and indestructible body. Now…" He raised his staff and shouted an order.

The men began to do a series of deep squats.

Despite possessing natural strength from the time he was a boy, the months in The Pit had depleted Verus considerably. The weight felt heavy and awkward from the moment he hefted it onto his back. His legs were stiff, and his knees hurt from the shock of exertion. The first six were by far the hardest. Once he reached ten, his legs began to feel warm and loosened up. At Drusus' command, they went even lower, instructors giving a strike across the back to those who did not go deep enough.

After several minutes of endless squats, Verus' legs and lower back burned. The muscles twitched in protest at the unexpected demands placed upon them. He was gasping for breath, each repetition taxing his lungs as much as his legs.

"Oi! No one told you to fucking stop!" one instructor shouted at a prospect who attempted to rest for a moment.

Verus' mouth twitched when he heard the slap of the vine stick, followed by a stifled cry of pain from the unfortunate fellow. Fearing the lash, the rest continued to follow Drusus' shouted commands. Verus' face was red, his eyes squeezed shut, teeth gritted, as sweat streamed down his face and body.

"And rest!" the chief instructor finally shouted.

The prospects all gasped with relief and dropped the stocks. Several men collapsed onto their backsides, only to be met with shouts and blows from the other instructors.

"Who in Hades gave you permission to sit down?"

Drusus gave them a minute to catch their breath before ordering them to shoulder the stocks once more. This time they were to perform jumping lunges. These proved to be particularly difficult. The stocks were unwieldy and already left them off-balance. Drusus kept to a slower cadence; the trainees letting loose a loud shout upon each repetition. Verus' legs and back were in agony. Just when he thought he could continue no further, Drusus would order them to execute another ten repetitions. Upon the order to rest, every man collapsed to his knees or backside. This time, rather than shouted orders and blows from their sticks, the instructors laughed at them scathingly.

"Weak, pathetic cunts won't last a minute in the arena," one snarled, as he spat at the exhausted men.

Drusus left the derision and corporeal discipline to his subordinate instructors. He calmly told the men to take water before continuing. Still gasping for breath, the recruits stumbled over to a series of large wooden buckets; in these, floated numerous wooden cups. They drank thirstily, while some splashed water on their faces.

There was then a half hour reprieve, while they were given breakfast. There was porridge, though it was wheat and thick, unlike the runny barley gruel from The Pit. Meat and fresh vegetables were also part of their morning staple, and they feasted hungrily.

A whistle was blown, and the prospects were herded back onto the training square. They were ordered to stride up and down the long row of stone steps that stretched from the ground to the top of the high encircling wall. The steps were deliberately set to be twice the height and distance as normal stairs. The men were directed to ascend with their hands on their hips, taking long, slow strides all the way to the top.

At the summit was an instructor who forcefully shoved them to the left, where they were to run a complete lap around the entire complex. Verus' legs were wobbly, and his breath came in gasps, yet he was first in his group to reach the top. He felt he was losing his balance and may pitch over the wall. The instructor grabbed him roughly by the tunic and cuffed him across the ear. With a few muttered profanities, he shoved him along. As they were not told how fast to run, he kept to a modest jog, regaining the feeling in his legs and slowing his breathing. The midday summer sun beat down on him, causing him to sweat even more. In just the first few hours of training, he'd pushed his body far beyond what he thought capable. And this was just the first step in a long journey to becoming a gladiator.

Their training continued until long after the sun turned red as it descended into the west. Verus' stomach was twisted in knots from all the times he started to dry heave. The instructors doled out extra lashes to any who vomited, so he painfully swallowed hard and fought against his body's violent protests. Every muscle fibre in his body throbbed in agony as the groan of the horn sounded the end of the day. All he wanted was his bed, yet Drusus and the instructors led them to a massive hall not far from the bathhouse.

Scores of other gladiators from the ludus were already assembling, sitting on wooden benches around numerous tables. Delicious smells of cooking meats came from behind double-doors on the far end of the hall. Tired, sweaty men banged on the tables, demanding to know where their supper was. The double-doors swung open, and numerous slaves wheeled in carts piled high with various meats, potatoes, cabbage, vegetables, with chunks of bread and other assortments.

Only when he was thrust towards one of the tables did Verus realise just how famished he was. He grunted as a pain shot up his back, when he slumped onto the nearest bench. Everything from his neck down to his ankles hurt. A wooden plate was unceremoniously dropped onto the table in front of him, along with a small cup. Servants commenced to heap piles of roasted beef and pork onto his plate, as well as chunks of bread and piles of cabbage. He ate ravenously, nearly choking several times before washing mouthfuls down with watered-down wine. The food was plain and lacked any sort of seasoning, but to Verus and the new prospects, theirs' was a meal fit for the Emperor himself.

On a table at the end of the hall, atop a raised step, sat Drusus and most of the instructors, medics, and other staff. Narcissus was conspicuous by his absence. As the owner of the school, it was clearly beneath him to have his meals with the rabble. Instead, he dined in his manor house, which sat on a small rise just outside the ludus' walls.

His hunger pleasantly satisfied, Verus let out a sigh and began to stand up, thinking it was time to leave.

An instructor grabbed him by the shoulder, forcing him back down onto his seat. He then grabbed a chunk of beef off the nearest cart and slammed it onto Verus' plate. "You're too scrawny. Eat!"

Verus did as he was told, though he was full and now in a state of discomfort.

'Eat!' was shouted from other instructors towards the newest members of the ludus; echoed by the gladiators. The irony was not lost on Verus. His nemesis in The Pit had been starvation, here it was gluttony. He could not even begin to fathom the cost and logistics involved for Narcissus to keep so many men fed to such a degree every day.

The sun had long since set by the time the gladiators of the ludus finished their evening meal. The new prospects were ordered to bathe before retiring to their beds.

"And to think, this was only our first day," Severus said, as he walked over to Verus and leaned his forearm on his friend's shoulder. "I don't know what hurts worse, my battered muscles or my engorged stomach."

"It could be worse," Verus surmised. "We could be back in The Pit battling starvation and disease."

"Yes." Severus held up his hand as he felt a raindrop splash his face. "At least we won't be sleeping out in this shit tonight." He winced and clutched his stomach. "Bugger all, I don't think that cabbage is agreeing with me. I thought it smelled funny…well, funnier than cabbage usually does. I'll be in the latrines for a bit before I bathe."

His eyes heavy, Verus nodded and stumbled into the bathhouse. It was especially crowded. For the first time, he got a real look at the physiques of those who'd been part of the ludus for some time. Though they varied in height, every man carried an unnatural amount of hulking muscle. While the sight was terrifying to the outside observer, Verus was too exhausted to be intimidated. Most of the veteran gladiators ignored him as he found a spot in the caldarium and let the heat soak into his battered body. He only stayed for a few minutes; just long enough to rinse away the sweat and grime from the day's training. He plunged beneath the surface for a moment, before scrubbing his fingers through his soaked hair. He thought about seeing if a masseuse table was available, but he was so utterly exhausted, all he wanted at that moment was sleep.

Squinting his eyes, he stumbled along the path that led to their dormitory. The cool night air gusted over him, and a faint boom of thunder sounded in the distance. He forced a smile, glad he would not be catching his death out in the rain! There was no lamplight to see by inside their flats, and so he had to fumble his way in the dark until he found his room. The clapboard shutter over the lone window was cracked open, allowing a breeze into the otherwise stifling room. Letting out a deep sigh of relief, Verus stripped out of his tunic, rolled it up into a ball, and laid his head against it as he slumped onto his bunk. He didn't even bother pulling the blanket over him. His first full day of training was over, and it felt like it had lasted a lifetime. He dreaded how his body would feel in the morning when it started again.

Within moments, he was fast asleep. And for the first time since his capture, his exhausted mind drifted off into oblivion, devoid of any thoughts at all; not even ones for his wife and son.

Time became a blur for Verus and the other prospects. During their second day, they did little except run and do various bodyweight exercises. On the third, it was all upper body strengthening; lifting heavy weights such as logs and rounded boulders. For the next three months, they did little except condition their bodies. He felt like he was a gladiator in name only, for he had yet to handle a single weapon. Every day, from sunup until sundown, they were either building muscle or expanding their lung capacity and endurance. Evenings were spent gorging themselves at the nightly feast.

Within the first month, Verus gained back all the weight he'd lost during his time in The Pit. By the end of the second month he was noticing muscles on his frame that he never knew existed. Even though his years as a blacksmith rendered him incredibly strong, his old forge could only give him a fraction of the mass he was steadily gaining. By the third month, he felt his newfound size was becoming a hindrance to his speed and mobility. After a morning training session, he expressed his concerns to Drusus.

"The people want monsters, titans of ungodly size," the magister stated. "And that is what we give them, no matter how impractical it may be." He glared at the prospect sternly. "And never forget, you were not an auctoratus when you came to us, but a slave. You should be thanking your gods that you are here. If we'd left you in the quarry, you'd likely be a rotting corpse by now, fit for nothing but the carrion birds. We're giving you a chance at immortality." Drusus scowled and waved him off.

Verus was quick to make himself scarce. The last thing he needed was to enrage the one man in the ludus he held a measure of respect for.

Despite their newfound strength and endurance, the months of savage training took its toll on the prospects. Three failed to maintain the standards demanded by Drusus and were taken away, never to be seen again. Verus suspected they were returned to the mines, or whatever hellish place they'd come from, likely after being brutally flogged. Of those who remained, Severus had managed to adapt well, even though his naturally slender frame struggled to put on sufficient muscle. Because of this, he was given additional rations, particularly meat and eggs, which the instructors practically force-fed him during each meal.

"At least I know I'll never starve here," he laughed, as he and Verus left the enclosure where they took their meals one evening.

"I know I should not complain, given where we came from," Verus said, refusing to mention The Pit by name. "Still, all this size they are forcing us to build; it's not practical."

"Then you need to make it practical." A voice came from behind them. It was Priscus, the hulking Caledonian colossus. Easily the largest and most fearsome fighter at the ludus, the recruits had kept their distance from him. Verus and Severus found his good-natured manner rather disarming.

He continued, "Have the masseuses thoroughly stretch your muscles every day, not just massage them. Once you start training with weapons, you will work on speed."

Verus gave a nod of appreciation. "Thank you…friend?"

"Sure, why not?" Priscus shrugged and slowly began to smile. "At least, until we have to face each other in the arena. You should be picking up the training swords soon. We'll see what you're made of then. Remember, it takes more than just strength and physical prowess to win in the arena. The question then becomes, can you develop the skill, instinct, and mental toughness?"

They would not have to wait much longer to find out.

Chapter VIII: Forged in Steel

The Gladiator Ludus
November, 78 A.D.
***

Verus' body and mind were conditioned to the point that he usually woke a few minutes before the morning horn sounded. With a loud yawn and stretching of his stiff body, he rolled off his bunk and fumbled for his sandals in the dark. He opened the clapboard shutter on his window and inhaled the smell of the previous night's rain. The leaves were changing colour; the autumn air making the mornings cool and brisk.

"They will have already brought in the harvest back home," he said quietly, letting out a melancholy sigh. He briefly recalled the scythe blade he'd been forging for poor Goson. Most likely it still lay where he'd dropped it; covered in rust and never to see a harvest.

Much to his regret, his thoughts about home became less and less since coming to the ludus. His every waking moment was consumed by his training and learning to become a gladiator. Anything else was merely a distraction. For all he knew, his village did not even exist anymore. And his family? Tamura and Fillon were his source of strength when he was languishing in The Pit. Yet even his wife's beautiful face, which he cherished seeing more than anything else in this world, began to fade. It was a strange paradox. Now, with at least a chance for life and the faintest hope of eventual freedom, he felt further from them than ever. His secret fear, however, was that he would forget them completely before he could win his freedom.

He had also ceased praying to his god, Safa. There was no point in asking for protection over his family; either he had saved them from the Romans or he hadn't. Verus reckoned he would never know either way. Besides, a Rhoxolani god of the hearth had no power here. In the ludus, thousands of miles from the Danube, was the dominion of the Roman gods.

As the sun broke over the hills to the east, Verus noticed that the stocks, boulders, and iron weights were missing from their drill field. These were replaced by rows of what appeared to be wooden swords and circular shields. The Dacian beamed. The time had come for the remaining prospects to 'graduate' into combat drills.

At the sound of the morning horn, the prospective gladiators rushed from their billets and onto the sand. Their initial excitement was replaced by a touch of disappointment, when it was noted that their swords were not metal but wood. One of the auctorati scowled as he hefted his weapon. What surprised all of them was just how heavy each sword and shield was.

With a shout from an instructor, they sprinted over to another section of the vast field. Here were rows of wide poles, six feet in height, planted vertically into the ground. Each was battered and covered in gouges.

"You have forged your bodies," Drusus explained, as the prospects each took up position at one of the tall poles in the courtyard. "But, that does not mean we will allow you to become weak. These weapons are twice the weight of an actual gladius and buckler. Only after you've mastered the training stakes, individual drill, and passed the final test will you be allowed to handle real weapons. And only then will it be decided which class of gladiator you are to become."

The early drills were very basic and repetitive. Their initial stance was staggered, with the leg on their sword arm side back. They were told to utilise the balls of their feet and not stand flat-footed. Most of the morning was spent conducting mobility and movement drills, while each man kept his face towards his training stake. Those who stumbled or failed to maintain proper posture were given a smack from the instructors' staffs along with a sharp berating. For Verus, it all felt very natural. Despite the bulky mass he'd been forced to add to his frame over the past few months, he was now glad he'd taken Priscus' advise. The daily stretching of his limbs and torso from the masseurs made him nimble and flexible despite his newfound size. As the drills continued relentlessly, he was grateful endurance and conditioning played such a profound role in their previous training.

Around midday, they were allowed to take water and a short meal of wheat porridge and cabbage before returning to the stakes.

Drusus now carried a metal gladius and buckler instead of his usual vine stick. "The gladius is the perfect weapon for close-combat. For centuries, it has been the blade of choice for the imperial legions. Do not let its short blade fool you, for it is the weapon that has conquered most of the known world. It is heavy enough that it can hack clean through limbs, and light enough to not impede movement or speed."

He handed his blade to Severus, allowing each of the prospects to feel the weight and balance of an actual gladius. Verus was impressed when the weapon came to him. The balance was superior to any sword he'd ever wielded before. He gave it a few practice thrusts. It felt like an extension of his arm.

"You've handled a blade before," Drusus noted.

"Once or twice," Verus remarked, passing the gladius on to the next man.

Drusus went on to explain that while the gladius *could* hack through limbs, it was primarily a stabbing weapon. They spent the remainder of the day and the entire next week practicing stabs and cuts against the training stakes.

The phases of their training appeared to be progressing quickly, especially compared to the slow months of nothing but physical conditioning. There was still plenty of this, though. Most evenings, when weapons training was complete, the stocks and stones were waiting for them. And though most of their waking moments were spent either training, feasting, or bathing, Verus kept an eye on the other training fields within the ludus. Given the intensity of drill he witnessed, he concluded that this phase in their training was to teach them the basics. He knew he would not truly learn how to fight in the arena until after he passed whatever final test Drusus had in store for them.

A month later, the day came to prove their worth. Verus was brimming with confidence. He'd heeded Priscus' advice and laboured intensely to maintain his speed and mobility, while not sacrificing the size the ludus had forced him to add to his frame. This, along with his natural athleticism, helped him master the training stakes in very short order. During one-on-one drills, he'd held his own against most of the instructors and was beginning to feel like a truly balanced fighter. He could utilise his speed against those stronger than him, and his strength against those who were quicker. More importantly, he remained focused, refusing to succumb to arrogance or overconfidence. He was still completely raw with very little training, and he was eager to learn. The only way he would be allowed to learn anymore was to pass Drusus' test.

On the morning of the test, the prospective gladiators formed a line, each carrying a practice gladius and shield. They knew nothing about their opponents, as these men all wore masked helmets. In fact, these were condemned gregarii, who Narcissus was giving a chance at redemption. Any who convincingly bested one of the prospects would be allowed to present his case that he be allowed back into the ranks of the regular gladiators.

Narcissus, Drusus, and a handful of instructors stood watching as each man came forward. Scribes were on hand to take any notes the lanista or doctors dictated. A martial stood ready to officiate each bout.

Verus was sixth in line, and he watched with anticipation as the first man came forward. He and his opponent saluted the lanista then faced each other. At the martial's command, their match commenced. Sword banged against shield, the bucklers occasionally clashing as each man fought to gain the upper hand. After a few moments, the prospect became overanxious and thrust wildly, missing his target completely, before being tripped onto his stomach with his adversary's sword point placed on the back of his neck. The lanista said nothing, but signalled for the men to depart and the next match to begin. This made Verus uneasy. He fought to control his breathing, lest his nerves get the best of him. The next four matches were an even split with two of the recruits besting their opponents, the others defeated.

It was now Verus' turn. He took a deep breath, slapped himself hard across the chest, and stepped out onto the sand. As he sized up his foe, the martial nudged them both with his staff, a reminder that they needed to turn and salute the lanista. Verus nearly panicked, fearing he'd offended Narcissus and would be subjected to his wrath before he even had a chance to prove himself. Thankfully, their master appeared to not notice this transgression.

Following a quick salute, he and his adversary turned to face each other. Verus settled into his fighting stance and inhaled slowly through his nose. A feeling of calmness came over him.

"Fight!"

The masked gladiator lunged at him, attempting to knock him off balance with his shield. Verus' back heel dug into the sand as their shields clashed. Keeping his shield high, he took a swipe at the man's lead shin, missing by mere inches. His startled opponent stumbled backwards. Verus executed a short bash with his shield, yet he kept himself from becoming careless. It was better to gage his opponent's fighting style and any potential weaknesses, rather than rush in for a quick 'kill'. As they squared off again, Verus kept his shield close, then started to rapidly feint with his gladius. He noticed that while his foe blocked or batted away strikes towards the body readily enough, he flinched each time Verus thrust his weapon towards his face. His subsequent counter-strikes appeared haphazard and desperate as a result. Sensing an opportunity, he feinted a thrust to the face. Before his adversary could react, he dropped low and swung at his shin. This time his weapon struck the man's calf. He yelped in pain and dropped his gladius and shield, clutching at the limb. Verus brought the point of his blade up beneath the man's jaw, halting just short of stabbing him in the neck. The martial's staff was quickly thrust between them and forced the men apart.

"Next man," Narcissus said, his expression passive. It felt somewhat anticlimactic for Verus. But this was not a real match, only a practice with wooden swords to see who might be ready to become a gladiator. Regardless, he was relieved he'd passed the test.

Chapter IX: A Monument Eternal

Model of the Flavian Amphitheatre
To the left is the Temple of Venus and Rome, and at the bottom is the Temple of
the Divine Claudius

Though progress on his greatest public work was moving at a painfully slow pace, Emperor Vespasian was pleased with the results thus far. Every stage had been ponderous and painstaking. They had settled on the site of Nero's old Domus Aurea for symbolic reasons. While the late emperor had been popular with the people, his massive 'Golden House' was an affront to any sense of decency. Particularly when so many citizens in various provinces of the Empire, and even in Rome herself, lived in abject poverty. Vespasian, who loathed vulgar displays of wealth that served no other purpose than to satisfy one's ego, decreed that any building projects undertaken during his reign would be for the benefit of the masses rather than himself. The world's largest gladiatorial amphitheatre would be his gift to the people.

It was a strange paradox that despite the popularity of the games, especially within the Roman nobility, lanistae and those associated with gladiatorial matches were considered *infames*, social pariahs who could not vote, hold public office, be buried in Roman cemeteries, and who were scorned by the very people who paid them to put on games for them. Because of this social stigma, most amphitheatres and ludi were constructed on the outskirts of imperial cities. Yet, because of the size and symbolism surrounding this work, the *Flavian Amphitheatre*, as it would be known, was set in the very heart of Rome.

Work began two years after Titus' triumphant return from the Jewish War, funded in part by the treasure and spoils taken from Jerusalem. But before anyone could even discuss construction, Nero's private lake had to be drained. Covering one hundred acres, this was no small task. It took surveyors and engineers several months to construct pipes and drainage trenches to channel the water back into the River Tiber, without flooding parts of the city. It was Titus who suggested leaving this infrastructure in place, should they ever wish to channel water back into the amphitheatre, so they could stage naval combats. Once the lake was drained, it was many months before the ground sufficiently dried and settled that the excavators could begin.

Originally, Vespasian hoped to dig out a *hypogeum*; the subterranean network beneath the amphitheatre, from where gladiators and wild beasts could be raised into the arena on lifts. This was soon discarded for the time being. The plans were drawn up by architects, should the Emperor decide to order its construction at a later date. But for now, the ground was scraped and levelled. Engineers ordered the construction of a large encircling ring of wooden scaffolding, from which the work would continue in earnest. By the end of the first year, the Flavian Amphitheatre consisted of an open flat space between the Caelian, Esquiline, and Palatine Hills, surrounded by a rather crude and vulgar wooden barricade.

The amount of stone required was astronomical, hence the plethora of orders placed to every stone quarry within three hundred miles of the Eternal City. Unbeknownst to Verus, one of the reasons why he was captured and sent to The Pit was to provide disposable labour to fulfil the amphitheatre's inexhaustible appetite for stone. Quarry masters needed slaves, and ambitious generals like Marcus Antonius Primus were more than willing to launch raids beyond the borders of the Empire to fill the need. There was another quarry at Tivoli, just twenty miles from Rome, which supplied travertine for the construction. It was here that most slaves taken during the fall of Jerusalem were sent. However, living conditions were abhorrent and accidents commonplace. Three years later, there was scarcely a Judean from the conquest left alive within the quarry. The chief designers reckoned it would take over three million cubic feet of stone to construct the outer wall alone. While it was easy to calculate the ongoing costs of construction in gold and silver paid to the engineers and architects, one could not put a price on the toll in human suffering.

"It's very modular," Vespasian observed.

He and one of the chief designers walked along the bottom row of the lower bowl, near the north end where the imperial box would be. A similar seating area designated for the Vestal Virgins was directly across, on the southern end.

"Yes, Caesar. As you can see, we've started on the third level, which is much like the second. And you'll be happy to hear that the superstructure will support a fourth level, should you ever decide to make the amphitheatre even larger."

"The view is magnificent." The Emperor paused and rested his hands on the intricately carved stone rail where his personal seat would be.

"We placed the imperial box on the north side, so you won't have your face directly in the sun," the architect noted. He then pointed to the four columns that jutted up from the corners of the imperial box. "While we have plans for a retractable roof consisting of sails, your own seat will have a separate canopy."

Most of the seating was simple benches, except for the lower tier designated for members of the senate. These were open platforms, as senators were expected to bring their own, far more comfortable, chairs. As another means of raising funds, Vespasian authorised the selling of these seats to senatorial families, with the cost increasing the closer they sat to the imperial box.

The second level of seating was reserved for members of the equites and the highest levels for the plebeian public. Interestingly, there were some professions that were banned altogether from the arena. These included gravediggers, stage actors, and, ironically, former gladiators!

"How many spectators will this hold?" Vespasian asked.

"With the current three-tiered structure, about sixty-five thousand. And, of course, we are making certain that plenty of latrines are available on every level. Last thing we need is drunken plebs pissing on the floors."

Though much of the amphitheatre was still under construction, with scaffolds and ladders obstructing the view, Emperor Vespasian could readily envision what it would look like in all its grandeur. Titus had grown impatient during the past couple years, and Vespasian overheard him demanding to know why they could not rush construction. 'The Emperor is not a young man,' he'd said; his greatest fear was his father would die before his amphitheatre could be finished.

Vespasian had chastised his son with good humour, telling him, 'I'm not quite dead!'

His health and constitution had always been strong, though he could understand his son's consternation. After all, the Emperor was just two months away from his sixty-ninth birthday. And if the architects believed they were still two years away from completion, just how much time would he have to personally enjoy this colossal gift he was leaving to the people of Rome?

Satisfied, Vespasian started making his way out one of the passageways called *vomitoria*. This rather vulgar name came from the observation that amphitheatres seemed to 'vomit' people out after the games were over. In a vast empire encompassing hundreds of ethnicities, languages, and cultures, such terms were regarded with revulsion and were distorted into various myths. One Vespasian found particularly amusing, was that Roman nobles had designated 'vomit rooms' where gluttonous guests could purge themselves after gorging during dinner parties. While drunken binges were common enough, the idea that a special room would be needed for them to spew up the contents of their stomachs was absurd.

The sun had set, yet work continued under torchlight. This consisted mostly of unloading the various carts of stone, as they could only travel within the city at night. The Emperor was surprised to find his younger son, Domitian, waiting for him, along with a century of Praetorian Guardsmen who escorted the Emperor everywhere he went. This was, perhaps, the most difficult aspect of his life to adjust to. He hated the idea of having armed guards follow him everywhere, finding it undignified. Though he understood the necessity, he had never gotten used to it; even after almost ten years upon the imperial throne!

"Hail, Caesar," his son said with a bow.

"And a fine evening to you, my son. I expected to find your brother waiting outside…"

"But not me," Domitian finished for him.

Theirs had always been a difficult and awkward relationship. His father was in his forties when Domitian was born, and Vespasian often viewed his youngest child as an afterthought. Titus was naturally the favourite, being the eldest. He'd been groomed for service in the army at a young age and had command of a legion when he was Domitian's age. There had also been a strong bond of affection between Vespasian and his daughter, Flavia Domitilla. She was also the only member of the family who Domitian felt showed him anything resembling love. Despite their six years difference in age, the two had been close. When she died unexpectedly at the age of twenty-one, both father and sons were completely heartbroken. As Vespasian and Titus were thousands of miles to the east, during the re-conquest of Judea, Domitian had had no one to share in his grief.

"As your consular colleague for next year, I thought it only proper," the young man said.

"Ah, yes, of course."

"I, uh, hoped you had enough confidence in me, that I might serve a full term rather than a symbolic two-month suffect consulship."

"You should be thankful you've been given the honour at all," Vespasian remarked, as the two began the slow walk back towards the imperial palace. The Emperor refused to be carried in a litter or chair, and on this occasion, Domitian thought it best to follow his father's example. "You're what, twenty-seven? And you've had five suffect consulships over the past nine years."

"It's not that I lack gratitude, Caesar. I understand that normally one is not even eligible for the consul's chair at my age. But my combined suffect tenures do not even equal one full-term. It's purely symbolic, and given to me only because I am the Emperor's son. I've learned nothing about actual governing and cannot help but feel like I'm a burden to you."

"Not this again," Vespasian grumbled. He sighed and said something he swore he would never mention to his youngest son. "I have enough issues, dealing with your brother's infatuation with Queen Julia Berenice, and what that will do to the imperial succession. The last thing I need is your incessant bickering about not being given enough responsibility."

"I am aware of Titus and his Jewish whore," Domitian sneered. "And I know, perhaps even better than you, that he could undo all we've accomplished should he try to make that harlot his consort."

"All that *we've* accomplished?" Vespasian immediately regretted his words; he could see his son wince, as if a knife had been plunged into his heart.

Surprisingly, the young man regained his composure quickly. "Is it my fault neither you nor my 'dear brother' have any use for me, other than parading me before the senate in some menial role you'd rather not take on yourselves? If you wanted to be rid of me, you should have sent me off to the legions."

"The legions are a place of honour for the Roman nobility, not a place to send unwanted sons." Vespasian quietly cursed himself again. It seemed every time he spoke to his youngest son, he only added to the strain of their relationship. And while he wished to rebuke Domitian for claiming the Emperor had no real use for him, he knew he was right.

Had he been more forward-thinking, Vespasian would have found Domitian a place in the legions under an experienced legate as soon as he came to the throne. This would have given the young man a chance to learn and to prove his worth. After all, Titus had served multiple terms as laticlavian tribune. And the son of his old friend and confidant, Trajan, was well into his second tour as a chief tribune. The younger Trajan was already being groomed for a legion command, and he was two years younger than Domitian.

"You've never trusted me, father."

"It's not a matter of trust," Vespasian countered. "But to be honest, son, I simply do not *know* you…and before you say anything, yes, I accept that this is my fault and not yours. All my hopes for the family have always been placed on your brother. You can imagine the magnitude of added strain, now that we are not just the Flavians, but the imperial family."

"Which is why you should have come to me for help," Domitian stressed. "I know Titus is your co-emperor in all but name. But what of the succession, Father? Who will follow Titus?"

"Unless he sires an heir…that would be you."

"Precisely. And if Augustus had to learn any lesson the hard way, it was to not pin all his hopes on one potential successor."

"Not plotting against your brother, I hope!"

Domitian laughed. It was difficult to tell whether it was intentionally maniacal or simply a matter of nerves. This was probably the first time he'd had any sort of substantive conversation with his father. It was as enlightening for both, as it was awkward.

"Not to worry, Father, I have no plans to usurp my brother once you're gone. I am merely looking out for the family's best interests, and by extension, Rome's. As you say, we are the imperial family, and we owe the citizens of the Empire a stable dynasty. We are both fools if we think Titus will ever sire a son, especially if he insists on pining for his Jewish whore."

"That 'Jewish whore' is an allied queen who supplied our army with coin, as well as thousands of troops, during the Siege of Jerusalem," Vespasian rebuked sternly.

"As you say, Father. But, you are no more keen to see Julia Berenice as Empress Consort of the Roman Empire than I am. And if you listen to the people, the term 'Jewish whore' is mild by comparison to what the masses think of Titus' lover. He should be so fortunate if they only turn on him to the same degree they did Marc Antony."

"Antony was married to the sister of Octavian when he began his affair with Cleopatra," the Emperor reminded him. "He betrayed his fellow triumvir, as well as Rome. One cannot fairly compare this to Titus' affair with Queen Julia." Vespasian gritted his teeth in frustration. As many vehement arguments as he'd had with his eldest son regarding his choice of lover and possible future consort, it was maddening that he was now defending Titus and Berenice against the antipathy of his youngest son!

"Since when is the mob ever fair?" Domitian countered. "Details of what transpired a hundred years ago are forgotten by all except the historians and their dusty books. Logic and reason are not

100

exactly traits shared by the masses. If they were, we wouldn't be able to control them so easily by building amphitheatres and race tracks. Believe me, Father, I have eyes in every corner of the city. I *know* how we control the mob."

"You're a shrewd and devious little shit," the Emperor remarked. "Have you become so paranoid that you need your own circle of spies and informers amongst the masses?"

"It's one of the reasons I'm still alive," Domitian said darkly. "You and Titus were three thousand miles away when half the Empire declared war on Vitellius. The pretender had plans to either dispose of or use me as a hostage. Were I a superstitious man, I would say it was the will of the gods that I survived. Tragically, Uncle Sabinus was not so fortunate."

Vespasian winced at the mention of his late brother, murdered by the Vitellians just prior to the Flavian army's capture of Rome. He suspected his son of grandstanding, as if he had somehow outwitted the Vitellians to save his own neck. In truth, a lot of it had been a matter of dumb luck. That Vespasian's rapport with his youngest son was lacklustre at best had, perhaps, helped save Domitian. Before his downfall, Vitellius even confessed that he did not see any real value to him as a hostage.

"I'll never fool myself into thinking there will be anything resembling love between us, Father," Domitian said bluntly. "Nor between me and my brother. Domitilla was the only one who ever loved and treated me like a member of the family. But unless Titus marries a proper Roman woman and produces viable heirs, I am the best hope for our legacy." He stopped and turned back towards the construction site of the amphitheatre. "But, at least you have your monument of stone. A thousand years from now, posterity will remember the Flavians."

Chapter X: The Gladiatorial Familia

The Gladiator Ludus
November, 78 A.D.
***

In all, twelve of the twenty initial candidates had passed the test to move on to the next phase of their training at the ludus. The rest would return to more basic drills and conditioning under Drusus' direct supervision. Any who failed a second time would be thrown in with the gregarii. Surprisingly, not everyone allowed to progress had won their matches. Four, in fact, were defeated by their faceless adversaries. Yet, their performances clearly impressed Narcissus enough that he felt they were ready to move on.

Immediately after their matches, those who'd proven their worth were ordered back to their rooms to gather all their possessions. The squalid billets they'd occupied were only for new prospects. Those who became permanent members of the ludus would live with those of their same gladiatorial class. As he found an empty room on the ground level of the main dormitory, Verus noted it was only slightly larger than the one he'd come from. However, it was noticeably cleaner and more well-kept. The mattress of his bunk was more comfortable, his blanket less threadbare, and he had an actual pillow stuffed with down feathers. There was also room for a small table and chair.

Verus and Severus were surprised to find Priscus waiting for them just outside. He was sweaty from recent training exertions with a large, fresh bruise forming on his right arm.

"You live in this building?" Verus asked.

"For now." Priscus then explained, "Those who perform well in the arena, and who earn enough coin, can purchase better accommodations. The harder you train and fight, the better your lot in your previously worthless lives."

"Good to hear," Severus replied. "I would have imagined you living like a king."

"After a few more matches I do intend to purchase better quarters. I watched you both fight this morning. Not too bad. Of course, you were fighting the scum of the ludus." His face twisted in a smirk at this last remark.

"And I see you had a bit of a rough go with your sparring," Severus retorted, noting the nasty bruise on Priscus' arm.

"This little thing? Worse happens to most of us every day. Better to be bruised and battered here than bleeding in the arena."

Verus furrowed his brow in thought, ignoring the banter between his companions. "So, who were those men we fought? Were they gregarii?"

Priscus nodded. "And their fate is arguably worse than the damnati."

"I've heard frequent mention of the gregarii, yet I've never actually seen them."

"Would you like to?" Priscus asked. "I know where they are housed. If anything will compel you to train hard and fight well in the arena, it is paying a visit to the scum of the ludus. Come."

A *gregarius* was usually a prisoner-of-war, condemned criminal, or rebellious slave who either failed or refused to be trained. A gladiator who fought poorly and embarrassed the lanista could expect to be disposed of this way. Their value was so pitiful that they were only allowed to fight as part of a larger pack. There was no chance for freedom, only the hope of delaying the inevitable. As Priscus' stated, their fate was no better than the damnati.

Priscus led his mates to a secluded corner of the ludus nearest the latrines. A set of crumbling stone steps led down into a large open chamber. Rickety beds were crammed next to each other and stacked three high. There were ten of these sets of bunks, along with a few small tables and chairs with legs that appeared to be falling off. The room felt claustrophobic and smelled of unwashed bodies.

"By Juno's twat, do these people never wash?" Severus asked in disgust.

"Why do you think their quarters are so close to the shit house?" Priscus added.

"It smells like we're back in The Pit," Verus noted with a scowl.

There were only a few fighters visible in the dimly lit chamber. Most were lying on their bunks with various appendages wrapped in bandages. About half the men were slovenly and unshaven. They kept together almost as if segregated from the rest.

103

"Even among the damned there are those of us who remain civilised," a voice said behind them. "We don't associate with unwashed barbarians, even if we do have to bunk together."

They turned to see a young man with black hair that was short and combed back. He was shorter than Verus and easily the skinniest person they'd seen at the ludus. He looked at them through squinted eyes.

"And how did you find yourself among these lost souls?" Verus asked.

"It's not that I lacked the ability to fight," the man explained, standing tall and defiant. "It's that I can hardly see a damned thing. Took a blow to the head during training. My vision went all cloudy and never fully recovered."

"Isn't there a class of gladiator that fights blind?" Severus asked.

"There is, but I lacked the skill for that. Or at least that's what our benevolent overlord, Narcissus, said. Personally, I think he felt I wasn't worth the effort, and so he cast me down here. I think he finds it amusing that in the frenzy of battle, I'm just as likely to attack one of my companions as I am the enemy."

"A cruel fate," Verus noted. "How long have you been down here?"

"Six months. I can still see enough to make my way around the ludus, find the bathhouse, what have you. If I stand uncomfortably close, I'll be able to recognise your faces, but not much else. I've fought in two pit matches and, somehow, I'm still alive. Half of those in the gregarii when I was sent here have been dispatched to Hades."

Verus felt a sense of familiarity in the man's accent. He spoke to him in Dacian. "Where was home, friend?"

The man's eyes grew wide, his face contorting into a long-absent smile. "Sarmizegetusa," he said. "And you?"

"About six days' southwest of there," Verus replied, still speaking in his native dialect. He added sadly, "My village likely does not exist anymore."

"Ah, so you were also captured during a Roman raid."

Verus was aghast to learn the imperial legions launched many similar raids like the one that destroyed his village. The nearly-blind Dacian, named Dadazi, explained that the Romans needed massed numbers of slaves to work the mines.

104

"The Emperor's building projects, especially his new arena, required far more stone than the quarries could produce. So, his generals on the frontiers go out and acquire fresh slaves."

"That is what happened to me," Verus explained. "I spent ten months in a place we called The Pit before being given a chance to make my pact with death."

"I avoided being sentenced to the quarries," Dadazi explained. "The soldiers who captured me said I fought well, and they had something better in mind. Despite my blindness and the squalid conditions we live in, I suppose they were right. I have no delusions about winning my freedom. Even if I did, what then? Gregarii don't earn coin for spilling blood in the arena. Like the damnati, we continue to fight simply to delay our inevitable deaths."

It upset Verus to see a fellow Dacian reduced so low. There was nothing else he could say. He placed a reassuring hand on the man's shoulder before he and his companions left the depressing dormitory.

"If we ever think we're expendable, all we need to do is pay them a visit," Severus observed, taking a deep breath as they stepped back out into the open air.

"Such a depressing place," Verus said. "Scarcely a step up from The Pit. I was surprised how few there were."

Priscus shrugged dismissively. "There were a few more when I first arrived, and I suspect Narcissus will be looking to swell their ranks just prior to our next games."

"Is it only failed tirones who get sentenced to the gregarii?" Severus asked, drawing a booming laugh from the large Celt.

"By Jupiter's cock, no! One way of knowing when we have a match coming up is when the courts dump their trash on us. Incorrigible slaves, criminals sentenced to death but who aren't worth the effort to train; those are who we will see fighting for their lives as a disorganised mob. That fellow you met, Dadazi, is the exception. I pity him. I watched him train and thought he showed real potential. We were supposed to fight our first bouts during the same matches, when he took that terrible crack to the side of his head. Thought he was dead, at first. That he's half-blind and still survived two pit brawls tells me we lost a potentially great fighter. He's lost so much size, I don't think he bothers to eat much anymore. Poor bastard has given up on life."

105

Having passed the first test, Verus, Severus, and the other candidates were now *tirones*; full-fledged gladiators who had yet to prove their mettle in the arena. They would now train with the other members of the ludus under the tutelage of a mostly new cadre of instructors. Drusus still made his presence known, though his was mostly an oversight and supervisory role. Occasionally, a few new prospects would arrive at the ludus, and these demanded most of his attention.

The tirones would quickly learn that the *gladiatorial familia* had a very strict hierarchy. One was expected to know his place. Tirones were towards the very bottom and would remain so until they fought in their first match in the arena. Their station was only higher than the gregarii and damnati.

At the very pinnacle of the hierarchy were the *primus palus* and *secundus palus*. Modelled after the most senior rank a Roman legionary could aspire to, *centurion primus pilus*, the primus palus was the most revered and senior combatant at the ludus. A free man, he was most often an auctoratus who completed his contract. On extremely rare occasions he might be a slave who'd won his freedom. Regardless of background, he was always a legend in the arena. Many victories to his credit, he could fill the stands of any amphitheatre just by mere mention of his name. For him, the ludus was his very livelihood, and he had no interest in returning to 'normal' society. Because he was a freedman volunteer, he could come and go as he pleased and usually lived away from the ludus with his wife and family. He could negotiate who he fought and what his fees would be. Drusus had been the ludus' primus palus for several years before permanently retiring from active combat due to injuries and advancing age.

Something Verus found interesting was that the primus palus position at their school was currently vacant. The previous holder retired from competition just before his arrival. The secundus palus, who was simply another volunteer of great renown waiting to step into the primus' position, had bled to death after suffering a horrific gash to the thigh during his last match. And despite the protests of numerous magistrates and game sponsors, Narcissus was content to leave the positions open until someone earned the right.

The most common class within the ludus were the *veteres*; gladiators who survived at least one combat in the arena and were considered veterans. A sub-group of veteres were the *missiones*. These were fighters who suffered defeat in the arena yet given a *missio*, meaning they fought well and were spared from death. Though missiones were rated lower than other veteres until they had at least one victory in the arena, they were still rightly feared and respected. Beneath the veteres were the untested tirones and then the gregarii. Each tier within the hierarchy always made certain those beneath them knew their place.

Within the gladiatorial realm, a fighter's reputation depended on more than just his number of victories and defeats. A man who was unbeaten but had only fought against weak combatants that were one step away from the gregarii, were rated lower in the hierarchy than a gladiator who might have an equal number of losses and wins but always fought against the best. Much of this was luck of the draw, for with the exception of the primus and secundus palus, a gladiator did not get to choose his opponent. On the evening after their final test, Verus overheard a rumour that Drusus had won an astounding thirty-two victories in the arena. No one knew how many times, if any, he'd been defeated; and none dared to ask.

The most feared residents of the ludus were the *Damnatio ad Gladium.* The literal meaning was those condemned to 'die by the blade'. These were murderers, thieves, rapists, or any others convicted of a capital crime. Rather than execution, they were sentenced to an eventual death in the arena sand. There was no missio for them if they lost, nor could they be awarded the rudis and palm. Their sole worth was measured in how much entertainment they could give to the masses before their inevitable, bloody demise. This also meant they did not enjoy any of the freedoms or privileges enjoyed by other members of the ludus. They were kept locked in small, cramped cells, where they slept and took their meals, only coming out to train. Their life expectancy was extremely short. Other gladiators hated being paired against the damnati, for they fought with the desperate ferocity of men who, literally, had nothing left to lose.

Unfortunately, potential for advancement out of the tirones often came slowly. Despite their immense popularity, gladiatorial contests were uncommon. In part, due to the costs involved in hosting even a handful of pairings. And when a sponsor did come to the ludus, there was no guarantee of a tiro getting selected for a match. Of course, an auctoratus was delusional if he thought he might hide out his entire contract without fighting in the arena. The cost of feeding, housing, and training gladiators was immense. The lanistae were determined to get a substantial return on each gladiator they invested in. It seemed the only certain thing in a gladiator's life was uncertainty.

Each day came and went like the last: endless training, sparring sessions, strength exercises, and other forms of physical conditioning. The stronger and more fit a gladiator became, the harder the instructors pushed him. It was only when the sun was glowing red in the west that training would cease, and everyone would head to their dining area for another herculean feat that was the gladiators' supper.

One thing that became readily apparent was the hierarchy at mealtimes. Veterans had the first pick of meat, breads, and fresh vegetables. They were also the most closely watched by the doctors and medics who would often grab handfuls of food off serving platters, particularly hunks of wheat bread and thick cuts of meat, practically force-feeding those they felt were not consuming enough.

"Wheat is the staple of our diet here," Drusus explained to some of the tirones, as he paced behind their table. "It digests slowly and will give you energy throughout the day tomorrow."

"I don't give a damn what it is," Severus said, as soon as their senior instructor had walked past. "It's free, and there's lots of it!"

"I've eaten more in a single day here than I did in an entire week in The Pit," Verus remarked.

What surprised Verus most was that, except for the damnati, gladiators who were at least tirones could come and go freely from the ludus. Granted, there was very little time for this; however, about once a week they were given a day of rest. To an outsider, it may have seemed strange that slaves did not attempt to run. For most, being a gladiator was the only chance at 'life' they had. The training was brutal, and there was the ever-present threat of death in the arena. And yet, they had a roof over their heads each night and, as Verus noted, more food than they could possibly consume. Slavery in the arena was far preferable to the 'freedom' of starvation in the gutter.

For Verus, there was the natural temptation to flee to his home and family, albeit they were thousands of miles away. If he were to run, how would he get there; walk half the length of the Roman Empire while stealing food along the way and hoping he did not get caught? It was a possibility, of course. And if he was captured, he could expect a far worse fate than anything that awaited him in the arena. The Romans had a penchant for torture. To them, it was an art form. Verus also saw this as an opportunity. A gladiator could make his name and fortune. If he fought well enough to earn his freedom, he could return to Dacia a very wealthy man.

All these thoughts flooded into his mind as Severus took him to one of the markets not far from the ludus.

"There's someone I want you to meet," his friend explained.

They worked their way through the stifling crowds. It was suffocating for Verus, yet Severus seemed right at home. It was nothing short of astounding that he could find his way so seamlessly through the chaos of humanity. At last, they came across a small vendor stall with a faded blue canopy, near one of the many shrines to the various Roman deities. A broad grin creased Severus' face as he spied the woman selling an amphora of oil to a well-dressed citizen. A length of cloth held a small bundle against her chest.

"Claudia!" he called out, startling the woman. Her eyes grew wide in disbelief, and tears of joy ran down her cheeks.

"Severus?" she asked breathlessly, forgetting about her client for the moment. "Severus!" Clutching the bundle with one arm, she wrapped the other around her husband's neck, kissing him repeatedly. "Wh…what happened to you? They sentenced you to the mines, and I thought you were dead."

"And I probably would have been, if Nemesis had not found a use for me."

"You're huge," Claudia remarked, clutching at one of his thick arms.

"They made me a gladiator," Severus explained.

Claudia appeared not to hear him and was drawn to the bundle she carried. She pulled back the cloth to reveal the face of a sleeping baby. Severus beamed as he placed a hand gently on the child's head.

"Your son, Lucius," Claudia said.

"My son…" Tears now came to Severus' eyes. The child he thought he would never know, yet already loved with every fibre of his being. Claudia handed the babe to him. Severus' hands trembled with emotion. He then remembered his friend. "Claudia, this is Verus."

Claudia gave a friendly smile which Verus matched.

"An honour to meet you," he said.

"I can't place your accent," Claudia said, her ear cocked towards him. "Where was home for you?"

"Dacia," he replied sadly. "My people, the Rhoxolani, live north of your borders, yet I found myself here." He felt rather awkward and wished to give Severus some time to spend alone with his family.

For the moment, Claudia returned to finish her transaction with the impatient client.

"Think you can find your way back to the ludus?" Severus asked.

"No idea. I suppose if I keep the sun at my back, I'll find it eventually."

It took the better part of an hour for Verus to work his way through the congested streets and up one of the surrounding hills. He found himself in a large open-air garden near a cluster of residential flats. The ludus was below him about a half mile away. To the west, he could clearly see the towering hill with the magnificent temple to the god, Jupiter. There were, in fact, many temples and shrines atop the hill, yet the Temple to Jupiter dwarfed all of them combined.

The sprawling metropolis that was the heart of civilisation was completely foreign to Verus. From above, there was a certain beauty to be found in the city of Rome. The architecture was stunning and not just the magnificent temples. Even from a distance, he could see the palatial splendour of the manor houses belonging to the imperial elite. With their ornate stone pillars, tiled roofs, and each with its own set of gardens, even King Duras of Dacia did not live in such magnificence! Of course, these contrasted sharply with the vast sprawls of humble flats belonging to the rest of Rome's populace. Verus noted that the three-level insula block behind him was only a fraction of the size of a single palatial home and likely housed thirty families instead of one.

His countenance darkened as his thoughts returned to his own home; the home which this empire had ripped him from while slaughtering his people. While the swarms of citizens he watched had not been the ones who attacked his village, nor could many of them even find Dacia on a map, they were still enemies of the Rhoxolani. Verus knew he should hate the Romans. And yet, his passionate loathing for the imperials had all but evaporated. Not only were there no more feelings of rage, but soon he would be fighting in the bloody arena for the very amusement of his people's enemy. Perhaps it was a sign. Between The Pit and the gladiatorial ludus, they truly had broken his spirit and bent him to their will.

Chapter XI: The First Match

The Gladiator Ludus
December, 78 A.D.

Provocator-class Gladiator

"At last!" Narcissus said excitedly, handing the scroll to Drusus.

The two were sharing breakfast at Narcissus' manor house overlooking the ludus. It was a brisk December morning, and most of the populace was rapt with anticipation for the upcoming week of Saturnalia, later in the month.

"Ah, Gavius Atticus wants to sponsor some of our gladiators," Drusus replied as he read the letter.

"Yes," Narcissus remarked. "The man who served as suffect consul two years ago. He wishes to commemorate his daughter's marriage to Acilius Strabo with both a chariot race and a series of gladiatorial matches."

"How many pairings?"

"Eleven." Narcissus handed his magister another parchment bearing the request details.

"The coin he is offering will not pay for our finest," Drusus noted. "We can, perhaps, give him two feature matches and a few showcases with some of our fresh talent."

"Agreed. Atticus may have sat in the consul's chair, but he is a man of limited means. Still, when it comes time for negotiations, I'm certain I can squeeze a few more sestertii from his purse. He's asked for ten of our newer gladiators to face off against ten novices from the ludus of Annius Proculus."

"A chance for us to make good on our investment of that lot from Cottanello. And what about that big fellow we retrieved from Britannia, Priscus? It's been almost a year since he last fought.

"His potential is downright terrifying," Narcissus remarked. "Especially since you've been working with him. I just worry about him killing his opponent."

"He's become more disciplined since coming here," Drusus reassured him. "He knows he can win greater fortune and fame by staying within the laws of the arena. But I agree, his strength alone is enough to tear a man's head from his shoulders. And he's quick."

"I suspect he'll make an example out of whoever Proculus pits against him. But since he only has one match to his credit, I doubt Atticus will want him in the feature bout."

"And unfortunately, we still have no primus palus," Drusus added, much to Narcissus' annoyance.

"What in the bleeding fuck would you have me do about it?" the lanista asked in irritation. "It is an unfortunate circumstance that most of our veteres are still lacking in experience. Would you have me offer freedom to a fighter with only four victories, just so we can say we have a primus palus? My reputation would be ruined! And you know I am not about to grovel to any retired gladiator that hasn't already decided to continue fighting."

"Fair enough," Drusus replied, raising his hands in resignation. "I was just making an observation."

"If you had a few less grey hairs, I'd ask you to come back for one last match," Narcissus said with a wicked grin.

"Yes, well, thankfully you can only *ask* me to come back," the instructor said with a tired smile. "Not that it hasn't been tempting. But I was too old for bleeding in the sand ten years ago."

Negotiations for a gladiatorial contest were tedious but necessary. In addition to the sponsor—also known as the *editor*—and lanistae, an accountant and lawyer attended to make certain all proprieties and laws were observed, as well as to assume responsibility for the necessary deposit made by the sponsor. Because gladiators were using actual weapons there was substantial risk, even if the sponsor had no intention of having any of the fights go to the death. As such, he was required to put down a deposit, to be held by the accountant, to pay the cost of any combatants who died in the arena. And while there were generally accepted rates, these had never been set into law by the imperial government. This meant a lot of negotiation over the worth of a class of combatant.

"If you want two groups of ten gregarii to fight until one side is annihilated, it will be a thousand sestertii each," Narcissus stressed.

The bronze sestertius was the most common currency used and valued at one-quarter of the silver denarii. Proculus nodded in agreement. The two men were hated rivals, yet on this day of negotiation, they were best of friends.

"This is thievery!" the former consul grumbled. While he found it beneath him to even speak to infames like Narcissus and Proculus, he preferred negotiating the terms of the games' cost personally rather than tasking one of his freedman clerks.

"That is the going rate," Proculus spoke up.

"To Hades with that," Atticus snapped. "You cannot tell me that a bloody slave, whose only worth is making a nice corpse in the sand, is worth more than an imperial soldier's annual wages!"

"Dead, they are," Narcissus surmised. "And since you're wanting mostly tirones for the actual matches, I'm sure we can settle on say…four thousand sestertii each." He shot a glance to the other lanista.

Though intense rivalry existed between the various ludi, when it came time to suck the last copper and silver coins from the rich patricians sponsoring the games, they were inseparable allies. The lanista gave an almost imperceptible nod of concurrence.

"If you wish for veterans, our minimum is six thousand for those with at least two victories," Proculus said.

After much grumbling, the lanistae relented and reduced their rate on tirones to 3,000 sestertii each and 5,000 for veterans. This was, of course, only the deposit to be paid to the lanista in the event a fighter was killed. There was also the matter of the fee for using their gladiators, which was one third of their overall value. A portion of this would also be paid to the fighter, depending on whether he won or lost and if he survived.

"I can offer you a pairing of women for scarcely the cost of two gregarii," Narcissus added, as the negotiations were reaching their conclusion.

"Not for me, thank you," Atticus said, his voice etched with irritation. Even if there were no fatalities aside from the gregarii, this spectacle was going to cost him a fortune. "I want these games to be remembered as a classic spectacle, not some vile freak show."

Narcissus gave a shrug, muttering that it was a shame. While women gladiators were a rare novelty, most games had at least one such pairing. Narcissus had spoken in the past about pairing one of his women against a man. This was scandalous, to the point he could have his license revoked by the imperial state. Though gladiatorial matches were almost as old as Rome herself, the first female combatants only began appearing in the arena during the previous twenty years. They were usually incorrigible slaves whose masters could no longer control them. The only time a freewoman fought in the arena was if she was a young and impoverished divorcee who preferred a life of violence to one of prostitution. All the same, they were considered a novelty attraction and rarely taken seriously. Within the gladiatorial games, for every hundred pairings there might be one or two involving women. For those with more perverse tastes, dwarves or those with various physical handicaps were compelled to fight each other. But these were even rarer than contests with female gladiators.

"I think we are finished," the accountant said at last.

Negotiations had taken two hours, and everyone was anxious to leave, particularly the former consul. He reckoned he would take a lengthy bath to wash away the contagion of having lowered himself to dealing with these disgusting men.

The accountant, also an imperial magistrate in charge of licensing the games, addressed the lanistae. "I will have your fees. These will be paid at the end of the contest, as well as the deposits for any unfortunates who end up meeting Charon on the River Styx."

115

The news of the pending match quickly reached the men of the ludus. Priscus was especially filled with excitement when told he would be fighting.

"This is only my second fight," he explained to Verus and Severus. "I wonder if they'll give me another retiarius? Or will they find me a better challenge? I completely thrashed the last man who fought with net and trident."

"I don't care who I fight, so long as I get a match," Severus remarked.

Claudia had managed to survive during his absence by opening an olive oil stall, but she and little Lucius were struggling to keep their tiny flat and enough food to eat. He needed a fight if he was to help provide for his family.

A handbill had been drawn up listing the pairings and each gladiator's class and number of victories. Under this last column, almost all the fighters had 'tiro' listed next to their name, meaning this would be their first contest in the sand. And because most gladiators were illiterate, the doctors would read the handbill to them. Verus quickly forgot the name of the man he would be fighting, but he was a murmillo-class; a heavily-armoured gladiator fighting with a gladius and large, rectangular shield.

While there were many classes of gladiator, most at their ludus fought as *provocators*. These wore a large helmet, with either a covered or open face, a padded manica on the left arm, a wide leather belt around the middle, and a single greave to protect their lead shin. A metal plate came off the shoulders to protect the upper chest. It was up to the individual combatant whether they carried a rectangular shield, similar to the legionary scutum, or small circular buckler. All wielded the gladius as their primary weapon.

Priscus was thrilled when he heard he would be fighting against a heavily armoured murmillo with three victories to his credit. "Slow-moving bastards wear too much shit."

Severus was just relieved to see his name on the list. He would be fighting a *secutor*, the same class as him. Secutors, also called *chasers*, were a medium to light class who fought with a gladius and smaller rectangular shield. Most often they were paired against the

116

minimally equipped *retiarius*; light fighters armed with net and trident and very little armour.

For the eleven men who would be fighting in the games, Drusus kept the training light throughout the week leading up to the contest. The day before was one of rest. During the mid-afternoon he came and ordered them all to bathe and don their best tunics.

"Our best tunics?" Verus asked.

"Of course," Priscus said excitedly, "tonight is the feast!"

"What feast?" Severus persisted.

"The night before any games the sponsor always holds a large banquet," one of their mates explained.

"And if Aphrodite smiles upon you, one of the ladies will show her *appreciation*," another spoke up.

That evening the gladiators from the ludus made their way to the manor house belonging to Atticus, the former consul. Only the main combatants were invited; the gregarii were confined to their dormitory, though they were given an extra portion of meat at their supper. And while the carrying of weapons was prohibited within the city, permission had been granted for a dozen armed guards to act as escorts to keep the unruly and overeager crowds at bay. Narcissus left several hours before his charges. And so, it was Drusus who led them through the crowded streets along Aventine Hill, south of the imperial palace. The sun set early in the Roman December, and it was well after dark by the time they departed in mule-drawn wagons.

The outer gate to the estate was flung open, and the men dismounted the carts. Verus had only previously seen the palatial homes of the wealthiest Romans from a distance. Most of the city was covered in humbler flats belonging to the poorer classes of society. The garden alone held him in awe at the displays of wealth owned by a single man. The hedges were neatly trimmed, the grass cut short; flowering plants, fountains, and statuary lining the path leading into the main house.

"Ah, our noble guests," the freedman in charge of the household staff said. He bowed as he greeted the assembly of gladiators.

They were led into the foyer. Oil lamps hung from copper chains; their light reflecting off the polished tile floors. Painted frescos adorned the walls and even the ceiling. Music from lyres and flutes resonated from down the hall along with the sounds of drunken merriment.

The freedman led the band of fighters into the large dining room, where about twenty noblemen and their wives lounged on couches. Surprisingly, there was about twice as many women who were unaccompanied. They mostly ranged between early thirties to mid-fifties in age. All wore elegant stolas and were adorned in expensive jewellery and makeup. Furthermore, they were eyeing the gladiators lasciviously.

Atticus rose from his couch, clapping his hands to silence the musicians and revellers. "My friends!" he called to the gladiators. "As you can see, you have your own table for this humble feast."

It surprised Verus to see the former consul's guests fawning over them as if they were conquering heroes, when at any other time he would spit on them. Drusus told them to enjoy themselves, but cautioned against ingesting too much wine, lest it affect their performance the following day.

The feast itself was spectacular with greater quantities of fine foods than Verus had ever laid eyes on. Some of the courses he found rather revolting, such as roasted dormice. However, there was plenty of lamb, goat, pig, as well as assorted fresh fruit, vegetables, and various nuts than the Dacian had never heard of.

As the evening wore on, many of the gladiators became better acquainted with the various unattached women.

Verus grinned as he watched Priscus being led away by a rather fetching younger noblewoman, whose stola failed to hide her shapely hips and breasts. "I wonder who she is."

"Probably some widow or divorcee," Severus speculated. "Those are usually the desperate types who take pleasure in our more intimate company. Something exotic about sleeping with a fellow on the night before he leaves his bloody corpse in the arena."

"I think Priscus is the last of us who will end up as a bloody corpse."

"Even better," Severus said. "If he wins spectacularly tomorrow, she can tell all her friends, 'that fellow ploughed me like a rutting stallion'." He thought for a moment and added, "From what I've heard about these feasts, it is not uncommon for the host's wife to satisfy herself this way."

"And he would be fine with that?" Verus was appalled at the idea, though Severus appeared nonplussed at the concept.

"We're all slaves here, even those of us who were born free. And under Roman law, it is not considered adultery if one chooses to satisfy their carnal lust with a slave. Which is why I have been waiting for that fetching beauty over by the bust of Minerva to come and introduce herself."

"But your wife is just across the city," Verus protested.

"Yes, but she is not here," Severus stressed. "Trust me, she has taken her share of men and women since I was first sent away. I think she will be happy to hear that I've been used as some patrician's plaything. If you will excuse me…" Severus laughed and smacked his friend on the shoulder, deciding to take the initiative and introduce himself to the young woman who'd been glancing his way all evening.

There was no shortage of noblewomen seeking a few hours of company with one of the gathered arena combatants. After the games on the morrow, the survivors would be regarded as scum once more. Even the most famous to ever fight in the arena were still infames. Yet, for the briefest of moments, they became like gods. It was a perverse paradox Verus would never understand.

Verus did not remember falling asleep that night. For the first time, he failed to wake before the sound of the morning horn. After a short breakfast, the combatants were hustled into a waiting cart. Special permission was granted for the wheeled transport to be used during the early hours, and a company from the city's urban cohorts provided escorts to keep the streets clear. The arena itself was in an obscure neighbourhood on the outskirts of the city, about half a mile north of the Forum of Vespasian. It was small with capacity for perhaps six hundred total spectators. About a hundred seats were occupied by Atticus, his extended family, and that of his future son-in-law. The rest were open to the public, with priority given to any members of the senate or equites who wished to attend.

Combatants were kept in a pair of chambers on the east and west wings of the arena. Armourers and medics had arrived about an hour before the gladiators. Drusus then briefed the men on what order they would be fighting in, and ordered the first to get ready. Some of the gladiators gathered around the barred windows looking directly out onto the sandy pit. Verus, however, refrained from watching any of the other contests. His was to be the fourth match of the day. Priscus would be in the opening bout, immediately prior to the gregarii. Narcissus intended to use his prized gladiator as a means of setting the stage for the rest of the afternoon. Five pairings, plus the gregarii brawl, would be contested this day, with the remainder on the morrow.

While the chamber they occupied was quite large, it was crammed with other gladiators, instructors, armourers, medics, and staff. The gregarii were escorted past the senior gladiators, who leered at them, and told them 'not to shame the ludus!' Narcissus had told all the gladiators before they departed for the arena, "Embarrass me, and I'll make you wish you'd died in whatever shithole I found you in!"

From his place near the sponsor's box, Narcissus watched the opening contest with anticipation. He left the actual supervising of his combatants to Drusus while he mingled with the patricians and other noble guests. It gave him no small measure of satisfaction that the same men who now praised and thanked him for bringing his gladiators, would spit on him any other day. And though it was a serious breach of protocol, he even took the occasional wager. This was to be expected, though no lanista would ever place a bet against one of his own gladiators. The idea that a fight could be fixed would undermine the entire games and ruin the reputation of the ludus, not to mention landing the offending lanista in serious trouble with the law.

Most of the wagers were friendly in nature and only for a few dozen sestertii. Narcissus did, however, manage to convince a pompous old senator, who'd once called him 'an infamis cunt', to wager the princely sum of a thousand denarii on Priscus' bout. The arrogant nobleman had never laid eyes on the Caledonian and only knew he had a single victory in the arena. When he saw the monstrosity stride out onto the sand, his face turned pale. Narcissus smirked contentedly.

Priscus' opponent, a heavily-armoured provocator, was a big man in his own right and just a couple inches shorter than the Caledonian. He wore a bronze plate over his upper chest and a wide studded belt around his midsection. His sword arm was heavily wrapped, and a single greave protected his lead shin. His face was completely obscured behind his encompassing helmet. In addition to his gladius, he wielded a curved rectangular shield.

In contrast, Priscus wore an open-faced helm with a light leather cuirass protecting his upper torso. He also elected to not wear any sort of protection on his sword arm, stating it would hinder his mobility. His choice of shield was a small circular buckler.

At the martial's order, the fight commenced. Given his opponent's comparable size, Priscus elected not to attempt to bowl the man over with a clashing of their shields. Instead, he circled to his right, occasionally feinting with his weapon, testing his adversary's speed and reaction ability. The provocator was an experienced fighter. He, too, took the time to measure his opponent and test him with occasional blows from his shield.

Both men knew they could not spend too much time feeling each other out, lest the crowd become restless. Priscus thrust his gladius towards the right side of the man's helm, only to have his blow deflected by the provocator's shield at the last moment. He rightly suspected that the man's helmet, with just a few holes to see through, left him virtually blind on the flanks. He caught his adversary off-guard by lunging forward, allowing their shields to clash. He then chopped the man's shin with his blade. And while the greave absorbed most of the blow, it caused the provocator to yelp and stumble backwards. Giving him no time to regain his footing, Priscus lurched to his left, stabbing at the man's exposed belly. With alarming speed, he then kicked the provocator's rear leg out from under him, sending him flying onto his back. Before the martial could restart the match, Priscus kicked his opponent's shield away and placed the point of his gladius on the man's throat. This elicited a voracious ovation from the crowd. Priscus looked towards the sponsor's box. Atticus slowly stood and took a cursory glance at the

121

crowd before raising both his hands. Priscus stepped away, while his defeated opponent stumbled to his feet, his head bowed in shame.

Narcissus' expression remained unchanged, though he gave a slow nod of approval. The Caledonian beast he'd brought back from Britannia was finally proving his worth.

The gladiators from Narcissus' ludus gave a loud cheer as Priscus strode through the gate, arms raised in triumph, as he let loose a victorious roar. He locked eyes with Verus for a moment. Priscus brought his gladius up to his chest in salute before continuing to where slaves awaited to help him out of his armour.

Sounds of shouting and the clashing of many weapons echoed from out in the arena as the gregarii brawl commenced. Some of the gladiators walked over to the barred windows to heckle the mob of misfits. Their collective lack of skill was evident in how they handled their weapons. Severus, whose match was not until the morrow, watched with amusement, losing count at the number of times fighters left themselves exposed by swinging their swords wildly. Their equipment was far inferior to that of regular gladiators; consisting of rusted and half-broken bits of armour and weaponry that had long outlived their usefulness.

"One has to admire their tenacity," Severus said appreciatively.

Since they did not know any of the gregarii personally, it was impossible to differentiate between the two sides. And there was no sense of cohesion or order like there would be in professional armies. Within less than a minute all combatants were engaged in a furious and chaotic frenzy.

The advantage would be quickly decided by whichever side managed to fell an opponent first. And because this brawl went until one group or the other was destroyed, there were no martials or overtures made to spare the fallen. Severus winced as one man took a hard chop between the neck and shoulder, driving him to his knees. The man's screams were drowned out by the roar of the crowd, as well as the continuing clash of weapons and shields. His adversary, knowing the man was done for, did not bother to finish him even as the poor wretch writhed about in agony; his life's blood gushing from the hideous wound. Instead, the victorious fighter scampered behind another pairing, stabbing a rival gregarious in the back. This elicited a harsh chorus of boos from the crowd. In a fight for their very survival, no one on either side gave a damn about giving their opponents a sporting chance.

Within minutes the brawl was over. While the regular gladiators despised the gregarii out of principle, there were a few cheers and accolades when it was determined their fighters had prevailed. Every gregarious from their rival school lay dead or maimed. Six fighters from Narcissus' ludus had fallen as well. Two of the four remaining clutched at their bloody sides and arms, having taken a terrible mauling in gaining their victory.

"And what prize awaits them?" Severus asked aloud.

"They're allowed to live another day," a veteran gladiator said dismissively.

It was another hour before it was Verus' turn. He closed his eyes and took slow, deep breaths as the armourers fitted him into his breastplate and greaves. A combination of nerves and excitement coursed through his veins, and he struggled against the trembling in his hands. He wasn't scared, per se, though this would be his first time fighting with actual weapons and not wooden training implements. While most matches were ostensibly not 'to the death', much depended on the bloodlust of the crowd and the wealth of the sponsor. If this man was a former consul, then he could likely spare a few hundred denarii to sate the desires of the mob. And of course, there was the inherent risk of fighting with actual weapons, while only wearing a minimal amount of armour. Verus shook his head and forced such thoughts from his mind. If he met his end this day, then so be it.

"Verus!" Drusus called to him. The gladiator gritted his teeth and nodded. With forced confidence, he walked briskly past the magister, who gave him a reassuring smack on the shoulder as he strode into the arena.

The crowd cheered as Verus' name was announced. The sands were black and sticky from the blood of the fallen gregarii earlier. As a provocator, Verus was equipped identically to Priscus, even going so far as to elect to wear an open-faced helm.

123

The man he faced was a murmillo-class wearing a large, plumed helmet with a grill visor. His sword arm was protected by a mail manica, and bronze greaves covered his shins. He wielded a gladius and a large rectangular scutum shield, much like that carried by imperial legionaries. He also wore a similar cuirass of segmented plate armour to protect his torso. This suddenly disrupted Verus' focus. The shield was heavily battered and painted blue; the same colour as the legion that had attacked his village. Suddenly, he was no longer standing in the sand of the arena, but back in Dacia, facing the onslaught of the Roman army…

The rap of the martial's staff across his chest snapped him out of his disturbing reverie. Verus cursed that he was wearing an open-faced helm, for it revealed his face was already red and sweaty. He swore he could see his opponent sneering behind his mask. With a signal from the martial, both men turned to face the sponsor and raised their weapons in salute. The crowd let loose a raucous cheer which helped calm Verus' nerves. The two then turned to face each other, and he noticed the murmillo's stance was almost identical to that of a legionary. The issue when fighting a man wearing so much armour and carrying a scutum was that there were so few vulnerabilities to strike. Verus knew he would have to use his speed and hope this man was not quicker.

As the martial snatched his staff away, the battle commenced. The murmillo stalked him, half-stepping forward and forcing Verus to circle. Their shields came together, and Verus attempted a thrust at the man's neck, only to have the scutum knock his arm upward, the point of his gladius deflecting off his foe's helmet. He leapt backwards, as he anticipated the murmillo would tilt his shield and attempt to jab him with the bottom edge. A loud cheer echoed from the crowd, causing Verus to smirk as he attacked once more. He thrust his gladius high, trying to keep the man distracted by having to continuously protect his face. He kept his own shield close and tried to watch the murmillo's sword arm in his peripheral vision. A couple of thrusts were deflected off his shield, yet they lacked conviction. He was suddenly aware that his opponent had to move very little to protect himself with his large shield. He simply had to pivot while maintaining a solid base with his feet. Conversely, Verus needed to exert a lot of speed and energy to maintain his assault.

124

Then with a heavy punch, the murmillo landed the bronze shield boss against the side of Verus' helmet. Verus stumbled backwards, narrowly avoiding a strike to the stomach from the bottom of the shield. His opponent lunged for him, keeping his shield near his body, sword arm back ready to drive his gladius home. Verus tumbled to the side, his head still spinning as the murmillo's charge missed him completely. His vision clouded, he still managed to see the murmillo was off balance. He staggered forward and thrust his weapon towards the man's exposed flank. The point stuck in the wide studded belt, the blade snapping in two. Verus was horrified by this turn of events. Before he could react, the murmillo slammed the bottom edge of his shield into the exposed lower stomach sending Verus onto his back, the wind taken from him. The murmillo did not even bother to stand over him with his weapon aimed at his throat. Instead, he raised his arms and shouted in triumph as the sponsor stood and applauded. Verus was helped to his feet by a pair of slaves. He shoved them off and stormed back to the gate that led to his team's armoury. His months of relentless training and physical punishment, ended by the breaking of a shoddy weapon.

Chapter XII: Redemption or Death
***

Seething with rage, with the adulations of the mob still echoing from the stands, Verus threw the broken weapon onto a table and practically tore the helmet from his head. "What is this *shit?*" he bellowed at the armourer. "Are you *trying* to get me killed in there?" Verus had to be restrained by a pair of gladiators, as he threw his helmet at the man. His face was red with fury.

"I don't know how this could have happened," the armourer said, almost nonchalantly. He picked up gladius. It was a perfect break running straight across about two inches above the pommel. "Beastly bad luck."

"It cost me the fucking match and almost my life!" Verus snarled.

"Hold!" the voice of Drusus echoed, as he walked into the chamber. "What is all this about?"

"This…" Verus said, wrenching himself from the clutches of his mates and snatching the weapon from the table. "This piece of shit cost me the match."

"No," Drusus said, shaking his head. "Your carelessness cost you the match. Had you not allowed the murmillo to send you careening onto your ass, the martial would have stopped the match. You both would have continued bare-handed. Keep in mind, this is not a mindless brawl, whatever it may appear to the mob. Know the laws of the arena and use them."

He then slapped Verus on the shoulder. It felt like part rebuke and part reassurance.

While he understood the magister's intent, it did little to assuage Verus' anger. Not only did he feel cheated, but as a former blacksmith, he knew the weapon he'd used was of shoddy craftsmanship. Dropping the broken blade, he retired to another room where the medics were waiting to examine each combatant as they left the arena. Verus wasn't aware of it, but he was bleeding from the back of his leg. He had no idea how he'd received the injury; whether the murmillo had landed a strike he could not recall, or if there was something more than sand on the arena floor and he'd cut his leg during his fall.

The medic ordered him to sit on the edge of a long table with his leg propped up on a stool. "That's not too bad," he noted. "Just a minor flesh wound."

The door opened. Priscus walked in, his face impressed with concern. "I saw your match. You fought well. That murmillo had you reeling for a time, but you were starting to learn his tells. His balance was poor. Had you gotten back to your feet, I think you could have taken him."

"Until my damned weapon broke," Verus grumbled. He ran his fingers through his hair in frustration. He winced as the medic began to clean the wound with a pungent smelling liquid. "I can't believe I'm beginning my career as a gladiator with a loss."

"Your opponent did not even bother waiting to see if you were to be spared," Priscus recalled. "Everyone knew you gave a good showing out there. That is all that matters."

"Easy to say, for the man who's never tasted defeat." Verus scowled.

Priscus' face broke into a twisted smile. "You really think I've never been beaten? Remember, I was fighting for years in Britannia before I came to Rome. Granted, these were less-than-organised bouts in the far north, with neither martial nor rules to abide by. And, I was just a boy when I started fighting. It was the only thing I was good at. It kept me alive, and the local warlords amused for a time."

"Did you lose your first match?" Verus asked, his brow creased. He could not envision this monstrosity ever being defeated.

"No, but I lost a few after."

"How many?"

"More than a couple," Priscus replied evasively. He raised his hands from his sides and glanced down at his own body. The muscular frame bore numerous scars, some of which ran deep. Verus wondered how his friend had not bled to death. "But, as I am still here, I would also say 'less than too many'. Those who bested me never forgot who I was; I saw to that. And I was fortunate enough to avenge my first two defeats. Those poor bastards did not live long enough to learn from their mistakes. And trust me, that murmillo will never forget you. In a fight without rules...and with a better weapon, you likely would have killed him. He *knows* this, and so does the crowd. Now quit feeling sorry for yourself. You're a veteran now."

"A missio," Verus corrected. "I'm sorry, but I cannot leave here with nothing but a loss to show for it."

Priscus shrugged. "Well, maybe they'll give you another match, provided the medic says you're fit to fight. But be careful what you ask for. A sponsor may not prove merciful if you are defeated twice in a row."

"He what?" Atticus asked, utterly perplexed.

"He wants another chance to prove himself," Narcissus said, casually taking a sip off his wine.

The two lanistae were invited to dine with the sponsor and his other guests. While this was met with chagrin by the friends of the former consul, Atticus treated the gladiator owners cordially.

"He's a damned slave, so I don't give a cup of piss what he wants," he retorted.

"And what if *I* requested it?" the lanista asked.

Atticus scoffed. "You're an *infamis.* What you want rates scarcely more than a slave," Atticus countered. He paused for a moment and addressed the other lanista. "What say you? Do you have a fitting opponent for this upstart?"

"I have," Proculus replied. "And if your excellency wishes, I will see to it that he is taught a harsh lesson for his impudence."

Atticus glared at Narcissus. "Alright, I will authorise the match. But know this, if your man doesn't bring the arena to its feet, I don't give a damn what it costs to replace him, the sand will drink his blood."

That Atticus had been offended by Narcissus' request was unknown to all except the few who'd witnessed it. Instead, the former consul decided to play up the crowd the following day, adding to their adulation, by offering them a bonus match at the end of the games.

"Two combatants now return to the arena for your pleasure," the master of ceremonies announced. "Two men who fought their first matches during yesterday's contests and have proven worthy to fight for you once more." He waved his hand to his right. A man carrying a trident, with a net draped over his left shoulder, strolled confidently onto the sandy floor. "From Thrace, a retiarius whose bout you will recall was won in spectacular fashion. Gavius Atticus presents to you, Baztisa!"

The Thracian raised his spear, letting loose a bellow of fierce rage. The crowd roared its approval. The master of ceremonies raised his hands, silencing the mob, as the far gate opened.

Verus stepped determinedly out onto the sand.

"And from Dacia, a provocator. Though defeated yesterday, he fought with such valour that our gracious sponsor saw fit not only to spare him, but to give him a chance for redemption in a special match to close the games. Will he find his honour restored? Or will he have to beg for mercy? Gavius Atticus is pleased to give you, Verus!"

As he glared at his opponent, oblivious to the master of ceremonies, Verus managed to catch his own name being called and was surprised at the ovation he received. It seemed the hoards did appreciate valour, even in defeat. Gritting his teeth, he made a silent vow. He would not leave the arena bested twice in a row. If he fell, he would not raise a finger to ask for mercy.

Slapping his gladius twice against his shield, he snarled. He and the retiarius stalked towards the centre of the floor. Turning to execute the required pre-match salutes, Verus spotted Narcissus seated next to the consul. His hand was held against his face thoughtfully. The other lanista appeared to be snickering at the prospect of this match.

Retiarius-class Gladiator

"Ready...fight!"

The Thracian began to swing his weighted net in circles over his head, probing Verus' defences with his trident.

He leapt out of the way of a sweep of the net. For Verus, there was none of the nerves or excitement from the previous day, only determination bordering on rage. Fighting as if he had nothing left to lose had stripped him of all fear and apprehension. *Do not lose your focus*, he silently chastised himself.

From the few practice sessions he'd had against a retiarius, he knew the biggest danger was not the trident, for it was only effective so long as the fighter could keep his opponent at a distance. Once inside its reach, with no shield to protect him, and no real protection to speak of, the man was essentially helpless. The net, however, posed an unusual threat. Provided its wielder was competent in its usage. A retiarius was devoid of both shield and helmet with only minimal armour; however, the net could easily trip up, or otherwise incapacitate, a reckless opponent.

This Thracian was wielding the net with great speed and balance, almost like a whip. It became apparent he was using the trident to set Verus up to be tripped or to throw the net over him. Twice he ensnared his shield. Verus was able to wrench free just before the man could stab him in the ribs. Verus knew he would be hard pressed to get close to his foe without being skewered or completely entangled in the net. While continuing to circle and maintain his distance, he worked his left forearm lose from the strap that held the shield in place.

With a quick overhand snap, the net wrapped itself around Verus' shield. He held in place for a brief second and, as the retiarius twisted his body, intent on pulling Verus off his feet, he simply let go. The Thracian fell onto his side, his trident stuck awkwardly in the sand and wrenched from his grasp. Letting loose a howl of fury, Verus leapt forward. Before the Thracian could recover, he kicked him hard in the side of the head with his shin greave. His opponent's eyes rolled into the back of his head, a slumped onto his back. Verus' face was red, his teeth gritted. He let loose a howl of triumph, as he stood over his fallen adversary.

The throng of onlookers were on their feet, applauding and shouting his name over and over. Atticus was also standing and clapping, showing his approval. Even the ever-passive Narcissus was applauding his fighter's performance. The rival lanista was the only man not cheering. He shrugged indifferently, accepting whatever the sponsor decided. Verus looked to Atticus. He turned his thumb down, signifying 'leave him on earth', and then raised both hands, signalling for the arena staff to help the fallen gladiator away.

With his fury subsiding, Verus' breathing slowed, and his complexion returned to normal. He let out a sigh of relief. Atticus was clearly pleased; his anger at the gladiator's impudence replaced with ecstasy. He listened to the cheers and adulations of the crowd. This bonus match had earned him additional favour, eclipsing that of the previous days' contests. Across the sand, he saw the retiarius being helped to his feet. The man was clearly disoriented and needed assistance walking. However, he managed to turn to face his adversary. In a sign of respect, Verus held his gladius against his chest in salute. The man cocked a half-smile and nodded in return, before he was assisted out of the arena. Each man left the games with a win and a loss, but it was Verus the crowd would remember.

Verus stepped back into the waiting chamber. He was greeted with cheers from his fellow gladiators.

131

"That was pure fucking balls," Severus said, clasping his hand and grabbing him by the shoulder. "I thought I fought well, but after what you just did, no one is even going to remember my name."

The fighters parted. Their senior instructor quietly made his way over.

"I'm not entirely certain whether your actions were brave or foolish," Drusus remarked, his arms folded across his chest.

"Possibly both," Verus said. "I couldn't get close and knew he was trying to snag my shield, so I took a chance."

"What would you have done had it not worked?" the instructor asked, with a measure of persistence.

"Improvised...or died."

Drusus nodded and signalled for the man to follow him, wishing to speak in private.

"I would say that your victory was a matter of both skill and good fortune," the magister observed. "Yet fortune is not something we can always depend on. I am not chastising you, for the crowd loved it. I dare say, your name is the one they'll remember, and not just because your second match was the last of these games. You're still young and new to the arena. In time, if you survive long enough, you'll learn to constantly be thinking three to four moves ahead of your opponent." He tapped Verus on the top of the head with his finger. "Remember, your mind is your greatest weapon. Win the mental game before the first blow is struck. You will never taste defeat, even if Fortuna should abandon you."

Some would have taken the magister's words as a rebuke, yet Verus burned them into his mind. He knew luck had contributed as much to his victory as skill. His opponent, like him, had only fought his first match the previous day. A more experienced retiarius would have anticipated his actions and never allowed himself to be thrown off-balance so easily.

As slaves helped him out of his helmet and armour, he was suddenly aware of a hulking presence standing behind him.

"Way to upstage the rest of us," Priscus said, his tone harsh. And yet, there was an unmistakeable trace of a smile across his face. "I thought I would be the one they'd remember after the thrashing I gave that poor Spaniard."

"Hard to believe he had three victories in the arena," Verus recalled, letting out a relieved sigh as his cuirass was removed.

"Still, I suppose it helped that my second match being the last of the games."

"True," Priscus replied with a brief frown of contemplation, "but I don't think anyone will remember your defeat from yesterday. They'll be talking about how you found victory, even when that Thracian snatched your shield from you."

That evening, prior to the daily feast, Drusus met with the combatants who fought during Atticus' games. Verus was handed two small leather pouches. In one were twenty-five brass sestertii; the most common coin in the Roman Empire with only modest purchasing power.

"For your efforts against the murmillo. The other is for your victory against the retiarius."

Verus' eyes grew wide, as he dumped out thirty silver coins. They were significantly smaller than the sestertii, but he knew their value was much greater. He held one up and looked to Drusus inquisitively.

"Those are denarii," the trainer explained. "Each one is worth four sestertii. Those thirty silver coins you now hold are worth about two months' wages of a legionary."

"All for one fight in the sand."

"One fight in an insignificant arena with only a few hundred spectators," Drusus added. "Those games were a small, private affair. Win a match in publicly funded games, particularly during one of the numerous religious holidays, and you'll earn ten times that amount. However, your opponents will be much stronger and far more experienced. And while Emperor Vespasian is not known for blood-letting, any imperial sponsored games run a significantly added risk, in addition to greater reward. Be especially wary if you ever get called to fight in any matches hosted by Titus, the Prince Imperial. He has a taste for blood and will not hesitate to punish a poor performance."

Chapter XIII: Veteres and Missiones

With their first matches behind them, the tirones became veterans of the arena. Of the eleven who'd participated in the games sponsored by Gavius Atticus, six emerged victorious with five defeats, including Verus. However, his gutsy display of asking for a second match, and then winning in spectacular fashion, gave the ludus seven wins against five losses. Two of the vanquished acquitted themselves poorly and were remitted for remedial training under Drusus' most savage instructors. Narcissus had personally admonished these men, stating that if they embarrassed him again, they would be flogged and condemned to the gregarii. The other two had performed well and were now counted as missiones; veterans who were defeated yet fought with skill and valour. Narcissus applauded these men, stating that they still brought honour to the ludus.

Those who'd won their matches had enough coin to purchase numerous comforts to make their lives better. Narcissus informed them that, with enough coin, they could even acquire one of the more 'luxurious' flats where the elite of the ludus lived. As a further reward, all who competed in the games were given four days of rest; more for those injured and under care of the medics.

The sun shone through Verus' clapboard window on the morning after the games. His injured leg was stiff and causing him great discomfort. The only relief he could find was in keeping his knee bent and the limb curled up as he lay on his side.

"Nothing a day or two of rest won't sort out," he mumbled to himself, intent on sleeping away the rest of the day.

His slumber was interrupted by a loud banging on his door. Without waiting for an answer, Priscus let himself in.

"Welcome to the veteres!" he shouted in his ever-booming voice. He stood next to the window and sniffed the brisk late-autumn air. "It is a fine day; too fine to be penned in behind these walls."

"Ah, yes, well…I had hoped to rest up today. My leg is a bit sore and all."

"Nonsense!" Priscus countered, giving Verus a hard smack on his leg, causing his friend to gasp and bolt upright. The Caledonian seemed not to notice. "Now that you have a few copper and silver coins weighing you down, you should find a few things to make your quarters a little more liveable."

Knowing it was useless to argue, Verus threw off his blanket and tumbled out of bed. He threw on his tunic, though his leg moved rather stiffly as he bent down to don his sandals.

"Nice little scratch you've got there," Priscus observed, noticing his friend's injury for the first time. "Still, nothing a stretching of the legs won't take care of."

The incessant cacophony of gladiators training echoed off the high walls of the vast ludus complex. New prospects were subjected to the torments of savage strength and conditioning, while tirones drilled rudimentary basics on the training stakes. Veteres conducted one-on-one instruction with the doctors skilled in their various specialties. The stench of dirt and sweat hung pungently in the air. At the gate, there was a constant flow of people coming and going; food vendors with carts full of freshly-killed livestock and mountains of grain sacks; iron and copper suppliers with raw ore for the smiths; plus, a handful of prostitutes, returning home to their brothels.

"Have you ever been outside the ludus?" Priscus asked as they walked along the narrow lane and out onto the busy street.

"Only once, during a short foray with Severus. I suppose the night of the pre-match banquet, and the fights themselves, don't really count. Strange that they let us practically come and go as we please."

"They know there is little chance that any of us would try to run," Priscus surmised. "After all, there's the matter of honour, even among brigands and scum-of-the-earth types, like us. We've all sworn an oath of obedience to the lanista. I have also seen what happens to a gladiator who breaks his oath and tries to flee. Let's just say it was a mercy when they finally got around to crucifying him."

Verus nodded in reply. For him, having previously been a slave previously condemned to the mines, the relative comfort and security the ludus offered was paradise by comparison. He could still recall the terrible nights spent in The Pit with no roof, and nothing except a ratty tunic to keep out the cold. These memories were most profound during the winter. Freezing rains would beat on his clapboard window, while he remained warm and wrapped up in a blanket on his reasonably comfortable bed.

In contrast to most slaves, gladiators were prized commodities, rather than tools of labour meant to be used until they broke and had to be discarded. They were well-fed and had better medical care than any outside of the nobility in Rome. Many of their medics came from the army with a wealth of experience in treating battle injuries and other illnesses. They also had a relatively comfortable bed to sleep in and a roof over their head. In an appalling paradox, Rome was the richest and grandest city in the world, yet there were thousands of terribly poor and impoverished citizens living on the streets on the verge of starvation.

And, of course, there was the matter of women willing to pay well for their 'services' outside of the arena. Once a gladiator became a veteran of the sand, his name was circulated among the divorced, widowed, or otherwise lecherous Roman ladies. While Verus was certain he would never see his wife again, he had thus far declined any such advances. Severus, however, was quick to exploit his newfound popularity; even taking the occasional lady companion to share with his wife.

In short, the life of a gladiator was harsh and unforgiving, the embrace of death ever-present. Yet, if one was strong, of stout courage and fighting prowess, he could make a far better life by selling his body and soul to the sand of the arena, than he ever could as a 'free' pauper on the streets.

They saw many of these poor wretches as they forced their way along the city streets. Verus had no idea where they were headed, and was simply following Priscus' lead.

"You asked me once about the gods of my people," the Caledonian said. "So I ask you, which gods do you pray to?"

"My household patron has always been Safa, the Rhoxolani God of the Hearth," Verus explained. "It was he who I made my pact with, that he would protect my family in return for my suffering in their stead."

"That doesn't sound like a benevolent deity to me," Priscus scoffed. "Sounds like a right little shit."

"It was I who made the offer; nothing was demanded of me. The Romans were attacking our village, and all I wanted was for my wife and son to be safe."

"And do you know if this Safa kept his end of the bargain?"

The question was one which Verus had asked himself every day since his initial capture. All he could do was shake his head. "I did not see them after I was captured, so I can only assume they escaped or were killed." These last words left a lump in his throat, yet he found it cathartic to let loose these fears that had consumed him for the better part of a year-and-a-half. He continued to speak quickly, lest he lose his nerve. "Even if they are alive, what fate awaited them? Our village was destroyed, with most of the people taken into slavery. The only hope for my wife…"

"Is to find another man's bed to share," Priscus finished for him. His words were coarse, though there was no mockery or malice in his voice. If anything, Verus felt a trace of compassion in his friend's words. What he said next cut like a scythe, severing Verus' ties to his old fate. "If that is the best that your gods can do, then what good are they?"

"Utterly useless," Verus muttered, shaking his head. Priscus clasped him on the shoulder.

"Good man."

They soon reached a market stall, where a well-dressed man was selling a variety of small statuary, as well as numerous oils and incense burners. Priscus grinned as he found what he was looking for; a marble statue a woman in a stola, wearing a crown, with an orb clutched in her outstretched hand.

"Ah, this is the one you want."

"Who is she?" Verus asked.

"My patron deity, Invidia; more commonly known by her Greek name, Nemesis, the goddess of retribution. Her name means many things in different tongues, though my favourite is 'the inescapable'. Many gladiators pray to her, and she has favoured me far better than any gods from my past life."

"You do not fear enraging the gods of your people?"

"Piss on them," Priscus scoffed. "They were never there for me in the old country. The gods of the Picts and Caledonians are feeble cunts. I first prayed to Nemesis the day before fighting at an arena near a Roman fortress in southern Britannia. She served me well and brought me here. I will continue to pay homage to her, until she fails me or decides I am no longer of any use to her." He gave a wicked grin and added, "We have an understanding, you see."

His words seemed blasphemous to Verus, but he could not argue with his friend's reasoning. He recalled the tales of tragedy and hardship Priscus told him about his previous life; that he was a lost soul, devoid of meaning. He now had purpose and, since finding his new deity, his reputation began to grow within the arena.

Verus decided that Safa had done all he could for him, if indeed he'd actually kept his part of the bargain to protect Tamura and Fillon. The pantheon of Rome ruled here. And so, he paid fifteen sestertii for the marble statue of his new patron deity.

Following their four days of reprieve, the new veteres returned to the endless days of training, readying for their next match. There was far more one-on-one instruction from the various doctors. They helped their charges improve their strengths while countering their weaknesses. They were further able to specialise their skillsets to whichever class best suited them. The vast majority of gladiators fought with sword and shield, with the only differences between some classes being what type of helmet or other cosmetic effects they wore. Some of these Verus found to be rather silly, such as the pair of feathers that adorned many of their helmets. He learned that many of the classes were more about spectacle, rather than practical. One class that he'd heard about, but yet to see, was the Venator; lightly armed gladiators with only helmet and small shield. They carried either a long carving knife or spear, and their specialty was fighting wild beasts.

Of the other veteres who'd either won their initial matches or were granted the missio, one elected to train as a retiarius, fighting with trident and net. Two of the larger men became murmillos, favouring heavy armour while sacrificing speed. Conversely,

Severus elected to continue training as a secutor, who wore minimal protection and relied almost exclusively on quickness and agility.

As for Verus, he found it best suited him to remain a provocator. The name literally meant 'challenger', and with its upper breast plate, single greave, and arm manica, he felt it offered the best balance between protection and mobility. He also preferred a circular bucker as opposed to the larger, rectangular scutum for a shield.

Something he could not bring himself to admit was that his struggle against the murmillo-class was less physical than it was psychological. He had faced heavily armoured opponents in training, but none of these men carried painted shields that resembled those of the imperial legions.

"Against a murmillo, you will have to rely on your speed," an instructor told him. "He can simply hide behind his large shield, exerting very little energy, while you exhaust yourself if you use brute force to try to get past all his armour."

He then led Verus through a series of drills meant to counter the added weight and armour of these classes. He was even ordered to spar while wearing the grilled helm of a murmillo, so he might learn its weaknesses and blind spots. The neck, lower abdomen, and upper legs were the only real vulnerabilities. The key was using all the added weight from their armour against them, as well as the visual impairments brought on by the ridiculously large helmet. Learning to battle against this class was by far the greatest challenge Verus faced, coupled with the knowledge that not every murmillo fought exactly the same.

And while he was confident he could more than hold his own against the retiarius, having defeated one in his last match, he spent many hours training against them as well. Not every gladiator who fought with net and trident would fall for the same trick Verus had last pulled. Furthermore, when training against fighters of similar class as him, such as the secutors for fellow provocators, there was a plethora of techniques to learn, depending on if the man he was facing happened to be quicker, stronger, or better skilled than him.

Verus may have been a veteran of the arena, but there was still much he needed to learn, if he ever wanted to win his freedom.

In late December, all training ceased for a period of seven days. This was in observance of the Roman holiday of Saturnalia; referred to as 'the best of days' by ancient poets. The Emperor and members of the senate sponsored a handful of gladiatorial matches throughout the city. However, a requirement that only fighters with at least four victories could compete prevented Verus, Severus, and Priscus from fighting.

Severus attempted to explain the religious origins of the week-long celebration, stating that the holiday was in honour of Saturn, the God of the Harvest. Verus could see little in the way of religion that had anything to do with what the citizens of Rome were celebrating. It seemed as if the entire world was turned upside-down; slaves becoming masters, minor crimes and mischief overlooked…and, in fact, encouraged. Despite the chill of the winter nights, many revellers wandered the streets in large groups completely naked, singing a plethora of rude and amusing songs. Trees were decorated with brightly coloured streamers, as well as biscuits shaped like people and animals, as well as gold and silver stars. Severus explained that the biscuits were symbols of fertility, while the stars were to honour the rebirth of the sun god, Sol Invictus, on the winter solstice.

"Something for everyone on Saturnalia!" Severus proclaimed.

Most surprising of all were the effigies of the Emperor and other members of the nobility that were carried through the streets, often twisted into inappropriate positions and spanked with wooden paddles or other implements. Much to his astonishment, Verus learned that Emperor Vespasian enjoyed seeing these mockeries of himself. He had a self-deprecating, not to mention crude and somewhat juvenile, sense of humour. He often stated the people should be allowed to express themselves freely and openly, even at his expense.

As for the gladiators, they often found themselves taken into the homes of the Roman elite, staging wrestling matches or mock fights for the amusement of the revellers. And while they were given freedom to do as they wished until the end of the festivities on 24 December, Narcissus demanded that all gladiators return to the ludus each morning and be accounted for. On the 25th, their heads pounding from endless bouts of drinking and cavorting, the gladiators resumed the grind of endless training once more.

Chapter XIV: Lady of the Sand

Rome
February, 79 A.D.

Female Venator

The endless months of living and training in the ludus had completely immersed Verus into the life of a gladiator, drastically altering not just his physical body, but his very spirit. This was his fate. As the days and weeks went by, he eventually cast off any fealty he once had for this former divine patron, Safa, and pledged himself completely to Nemesis. In a perverse twist of fate, the Romans had murdered and enslaved his people, while ripping him away from his family, yet he fought in their arenas with relish, and now subjugated himself before their gods. The deities of the Rhoxolani were dead to Verus. The gods of Rome lorded over all, and they could dispose of him as they saw fit.

This forging of the spirit, of being bent to the will of the ludus, reflected in his growth as a gladiator. He fought harder than most during training, while conducting personal sessions with various instructors; even after the day's training was complete, and he was already exhausted. Drusus quickly put a stop to these, admonishing

Verus and the instructors alike that he risked savaging his body to the point of breaking. However, he relented in allowing Verus additional provocator training in lieu of some of the other tasks, even going so far as to personally instruct him twice a week.

Despite this total immersion into life in the ludus, it wasn't until the month of February that the opportunity arose for Verus to fight again. Named after the purification ritual known as *Februa*, where evil spirits were exercised and the Eternal City spiritually purified, the city's governor, as well as the newest Plebeian Tribune, wished to hold a day of games to commemorate the ceremony. It was with rapt anticipation that Verus looked forward to this next match, though the games would be a much smaller affair than the contests sponsored by Gavius Atticus.

It was just after the Ides of the month that Drusus summoned those who would be fighting and read the handbill to them.

"You're fighting twice," he explained when he got to Verus. "Your first bout will be against a fellow who has thoroughly embarrassed his lanista twice already. Honestly, I do not understand why he is being allowed to compete in another single pairing."

"Will I have to kill him?" Verus asked.

His question surprised Drusus. "That is not up to me," he said coldly. "But I warn you against going easy on him, just so he can earn the missio. If you do, I will know it, and so will Narcissus." His words were calm, yet full of menace.

"For this reason, you are being given two matches," the magister continued. "Narcissus wants you to give the first man a sound thrashing and be done with it. It is your second opponent you should concern yourself with. He's a provocator; same class as you and very similar to the last man who bested you. I did a bit of research on him. He's an auctoratus with a year in the ludus. He has two victories and no defeats. I know how you struggle against the heavier classes, so be careful!"

Verus said nothing. He dreaded fighting a provocator, yet he was too ashamed to confess why. Did he dare tell his chief instructor that something so simple as a gladius and scutum shield made him flash back to the time he'd fought against imperial legionaries? It was absurd and embarrassing. After all, aside from the shield and weapon, a provocator bore little resemblance to a Roman soldier despite, supposedly, being mirrored after them. Their armour and

143

helmet were drastically different as were the patterns on the shields themselves. It made absolutely no sense, and Verus knew it. For reasons he could never explain, whenever he faced a similar fighter, even during training, his mind raced back to Dacia. He felt as if he were on the grassy field outside his home, staring down a wall of the world's most feared professional killers. He suspected his paring with a provocator was deliberate; a test from Drusus and Narcissus.

He also finally understood why he continuously forced old thoughts and feelings about his home from his mind. Thoughts of home were dangerous. They wrecked his focus, with flashbacks of legionaries swarming his village. If he wished to continue among the living, he had to kill his love of home.

Something Verus looked forward to was the feast the night before a match. On this evening, it was a much smaller gathering. The editor was a member of the equites, rather than the senate, and was celebrating his election as Tribune of the Plebs. The governor of the city had offered a sum of coin to fund these contests, as his way of honouring the Februa. There were fifteen total guests including the handful of unattached women.

The one person who Verus noticed immediately was a young woman lounging on a couch near Drusus. She wore a tunic instead of a stola, which was very much frowned upon in Roman society. From what Verus had gathered, the only women who wore tunics were either prostitutes of slaves. And yet, because she was on one of the couches, she was clearly a guest and not a servant. Her tunic was yellow with blue trim and belted around the middle like all the gladiators. Though most of the other fighters ignored her, Verus found himself more than a little curious. It's not that he was attracted to her, though her face was handsome, albeit a little plain. His inquisitiveness getting the best of him, Verus approached the woman.

She looked at him with a raised eyebrow and let out a bored sigh. "If you want to fuck, you'll have to wait until after the games tomorrow…provided we're both still alive and not too badly mauled."

This blunt assertion nearly caused Verus to break into a coughing fit and spill his cup of wine. "Come again?" he asked, utterly perplexed.

She sat up and apprised him, her hands resting on the couch. Her figure was extremely athletic, her arms and shoulders well-muscled. The right was marred by a deep scar that ran from the elbow up and around her bicep. She was fair-skinned with a smattering of tiny freckles around her nose and cheeks, and her dark blonde hair was pulled back tight against her head.

"Are you not looking for one last romp before bleeding to death in the sands tomorrow?" she asked, her head cocked to one side. "A pity. When I saw you come in with those other sweating heathens, I thought 'he'll do'. But, like I said, I only open up my legs after I've sufficiently thrashed some unfortunate bitch who thinks she's too good for the brothels."

"But does that not describe you, as well?" Verus asked with a coy grin.

The woman responded in kind. "Undoubtedly." She then motioned for him to join her.

The other guests were too busy watching Priscus and an equally large fighter from another ludus engaging in an arm-wrestling contest. Only Drusus seemed to notice Verus and his new lady friend, though he only shot them the occasional glance.

"So, did you become a lady of the arena willingly or were you a slave?" Verus asked. It might have seemed like an impolite question to the outside observer.

His newfound companion seemed to appreciate his directness. "My situation is a little more…complicated. I was not born a slave, though my lot in life was scarcely any better. At least a slave in a noble house has a place to sleep and knows they won't be starving to death. I was ill-suited for the brothels; the idea of being ploughed by every fat, hairy bastard with a few coins to get rid of did not sit well with me. It's a long story. Suffice it to say, about the only thing I've ever been any good at is fighting. Lucky for me, Drusus thought I had talent and took me under his tutelage."

"How does that work, exactly? I've never seen you, or any other women gladiators, at the ludus. Well, there were a couple of gregarii that *might* have been women, for all I knew."

145

"And you won't find any of us at a ludus," the woman explained. "Those with a cunt instead of a cock bear all the disgrace yet none of the glory. We've only been allowed to fight in the arena for about twenty years now. Emperor Nero found it exotic to watch two women try to disembowel each other. Titus, the Prince Imperial, also has a fondness for female gladiators, though he apparently always stresses that we must come from the lowest dregs of society. Juno forbid any of these soft, delicate, noble creatures bloody themselves for the amusement of the mob."

"About Drusus," Verus said, nodding towards their mutual acquaintance. "Are you two...?"

The woman gave him a confounded look and broke into a fit of laughter.

Just then, Priscus managed to slam his opponent's hand onto the table, ending their contest with a cacophony of voracious cheers from the assembled guests.

"Are we, what, lovers?" The lady gladiator struggled to contain her laughter. "Sorry to disappoint, but you're more his type than I am. Oh, he has a wife and family, though I suspect he utilised a 'hired cock' to sire his children. No, I am just a means to an end for him, kind of like you are. He pays for my flat, which is little more than a tiny room on the top floor of a squalid building that's just waiting to go up in flames. And he trains me a few times a week. In return, I provide the entertainment when an editor wants to watch a pretty young thing get dispatched to Hades."

"Are most women's fights to the death, then?"

"No more than yours. I've fought six times and only been bested once. That was my first contest, and I swore it was the last time some filthy twat would conquer me."

"It was the same for me," Verus recalled. "I lost my first match but was given a chance at redemption the very next day."

"Do you lust for revenge against the fighter who beat you?" the woman asked.

Verus shook his head. "No."

"Bloody hell, I did! I begged Drusus to let me fight her again. He said if I won a few bouts, he would give her to me as a reward. Well, given how infrequently we fight, it took two years for me to win three matches and satisfy him that I'd learned my lesson. When I fought that insufferable bitch again, I made certain she would not

146

leave the arena alive. She may have been granted the missio but a slash to a certain vein on the thigh is almost always fatal." She wore an evil smile at the memory.

For some reason, Verus did not find it unnerving. Was it arousal that he now felt? "And what of your opponent for the morrow?"

"Some wisp of a girl who thinks because her master let her play with his sword—in more ways than one—that she can fight in the arena. It's not a fair contest, really. But, when it comes to women, dwarves, and other 'novelty' fights, no editor gives a bucket of shit about whether it's a well-matched competition or not." She shot him a look. "So, what's your story? Are you a crazy bastard who volunteered for this, or were you dragged away from the courts in chains, to 'die by the blade'?"

"Neither. I...I was captured when the Romans raided my village." He then told her his story; how he was a Rhoxolani blacksmith living just north of the Danube; his capture, the ten months spent in The Pit, and his subsequent selection by Drusus and Narcissus to join the ludus. It was only at the end of his tale that he mentioned his wife and son.

"I am surprised you've not tried to escape," the woman remarked. "You've fought a couple matches and could readily find passage back to Moesia, Dacia, or wherever in the sodding world you are from."

"I've seen what happens to a gladiator who tries to run," Verus explained, telling her about a poor fellow who'd been caught and was sentenced to fight a wild tiger, without the benefit of weapons. "Besides, I have sworn an oath. I will only leave the ludus after I have earned my freedom. My capture was the price I paid to the old gods of my people for keeping my family safe. Yet I know not whether they have kept their end of the bargain, and so I have no more use for them, than they have for me. I've now sworn allegiance to Nemesis, at least for so long as I continue to fight in the arena."

His companion glared at him coldly. "If there are any gods...and that is a big, fucking *if*...they are nothing but deranged maniacs who delight in the suffering of us mortals. After my first victory, Drusus gave me a statue of Nemesis and said I should offer prayers and small sacrifices to her. I've spat on that cunt before every match and told her to piss off, yet here I am." Her face then broke into a wry

147

grin. "I admit, I would like to think she does exist, because that means I am a woman after her own vile heart."

Verus chuckled. "I'm sorry, but I don't even know your name."

"My name is 'Gladiator'," she replied in a raspy, mocking tone before letting out a sigh. "Vipsania; at least that's the name Drusus said I should have. Apparently, it was the name of Emperor Tiberius' first wife. I can't say for certain. I've never exactly been a scholar of history. Don't know why Drusus thought the name suited me. As for the name I was born with, it's not important."

"Vipsania," Verus said, with a nod of approval. "Pretty."

"I plan on still being alive, with my blood up, by this time tomorrow. If you manage to keep from getting yourself gutted, we should celebrate in a manner fitting of the damned."

"I told you, I have a wife."

"So you said." Vipsania seemed bored by this. "But tell me this, even if she survived being captured or killed, do you really think she's still waiting for you after all this time? If it's been two years already, she's likely found some other burly fellow to raise your son and satisfy her more wanton needs..." Her voice trailed off in embarrassment as Verus glared at her. She shook her head. "I'm sorry. I should not have said that. I can be a cruel bitch both in and out of the arena. I'm certain my eventual demise will be suitably brutal, and the world will be a better place for it. To be honest, I kind of look forward to it."

"You've said nothing that I have not thought about every day for the last two years. If my wife thinks me dead and has found another, then may Safa bless them. I hope he is a good father to my son. It is because of this I've often wondered what I will do, should I win my freedom."

"You could always challenge the bastard and kill him," Vipsania remarked casually.

"I hope I never have to fight again, once I leave the arena. Whether that means by my death or by earning the rudis, I don't care."

"A pity you're not more like your friend, Priscus," Vipsania said, nodding towards the hulking figure.

He now had his arm around the shoulder of his arm-wrestling opponent. Both were laughing loudly and quaffing mass amounts of wine.

"I think those two are fighting each other tomorrow," Verus remarked, trying to remember the other man's name.

"Best of friends tonight, mortal enemies tomorrow in the arena," the woman conjectured. "Should they both survive, they'll likely become brothers once more. And if one should die, I suspect the victor will drink to his fallen adversary."

"Will you drink to your fallen adversary, should you have to kill?"

"If she proves to be a worthy opponent." Vipsania then gave him an apprising look. "I like you, Verus of the Rhoxolani. You have a sense of nobility and honour about you. It may border on the naïve, but I still find it admirable. If there be any gods, may they grant you their favour in the arena tomorrow." She then added with a crass grin, "Of course, if you are skilled with a blade, you won't *need* their favour."

There was a sense of haste the following morning. Verus' first match was scheduled to take place just after sunrise. The arena was much smaller than the one he'd previously fought in. Only a handful of spectators were on-hand that early to witness the opening bout. His opponent was similarly armed and equipped, yet he was clearly overweight and ponderously slow. How he'd survived his months of training baffled Verus, and his condition alone spoke ill of the man's ludus. Verus recalled Drusus' directive to him the night before. He was to end this match quickly and decisively, saving his strength for the provocator later that day. However, he knew better than to concern himself with his second match when he had an armed opponent standing in front of him.

"Ready...fight!"

Before the martial had fully pulled his staff away, Verus lunged at his opponent, sending him stumbling backwards as their shields clashed together. The man managed to maintain his footing, and he came at Verus with a series of stabs from his gladius. Verus smacked these aside with his buckler and circled to his left into his opponent's sword arm. With a quick series of slashes and stabs, he cut the man in numerous places on both the body and sword arm. Only the mail manica prevented Verus from severing the limb. With a subsequent blow of his shield to the side of the man's head, he felled his adversary. Rather than attempting to regain his feet, the fallen fighter dropped his weapons and held up his finger, asking for mercy. It was a pathetic display, and the small crowd roared its displeasure. However, the sponsor allowed the man to be spared. As he left the pit, Verus wondered if his defeated foe would later wish he had been killed.

Around midmorning, with the stands now full of spectators, Verus heard Vipsania's name called. Though he rarely watched the other contests, he was rapt with anticipation as Vipsania and her opponent stepped out onto the sand.

"Ah, I see it's your lady-friend's turn to fight," Priscus noted. He joined Verus at the small window, his face held in a large grin.

Vipsania was armed like a provocator with a slightly smaller rectangular shield and a metal headband rather than a full helmet. She had explained to Verus that it drew more praise from the crowd when they could see her face. Although, whenever she fought an adversary with experience and actual skill, she wore a grilled murmillo helm. The woman she faced this day was slender and slightly shorter. She wore a secutor's helmet, a segmented plate manica covering her right arm, metal greaves on the shins, and an awkward fitting square bronze plate over her chest. She wielded a gladius and metal buckler, which she bashed together as her name was announced, inciting the crowd.

Though Vipsania spoke harshly of her opponent the night before, her stance and demeanour denoted that she did not take any adversary lightly. The two women circled and feinted for a few moments before attacking each other in earnest. The other woman possessed a measure of natural talent; however, she was raw and untrained compared to Vipsania. Most sponsors would never allow a new fighter to face an opponent who already had five victories to their credit. With female gladiators, however, there was little concern for rules of the arena or decorum. Had her adversary been properly trained with a couple of matches under her, she might have stood a chance. As it was, she was utterly outmatched from the outset. Vipsania was stronger and quicker. She picked apart her opponent with stabs from her gladius and blows from her shield.

It was her shield that felled her the hapless woman. Vipsania swung it in a high arc, catching her dazed opponent on the side of the helm. As she fell to her knees, Vipsania gave a howl of rage and bashed her repeatedly with the edge of her shield until the young woman collapsed unconscious onto the sand.

Rather than simply placing the point of her sword on the woman's neck, Vipsania grabbed her beneath the helmet and with a vicious jerk, ripped it from her head. The chin ties snapped, cutting the fallen woman's neck. This was an added humiliation. There was an even greater stigma attached to a woman gladiator showing her face than there was for men. The sponsor, as well as the defeated fighter's lanista, were outraged by this. Vipsania did not even wait to see the editor render his judgement before stalking out of the arena. This rebellious defiance drew even greater approbations from the gathered throng. They shouted her name over and over, as she held up the defeated woman's helmet like a trophy. The sponsor quickly regained his demeanour and held up his hands, nodding and clapping as if he approved of the display. The defeated fighter clutched her hands over her face as blood ran from her nose and mouth. Her body bore numerous cuts and gashes, and it was unlikely she would ever be allowed to fight in the arena again.

"I daresay, that vicious little bitch could give me a good run," Priscus said.

Even Verus was smiling appreciatively as Vipsania left the arena. He retired to one of the small side rooms, mentally preparing himself for his upcoming match.

Verus closed his eyes and took a deep, calming breath when his name was announced by the master of ceremonies. His gaze fixed straight ahead, he marched into the arena where he was met with cheers. He did not care that the crowd was less than half the size of that which had witnessed his first matches. For him, there was no crowd, only he and his opponent.

He gritted his teeth as the provocator's name was called. The man's shield was painted much like the murmillo he'd last faced.

Only difference was it was red with a yellow wreath encircling the metal boss. The man also wore an open-faced helm with cheek guards and a wide brim in the back. It was nearly identical to a legionary's, and Verus could not help but wonder if this was deliberate.

As the battle commenced, Verus' gaze became focused on nothing except his opponent. His mind even drowned out the shouts from the crowd. He instinctively remembered the drills he'd practiced for battling against these heavily-armed fighters. The massive shield alone meant Verus could not simply knock the man over. He needed to utilise his quickness and agility. He kept light on his feet as the provocator stalked towards him. Verus would thrust his gladius towards the man's face a couple times before quickly stepping to his right or left, to strike at his flank. He would deliberately establish a pattern which, in turn, made his foe anticipate his next move. Verus would then change his attack, often striking at the face or the lead shin to keep the provocator guessing.

Their battle continued for some time. Verus remained agile on his feet, never allowing his opponent to dictate the pace of the match. He'd cut him several times on the shoulder and torso, only to be bashed away by the man's heavy shield before he could finish him. Verus knew that patience was as important as skill in a contest such as this. With the frenzy of his attacks, he could only hope his adversary tired before he did.

It was fatigue which led the provocator to become desperate, and caused Verus to make a small yet nearly fatal error. He side-stepped to the left, hoping to catch the provocator with another jab to his exposed ribs when the gladiator unexpectedly charged. He launched his full weight behind his shield, smashing into Verus like a raging bull. Verus fell onto his bottom, his back smashing against the wall at the edge of the arena and knocking the wind from him. With a desperate blow from the edge of his shield, he smashed the unprotected shin of his adversary. The man screamed in pain as he fell on top of Verus. Unfortunately for Verus, his foe landed with his left knee pinning his sword arm and his own blade across Verus' throat.

"Hold!" the martial shouted, placing his staff across the provocator's chest.

The crowd was applauding loudly. The sponsor stood and raised his hands, ordering an end of the match. Though Verus had lost, it was the victor who was worse for it. As he rolled off Verus, the provocator clutched at his broken shin, grimacing in agony as his vanquished foe pulled himself to his feet. It was a bitter feeling leaving the arena in defeat, though not nearly as hateful as his first match. Judging from the reaction of the mob, not to mention his opponent still writhing in pain, one would think Verus was the victor rather than the vanquished.

Despite the loss, Verus was surprisingly calm as he returned to his ludus' room. His fellow gladiators were offering him congratulations rather than sympathies or admonishments.

"How are you feeling?" Priscus asked.

Verus sat and removed his helmet. He shook his head, utterly perplexed. "I don't know. I feel more confused than anything. I mean, according to the martial I lost, yet it doesn't seem like it."

"That man will be out for several months, if he ever fights again," Drusus said, as their fellow gladiators parted for him. "Yes, he won. And he might have killed you in a contest devoid of rules. That said, it is *you* who the people will remember." The magister chuckled and shook his head. "You're quite the figure, Verus. You seem to be the only gladiator whose reputation grows even in defeat."

It did seem strange to Verus. He'd now fought in the arena four times with two victories and two defeats to his credit. If one looked simply at the numbers, he was marginal at best. However, it was the way he won and lost that was earning him his growing reputation. He was beginning to understand what it meant to be a gladiator. It was spectacle and martial valour which counted, not just the number of victories or defeats.

"I would rather win than give the crowd an entertaining loss," he surmised. "And if I hadn't broken that fellow's leg, he could have readily sliced my throat before the martial stopped him."

"Tell me this," Drusus said, folding his arms across his chest. "Did you learn from this defeat?"

"Far more than my earlier victory," Verus confessed.

Despite his growing reputation, Verus knew he had to build a more impressive resume of victories, if he were to have any chance of earning his freedom. After all, that was the final prize. As a slave, no manner of coin won in the arena could earn him the palm and rudis. He needed to compete before a bigger crowd, and with the Emperor's colossal arena nearing completion, he would have his chance. However, if he were to fight before Vespasian, he first needed to win, both often and spectacularly. Drusus assured his gladiators that the closer the Flavian Amphitheatre grew to completion, the more often they would be called upon to fight in lesser shows. Potential sponsors, including the Prince Imperial, would soon be looking for the best gladiators; those worthy of fighting before the Emperor, senate, and people of Rome.

Two weeks after the last games, around the Calends of March, there was an unexpected visitor to the ludus. Narcissus was conducting his daily meeting with his magister and doctors when a servant opened the door to his meeting room and bowed.

"Your pardon, master, but you have a visitor. An old friend, as he put it."

"I was not expecting anyone to come calling at this hour," Narcissus said, scowling in irritation. He abruptly waved for the servant to show the man in. His frown turned into a broad grin as a familiar face stepped into the hall. "By Mars and Victoria!"

"It is good to see you as well, old friend and former master," the man said with a bow. His name was Gulussa, and he was well-known to every member of the staff at the ludus, as well as many of its senior veteres.

A black African originating from Numidia, he was above average in height with a bald head and smooth face. He was leaner than most of the gladiators living at the ludus, yet still very muscular. Little was known about his past before he became a gladiator, only that he was a Roman citizen. He came to the Eternal City penniless and destitute with an uncanny ability to fight. Signing on as an auctoratus, he fought sixteen times during his five-year contract, emerging victorious on thirteen occasions and winning his last six contests in a row.

"It's been what, two years since you earned your rudis?" Narcissus asked, forgetting about his meeting with the instructors for the moment.

"A little more than that," Gulussa replied. He wasted no time in explaining why he'd returned. "I hear you are still in need of a primus palus."

"*Need* is a relative term," Narcissus remarked. "Though you are correct, the position has been vacant for some time. I suppose you wish to offer your services?"

Gulussa shrugged. "If it's been too long since I last fought, and my thirteen victories are not enough, I will gladly pit myself against any man here to show I still have what it takes."

"You've lost a lot of weight," Drusus observed.

"As have you, magister," the African man replied. "All that extra bulk you make these men carry is practically useless in a real fight. I may not be quite as strong as I was when I last stepped into the sand, but I promise you I am much quicker."

"I would like to know why you've returned," Narcissus persisted. "I seem to recall you were counting down the days until your contract was complete, almost from the moment you arrived."

"True. I suppose it was only after I left I realised just how much I loved the arena; the place where I felt most alive. Does it really matter?"

"No," the lanista said, with a smile and shake of his head. "We'll find you a sparring partner to see how much you still retain. I take it you will not be requiring lodgings?"

"I have a modest flat about half-a-mile from here," Gulussa said. "If you can afford me, another victory or two at primus palus' rates, and I'll be purchasing a house on Palatine Hill."

This was met by laughter from all in the room including Gulussa. No matter how wealthy a gladiator or lanista became, he was still an infamis and greatly limited on where he was allowed to live within Rome. Both life and death were dictated by the norms of imperial society. Former gladiators and lanistae were restricted in where they could live, as well as be buried after death. However, men like Gulussa cared little for propriety. If he won even a couple of contests as a primus palus, especially if he managed to fight before the Emperor, he could afford to build himself a magnificent house and live out the remainder of his days in comfort.

Narcissus suspected it was more than just the promise of coin which brought the former gladiator back to the ludus. After all, a match during the opening games of the Flavian Amphitheatre could bring fame and immortality to the victors.

Chapter XV: Becoming a God

South of Rome
21 June, 79 A.D.

Emperor Vespasian

"By Mercury, what in Hades is the matter with me?" Vespasian quietly asked. "One would think my body didn't know today is the summer solstice!"

"You've been working too much," Titus chastised, as they rode their horses at a slow trot. The road leading south was normally very crowded, though the century of praetorian escorts kept the way clear for the imperial entourage.

Despite the warmth of the early summer sun, the Emperor felt a constant chill running up his spine. For this very reason, he decided to follow his son's advice and take a short holiday away from the capital. And so, they journeyed towards his favourite thermal springs in the Samnite provinces. Close enough to Rome that he could return quickly in the event of a crisis, yet far enough away from the chaos to allow him to properly rest. It was the ideal place to take a holiday. Even his granddaughter had compelled him that he was long overdue.

"You've not had a day of rest since Saturnalia," Julia had stressed.

Noting his father's pale complexion, Titus guided his mount over and reached across, placing a hand on the Emperor's forehead. It was cool and clammy to the touch. Vespasian would have normally smacked his hand away in irritation, yet he did not appear to even notice.

"You'll feel better, Father, once we reach the springs of Aquae Cutiliae," the prince reassured him.

"I certainly hope so," the Emperor grumbled. "I've been breaking out in cold sweats ever since we dined with Consul Junius Paetus. It must have been the damned fish we ate. I knew it was a bit 'off', and he's been shitting himself for the past few days. Whereas you, my boy, have been no worse for wear."

"I told you that fish smelled funny," Titus replied, shaking his head. "Which is why I stuck with roast peacock and dormice."

Besides a convenient location where he could take the occasional holiday, the natural hot springs of Aquae Cutiliae were a place of refuge for the Emperor whenever he felt ill. Many times, the curative powers of the mineral waters helped set him right. With another chill making him shudder, he hoped they would do so again. Now sixty-nine years of age, Vespasian had always refused to feel or act like an old man. His robust countenance had served him well during his years leading imperial armies into battle, as well as what was the most arduous task a man could be inflicted with - ruling over the vast Roman Empire.

"I never wanted to be Emperor, you know," he said, hoping any sort of conversation would take his mind off his weary state.

"So you've said, every day for the past ten years," his son replied with a forced smile.

"It's not like I had much success within the *cursus honorum*," Vespasian continued. "Thankfully, it was a full decade before you were even born when I was placed in charge of street cleaning in Rome. Who would have thought that keeping the roads of a vast city clear of rotting animal carcasses and mule shit would be so damned complicated?"

"Didn't Caligula once stuff dung and refuse down your toga?" Titus asked, breaking into a genuine smile.

His father laughed at the memory. "Indeed, he did, contrary to what some of the gossips say. It was well before he had the mantle of Caesar dropped into his unworthy lap. He called me an 'incompetent twat', grabbed a handful of filth from the street, and stuffed it down my toga, which he then used to wipe his hands."

"And you just stood there and took it, Caesar?" one of the escorting magistrates asked.

"I was a nobody then. I hadn't even conducted my first tour as a laticlavian tribune. Yes, I stood there and took it until he was finished. I then grabbed a glob of muck and smashed him across the face with it."

"I'm surprised that didn't earn you a place on his enemies list."

"On the contrary, he thought it was hilarious," the Emperor mused. "Years later, after he came to the throne, I was making ready to depart for my first tour as legate of a legion. He asked me if there wasn't a war I should be starting somewhere. He then suggested I instigate matters by slapping shit across the face of whatever barbarian chief was displeasing to Rome."

The group shared another laugh and Vespasian let out a sigh. "You know, I sometimes thought that fighting was the only thing I was ever any good at. My tenure as Proconsul of North Africa was a bleeding disaster!"

"That is why one of your greatest gifts, Father, is that you recognise talent and are willing to delegate."

"As Emperor, one has no other choice," Vespasian remarked. "Remember that, son. But make certain you surround yourself with competent people. You will be held responsible for everything that transpires within the vast borders of our Empire; even disasters fashioned by the gods. We cannot prevent calamity wrought by Jupiter or Vulcan. However, how we deal with such a crisis is how the people will judge us. And never forget, we serve Rome. Rome does not serve us."

It was early evening when the large complex of Aquae Cutiliae came into view. Consisting of multiple gardens, groves of fruit trees, several sport and recreation buildings and, of course, the baths built over the springs, it was an idyllic setting. For Vespasian, it had become like a second home. Yet on this day of the summer solstice, he felt none of the usual relief or contentment that usually came over him. Instead, his bowels suddenly twisted. He gasped and leaded over his mount, fearing that he would have an embarrassing incident before he could find the nearest latrine.

Red-faced and scarcely able to walk, the Emperor practically fell off his horse and stumbled into the *service building*—a euphemistic name given to the toilets at legionary fortresses. He considered it a small mercy that the chamber was empty. Feeling suddenly dizzy, he slumped onto an empty orifice as his bowels let loose.

Outside, Titus dismissed their escorts, stating he would remain and wait for the Emperor. His brother quietly walked up behind him.

"I have never seen our father like this," Domitian said, his voice betraying his concern.

"Nor have I," the prince imperial confessed. "Even when we were in Judea. Jotapata was a fetid, disgusting wreck by the time we took it, and I recall many of our soldiers falling ill as a result. In fact, there was not one man, myself included, who did not wind up with either fever or the shits at some point. Except him. I once told him that his constitution was forged in steel by the gods themselves."

Titus surprised himself by confessing these things to his brother. The two rarely spoke, and Titus tended to avoid him as much as possible. Some thought this was because he'd been carrying on a sordid affair with his sister-in-law. But this was, in fact, the least of their concerns. When Domitian approached his brother regarding the disreputable rumour, he encouraged Titus to continue sleeping with his wife. *'I want my brother and future Emperor to be happy,'* he had asserted. Recalling those words made Titus shudder. They still sounded creepy and perverse. And yet, even their father said little about the affair, as he hoped it would distract Titus away from his infatuation with Julia Berenice.

"Perhaps we shall be calling you 'Caesar' sooner than expected," Domitian remarked, almost casually.

"Don't be such an improper shit," Titus snapped. "The Emperor is ill. He is not dying."

"If you say so. Still, it is a good thing Father made certain long ago that the succession was properly sorted."

160

Titus' face grew red with anger. He turned and faced Domitian. It was clear his younger brother was vexed, despite his poorly chosen words and the callousness in his voice. He further sensed a hidden meaning in the young man's mention about the succession. Was it a rebuke of Titus for being unmarried with no designated heir? Or was Domitian implying that, as his brother, he was rightful heir to the prince imperial?

"Go away," Titus said, his voice calm but venomous.

"As you wish." Domitian gave a short bow.

Titus might have taken this as a form of mockery, but it was more likely due to his brother's natural awkwardness.

"By Juno's twat," his father swore, as he emerged from the latrines, his face pale and sweaty. "My guts are attempting to turn themselves inside out. It hurts like a bastard just to wipe my bottom. I swear there was more blood on the sponge than anything I ate or drank over the past two days. It's unbecoming, I tell you!"

Titus rushed to his father's side and placed Vespasian's arm around his shoulders. This normally would have been met with a stern rebuke, but the Emperor was so weak he gladly acceded to his son's assistance. Night had fallen by this time. Following the glow of oil lamps along the outer edge of the complex, they made their way towards the large house that was always reserved as the imperial residence. A pair of praetorian guardsmen rushed over to assist Titus, but Vespasian waved them off. Servants quickly opened the large double doors, and the two men limped their way into the atrium.

"Think you can make it upstairs?" Titus asked.

Vespasian weakly shook his head. "Not a chance in Hades. Just lay me down in one of the servant's quarters, and tell them they can use my bed."

The nearest room belonged to one of the groundskeepers. Despite being told he could sleep in the imperial quarters that night, he was distressed to see his Emperor in such a sorry state.

"This is so damned embarrassing," Vespasian grumbled, as Titus helped him onto the hard bed. His forehead was now hot to the touch.

"I'll stay with you," the prince said.

His father was already snoring quietly.

161

Titus found a rickety chair, which he set in the far corner of the room. He wrapped himself in a scratchy wool blanket and fitfully tried to get some sleep. He struggled against a growing sense of alarm and tried to supress what he knew to be the truth. This was not the ill effects of a bad piece of fish. Emperor Titus Flavius Vespasian was dying.

The following morning, Titus helped his father into the baths. Even the cold plunge did nothing to break his fever or change his deportment. Still naked and soaking wet, the Emperor practically had to be carried into the latrines, where he spent a large portion of the day.

"There's no hiding it anymore," Titus muttered as he listened to the sounds of his father's distress coming from within. His ascension would come soon, possibly within the next day or so. Summoning a scribe, he penned a hasty message. It was a summons for the consuls, leading members of the senate including Senator Nerva, as well as the praetorian prefect, Tiberius Alexander. He sealed it with his signet ring before having the praetorian centurion on duty sent to him.

"Take this to the senate with all haste," he ordered.

"By your leave, highness," the officer said, snapping off a quick salute.

There had been no hiding the Emperor's debilitating illness since their arrival. If everyone at Aquae Cutiliae, from the princes to the lowest slaves, knew about it, rumours had likely already reached Rome.

"And so, the next page in the annals of history is written," Domitian said, startling his brother.

"Damn it all, don't lurk behind me like that," Titus said curtly.

His brother ignored the remark. "Shall I be the partner in your labours, as you were to our father?" he asked instead.

"The Emperor has not yet passed on to the gods," Titus said, with a trace of reprove.

"Perhaps. But then, why the urgent message to Rome? You may think me callous, but the imperial family is never granted a time for mourning, or any of the other decencies enjoyed by common people.

162

I shed the last of my tears when we lost our dear sister. We have our duty, Titus, whether our father still breathes or not."

"You do not have to remind *me* about duty. I've been serving the Empire since you were barely able to wipe your own arse."

"And is that my fault?" Domitian was unable to hide his pained expression any longer. "Did I ask to be left behind while you and Father went about winning battles and glory for Rome? Is it my fault I am twelve years younger than you? Either of you could have found some use for me after I came of age. By Hades, I'm twenty-seven and still haven't done a shred of actual work, except be paraded before the senate as suffect consul for a couple months every year. You, dear brother, were commanding *legions* at my age!"

Titus was filled with indignation, though he stayed his tongue. He knew the two would have to sort out many issues once he became Emperor; not least of which was the matter of the succession. This, however, was not the time, and he made certain Domitian knew that. His brother then nodded in understanding and took his leave.

Once alone, Titus thought to himself, *By Jupiter, will that awkward retch really become my successor?*

Time was something Titus always assumed he had plenty of, particularly regarding finding a suitable heir. Before the Flavians, there had been no precedent for a son succeeding his father to the imperial throne. Augustus had no sons, and Tiberius' died long before him. Caligula's only child, a young daughter, was murdered along with him. And Claudius' son was underage at the time of his death. He was subsequently murdered on orders of his stepbrother, Nero, who became Caesar after Claudius. To top it all, none of Rome's previous emperors had living brothers at the time of their passing. Titus knew Domitian had the most legitimate right to be his successor. Even a son-in-law of proper birth would have less of a claim to the throne in the eyes of the senate and people.

"I've been a fool," he muttered. Suddenly, he was filled with regret for all the years he'd wasted pining away for Queen Julia Berenice. Though he loved her deeply, despite the years they'd spent apart, he finally understood that she could never be his empress consort. Not only was she a Jew, and 'foreign' in the eyes of the populace, she was more than a decade older and well beyond the age of childbearing.

More than anything, he knew he needed a son to secure the stability of the Flavian Dynasty. He quietly reassured himself, although Vespasian was not long for this world, he himself was still a young man. Titus was not even forty yet and in very strong health. If he lived as long as his father, he had plenty of time to sire and raise a suitable heir. He would, naturally, have to placate his brother in the meantime.

Vespasian always said the mineral baths of Aquae Cutiliae was his favourite holiday retreat, so he could return to the senate in a hurry if needed. Now it was the senate who hastily came to him. Among these was Marcus Cocceius Nerva; a close friend of the Flavians. For many years, he'd served as both mentor and like a second father to Domitian. Though lacking in military experience, Vespasian recognised his administrative talents and his knack for diplomacy. No doubt his oratory skills and tact would be needed in the coming days.

One man the Emperor wished to see more than any was his old friend and brother-in-arms, Marcus Ulpius Trajan. The two were very close and served on many campaigns together. Trajan had commanded the venerable Tenth Legion during the Judean War and was the man Vespasian trusted more than any. Trajan's son was quickly making a name for himself with the legions with a natural talent, greater than any would see in a generation. Regrettably, the elder Trajan retired from public life following his tenure as Governor of Syria and returned to his native Hispania. It would take at least a week for an imperial courier to reach him, and Vespasian did not have that long.

Titus was grateful for the senators that did manage to come to Aquae Cutiliae. Nerva, in particular, took much of the strain off the Prince Imperial, to include keeping the frayed nerves of Domitian in check. Two days after they arrived, Nerva sought out Titus. The prince was resting in one of the guest rooms, having not slept since before they arrived.

"Your highness," Nerva said breathlessly, shaking Titus awake. "You must come quickly. I fear the end is nigh, and Caesar has called for you."

Without waiting for Titus to acknowledge him, Nerva rushed into the room next door, waking Domitian. Their present quarrel quickly forgotten, the two brothers rushed past the senator and down the short hallway. As they flung open the door, they could hear Vespasian arguing with his attendants.

"Damn it all, help me up! An Emperor ought to die standing. I'll not introduce myself to Jupiter while lying on my sodding back!"

Titus bit the inside of his cheek, as he watched servants help his father to his feet, holding him upright. Vespasian's cheeks appeared sunken. He looked as if he'd aged twenty years in just the past few days.

"Ah, Titus, my dear son," he said, sounding tired. His breathing was laboured. His eyes constantly rolled, as if he might faint at any moment.

"I am here, too, Father," Domitian said quickly, clasping one of the Emperor's sweaty hands.

"Yes, so you are." Vespasian then addressed his eldest son. He no longer had the strength to raise his head and look him in the eye. "A pity I'll have to watch the games of our new amphitheatre from Elysium. Make certain you give the people something to remember us by."

"The Flavian name will echo through eternity, I promise you," Titus said earnestly. "And posterity will know that Vespasian was the greatest of us all."

"Come now, no false flattery, son."

"It's true, Father," Domitian said, squeezing his hand. "Thousands of years from now, long after the names Titus and Domitian are forgotten, the colossal amphitheatre of Vespasian will stand as your mark upon the world."

"Well, I had to leave posterity something to remember us by." The Emperor's eyes closed. His breath came in short gasps. He then broke into a fit of merriment, as if having one last joke that only he knew the punchline to. His head flopped back, eyes opening for a moment. With the last of his strength, he let loose as loud a laugh as either of his sons had ever heard.

"Oh my," he said, "I think I am becoming a god!"

Surprisingly, it was Domitian who removed their father's signet ring and placed it on Titus' finger. The younger Flavian pressed it to his lips and whispered, 'Hail, Caesar'.

Stepping into the atrium, the assembled senators noted the ring and the pained expression on Titus' face. All bowed deeply, while also saying the words, 'Hail, Caesar'.

The new Emperor walked slowly past them. He bowed his head and stared at the ring for a few moments. Whatever their differences, he knew his brother had been right. There would be no time for mourning the loss of their father; not true mourning. In that moment, the full weight of the Roman Empire came crashing down on Titus' shoulders. With a deep breath, he turned and faced Domitian. "I promise you, brother, you will be the partner in my labours, as I was to our father before."

Chapter XVI: A Promise Made

Rome
August, 79 A.D.

Murmillo-class Gladiator

The death of Emperor Vespasian was met with sorrowful lamentations from the people of Rome. The 'reluctant Caesar', who restored peace, dignity, and honour to the Empire was loved by many, and even respected by his enemies. Even Josephus, the former Jewish rebel who'd fought against him at Jotapata, wept at the news. As his eldest son stood over the funeral pyre, imploring the gods to welcome Titus Flavius Vespasian into eternity as one of them, word slowly began to make its way around the Empire. Titus now became the great hope for Rome, and the people waited to see just how he would carry on his father's legacy.

Soon after the passing of Vespasian, Verus was called upon to fight again. All of Rome was in a state of mourning, and many noblemen hosted private games to honour the Emperor's passing. In all, ten months had passed since his first two matches; the same amount of time he'd spent in The Pit. Under normal circumstances,

167

a gladiator fought roughly three times a year. Yet in those ten months, Verus had competed in twice as many bouts, amassing a record of four victories and only two defeats. Gladiatorial matches were now becoming far more frequent in and around Rome. With the Emperor's death, it was common knowledge that his son and successor would wish to commemorate him with a grand series of games in the new amphitheatre. Architects assured them that the colossal amphitheatre was within a year of completion.

Anxious to win favour with the people, as well as the new Emperor, more and more nobles started sponsoring contests. The intent was to find the best gladiators within the Empire, to provide Titus and the public with the best possible bouts for the grand games honouring Vespasian. And while Narcissus and the other lanistae were eager to provide matches to all their gladiators, there was a narrowing corps of veteres that seemed to be called upon more than others. In addition to Verus, Severus and Priscus were among these. Severus now had a record of four victories with one defeat; Priscus was unbeaten in six contests. There was little doubt that the Caledonian would be one of the feature gladiators in the upcoming games.

Gulussa, the new primus palus, had fought twice since his return to the ludus. The crowds and his fellow gladiators were quickly reminded why he had been a legend in the arena. Allowed to choose his own style and weaponry, he fought with a long spear and round shield, keeping a gladius strapped to his hip. His speed impressed even Verus. He watched him lunge at an opponent with his spear, only to release the weapon in mid thrust. Before his adversary could react, he tackled him to the ground, his gladius on his neck. Verus couldn't recall even seeing the African draw his blade! And while there were other fighters at the ludus with more matches, these four were clearly being groomed for the greater spectacle. It was, therefore, with mild surprise that Verus was informed of his upcoming bout in early February.

"They want me to fight again?" he asked.

"A talent exhibition," Drusus explained. "This one is being put on by Tiberius Alexander. I'm certain you've heard of him."

"The Jew who served with Titus in Judea," Verus remembered. "Wasn't he also Commander of the Praetorian Guard under Vespasian?"

"The same, though he has since handed his command over to a general named Cornelius Fuscus. As a close friend and confidant of the Emperor, Alexander is well-placed to influence who gets to fight in the eventual Flavian Amphitheatre games. You not only have a growing reputation, but you're among the few veterans healthy enough to make a good show of it. You, Priscus, Severus, and Gulussa will represent our ludus. There are others with more experience and victories than you and Severus, but they are recovering from injury or illness. Narcissus does not wish to risk their health or reputation. This is your chance to prove your worth on a larger stage, against stronger opposition. Take it as a gift from the gods, and do not waste it."

Excitement and nervousness made sleep difficult to come by in the days leading up to the match. When not training, Verus spent his time learning all he could about Tiberius Alexander. An important figure within the regime, not to mention one of Titus' closest friends, his Jewish ethnicity made him a controversial figure. That he'd violently supressed a Jewish rebellion in Alexandria and served with distinction during the Siege of Jerusalem did nothing to sway the xenophobic hate from certain factions within the senate.

Though his Latin had improved greatly over the past two years, with his accent fading considerably, Verus could not read or write. He therefore had to learn what he could from Roman friends such as Severus, or from spending time in the city. He was surprised when occasionally he was recognised by members of the public, and was completely taken aback when his name was shouted by admiring fans.

Something else that consumed much of his thoughts was Vipsania; *The Lady of the Sand*, as he referred to her. Though he knew her flat was not far from the home of Severus' wife, Claudia, he had refrained from trying to go see her. There was a sense of shame for thinking more about Vipsania than he did his wife and son. He was also thinking less and less about home, perhaps because when he did, the pain was too great. In many ways, it felt as if the ludus had consumed his very soul, forging it into something that was completely foreign to him. Was Verus of Rhoxolani dead? Had his very essence been replaced by Verus the Gladiator?

The day of the match arrived. Rather than being open to the public, the small arena outside the city was kept closed and under guard. Only members of the senate and equites were invited, along with a handful of magistrates and officials involved in organising the upcoming games. There were, perhaps, 300 persons in the stands during that sweltering summer morning.

"As you know," Drusus said, addressing his gladiators. "The man sponsoring these contests wields greater influence over the Emperor, and therefore control over your very livelihoods, than any man you've fought for. Each of you will be paired against the same class of fighter with similar skill and ability."

The matches were scheduled to last five days, with thirty contests on each day. On this first day, it was strictly 'light' and 'medium' fighters, such as secutors, armed with gladii and shields.

Severus was in the first pairing, facing a secutor who, like him, had four wins. Verus was to immediately follow, and so it was with great impatience that he was fitted into his armour. Anxious to see how his friend was faring, he snatched his helmet from a servant just as a loud shout came from the master of ceremonies, announcing the names of the first combatants. He ran to the half-open window near the door leading onto the sand.

Severus was more than holding his own. Verus watched his friend's fierce, yet concise attacks, surmising that Severus possessed greater skill than his adversary. He was, however, concerned that the enemy secutor kept circling, keeping his back to the eastern wing of the amphitheatre. It was only a couple of hours after dawn. As Severus readied for another assault, the sun broke over the edge of the arena, its glaring light blinding him. This was the moment the rival secutor had waited for. Severus did not even see the man's buckler until it smashed him upside the helm. He cried out when his opponent stabbed him in the side before the martial could intervene.

"Hold, damn you!" the martial shouted, slapping the secutor hard across the chest with his staff.

The crowd of magistrates and nobles which, up to this point, had been far more reserved than the usual raucous mob, let loose a combination of gasps and cheers. The triumphant secutor raised his crimson-stained weapon in victory. The stricken Severus writhed in anguish, bleeding from the terrible wound.

From his seat within the sponsor's box, Tiberius Alexander stood and raised his hand, signalling that Severus would be spared. However, the stricken gladiator could not stand. He lay on the ground, clutching at his side. Blood seeped between his fingers, dripping onto the arena sand. At a signal from the martial, four slaves rushed forward with a litter.

"No!" Verus shouted in horror. Mortified, he watched his friend being hefted onto the stretcher and carried away. He started for the entryway leading to the infirmary when a hand grabbed him roughly by the collar of his armour.

"Where in Hades do you think you're going?" Drusus asked sternly.

"Severus," Verus stammered. "I…"

His words were cut short by a hard slap across the face.

"Pull yourself together!" Drusus barked. "There isn't a damn thing you can do for him, and you're fighting next! Get your fucking head straight. Go out there and do what you've been training for since you came to the ludus." Verus gave a nervous nod. Drusus grabbed him roughly by the back of the neck. "This is your chance. If you fail, there will not be another."

Verus stood tall and firmly removed Drusus' hand from his neck. With a curt nod, he turned and made his way slowly, yet purposefully, towards the gate leading to the arena floor. He slapped his open-faced helmet onto his head almost as an afterthought. He checked the straps on his shield, drew his gladius, and gave it a few practice swings. He knew their opponents came from the same ludus. If he could not save Severus, then he would avenge him.

Without waiting for the master of ceremonies to finish announcing him, Verus stepped determinedly through the gate. His gaze, filled with rage, was focused on his opponent. He did not settle into his fighting stance right away, but simply glared at the man.

171

Only when the martial bellowed, *'Fight!'*, did Verus step one leg back and bring his shield to bear. The provocator he faced was of similar size, speed, and agility. And from what he'd learned prior to the match, they both had four victories in the arena. But none of that mattered now. Verus channelled his fury, determined to make an example of his adversary.

Drusus had taught him if he could out-think his opponent, he could best any man; be they bigger, stronger, faster, or better than him. As sword and shield clashed, it became apparent that Verus was quicker of the mind, if not the body. He remained two steps ahead of his foe, easily countering his strikes and peppering him with repeated gouges from his weapon, along with bruising blows from his shield, and the occasional kick to the leg with his protected shins.

The two fighters were supposed to be evenly matched, but within a minute, the other provocator was covered in blood from numerous superficial wounds. It was readily apparent that Verus was toying with him. The man grew desperate and even more frenzied in his attacks. Verus knew he needed to end the contest soon, for even an outmatched and desperate foe was still incredibly dangerous. Mimicking a manoeuvre he'd witnessed Vipsania perform, he executed a short side-step as the provocator thrust his sword wildly, before smashing the edge of his buckler into the side of the man's helm, dropping him to his knees. A subsequent blow to the head, followed by a hard kick to his exposed belly sent him sprawling awkwardly onto his back. Only half-conscious, he wasn't even able to raise a finger to ask for mercy. Verus stomped his foot onto the man's chest, raising his arms high while giving a howl of fury and triumph.

He waited long enough for Alexander to signal that the match was over before quickly making his way from the arena pit. He was covered in sweat, despite the relative brevity of his bout, and his hair was matted to his head when he wrenched off his helmet.

Despite his feelings of elation at having won what was arguably his greatest victory to date, Verus' chief concern was the wellbeing of his friend. Waving off the slaves who would normally help him out of his armour, he threw his helmet aside and ran back to the medical chamber. Severus was no longer crying out in pain. He lay still upon a table, eyes half shut in delirium. Orderlies had mopped

172

up a great deal of blood, but where he lay was stained and sticky. Priscus and Gulussa were there. Both men were sombre, their heads bowed slightly.

"Is he…" Verus started to ask, the words balling up in his throat.

"He's resting," the medic explained. "I had to give him quite the dose of poppies to make him sleep. It nearly killed him right there. I fear your friend is not long for this world. If it were a gash or broken bone, I could mend him. However, his injuries are internal. I fear his guts have ruptured, and he will soon die of infection. I suggest you say your farewells now. I doubt he will last the night."

In a profession where death was a constant companion, Verus knew the risk of maintaining friendships. That said, how could he not grow close to those who he lived, trained, ate, and spent almost every waking hour with? Besides, Severus had been with him since The Pit. He kept a very small circle of friends, namely Priscus and Severus, though in recent weeks Gulussa had spent much time training with the trio. He knew they were being groomed for greater things, once the Flavian Amphitheatre opened. But now they would have to continue without Severus.

It was Gulussa who Verus found sitting atop the high stone wall which overlooked the ludus. The Dacian had just come from the bathhouse, where he had tried to wash away the filth and grief.

Gulussa was the first black African Verus had ever met. He'd seen the occasional dark-skinned man or woman when wandering the streets of Rome. These, however, were few in number; mostly merchants from the furthest eastern reaches of the Empire or slaves imported from places like Gulussa's native Numidia. His fellow gladiator, however, was a Roman. His appearance was starkly different from Narcissus and Drusus. but he shared their native tongue, as well as much of their culture. Verus sat on the wall next to the primus palus, an awkward silence following.

Gulussa finally broke it. "I am sorry," he said, though his face and voice were impassive.

"Fate is a cruel bitch," Verus replied after a few moments. He went on to explain how he came to meet Severus. How, by a twist of fate, the lanista either never knew or did not care that he should have

173

been condemned with the damnati. That he'd been able to train and live like the rest of the gladiators, and able to see his wife and son, had given him hope. As much as he longed for his own freedom, Verus wished almost as fervently that Severus could overcome the cruelty of fate and be reunited with his family as a free man.

"There is no fate," Gulussa remarked. "People believe in things such as fate and the gods, because it gives them some measure of comfort to think there are powers, beyond those of the men, in control of the world." He shook his head slowly. "In all my years, I have found that those who place their trust in the gods, tend to die disappointed. After witnessing the first of many friends die screaming in agony, his guts splayed open, pleading with whatever deities he hoped would save him, I realised it was all for nothing. I decided not to put my trust in any divine powers. If they exist at all, they are utterly indifferent to the sufferings of men. I swore that if I fell in defeat, my very essence bloodily swept away to the blackness of oblivion, I would not give those bastards the satisfaction. Severus understood this. He did not cry out to any god as he lay dying, but to his wife. That is why I mourn for him."

Verus' next words choked up in his throat, as he struggled to speak. Finally, he managed. "And that is why we must look after Claudia and their son."

The following day, the sun shone bright, contrasting with the black garments worn by the procession of gladiators and instructors from the ludus. Even Narcissus joined them, wearing a black tunic lined with gold trim and a hooded cloak. On many occasions, Verus had walked past the gladiator graveyard on the outskirts of the city. He had never stepped inside its gated, low walls. Other fighters had died from injury or, more often, untreated disease. The ludus was very large, with nearly two hundred total combatants living in its dormitories. None of the others had been more than a passing acquaintance. For the first time since becoming a gladiator, Verus was saying goodbye to a friend.

Prior to being sentenced to the arena, Severus had been a lost and desperate soul. The ludus gave him discipline and purpose. And though she feared constantly for his safety, Claudia had often said

174

the school of the gladiator saved his life. No one ever mentioned the administrative error that kept him from being confined like the *Damnatio Gladiatorii.* This had given Severus the constant hope that he might one day win the rudis and palm.

On this day, Verus was dressed in black robes with the rest of Severus' friends. It was a bitter reminder of the hazardous nature of their profession; tomorrow was never promised, and fate was indeed a cruel bitch. Because of his work ethics and genial deportment, Severus had been popular at the ludus. This meant there was no shortage of mourners. Fifty men from the ludus, and even three women, accompanied the grieving Claudia to the cemetery. Among the women was Vipsania, who Verus had not seen in many months. She kept her black cloak close around her body despite the heat of the day. A sheer black veil covered her face.

Verus, Priscus, and Gulussa were among those asked to carry the body. As primus palus, it was Gulussa's right to stand with Narcissus and the other ludus staff during the interment. However, his loyalty was foremost to his fellow gladiators, and he gladly helped carry his fallen friend to his final resting place. Claudia walked beside them, while a younger woman, possibly her sister, clutched her hand, keeping her other arm gently draped over her shoulder.

Narcissus, Drusus, and about twenty of the ludus' instructors and staff stood in mourning garb near the grave. The loss of a gladiator, especially one of Severus' experience and potential, was more of a business than a personal loss. However, Narcissus maintained a sombre tone out of respect. He spoke briefly, asking the gods to welcome their fallen brother into the gates of Elysium. Claudia wept uncontrollably as her husband's shrouded body was lowered into the grave.

Verus placed a hand on her shoulder. "All of us made a promise to Severus; if anything happened to him, we would always look after you and your son. You are a part of our family, Claudia, and we will always protect you."

His words suddenly made Verus long for his own family and home. A chill ran up his spine, as he suddenly saw Tamura's face reflected on Claudia. He closed his eyes and swallowed hard. It was the first time in many months that he was able to visualise his wife's face. And then, in an instant it was gone again.

Shaking his head, he turned his attention to Severus' headstone, as several men hefted it off a cart. It read:

G SEVERVS
SECVTOR, IV VICTORIAS ARENAM
MORTVS, ANNVS PRIMVS, IMP TITVS FLAVIUS
XXIX ANNORVM AETATIS

Gaius Severus
Secutor, Four Victories in the Arena
Died in the First Year of Emperor Titus Flavius
Twenty-Nine years old

Chapter XVII: A Promise Kept

Rome
April, 80 A.D.

Secutor-class Gladiator

The months following the ascension of Titus to the imperial throne were fraught with tragedy. Less than two months after his ascension, and just days following the death of Severus during Alexander's gladiatorial matches, the volcanic mountain of Vesuvius erupted, with the fury of Vulcan spilling forth from the bowels of the earth. The cities of Pompeii and Herculaneum, 150 miles to the south of Rome, were consumed by the hellish wrath of the gods. Thousands were killed; their contortions of agony frozen in time for all eternity as they were engulfed in molten pumice and ash. Even in Rome the aftershocks could be felt. Verus and his fellow gladiators had stood atop the walls of the ludus, able to see a faint column of smoke. Ash fell upon Rome and much of Italia for weeks after. Emperor Titus spared no expense when it came to providing aid for the twenty thousand survivors who lost everything. The charred ruins of the ancient cities near Vesuvius were abandoned.

The remainder of the year mercifully passed without further calamity. Verus again became absorbed in his life as a Roman gladiator. He fought just one time over the next ten months. This was against a murmillo; the class of heavy fighter which had been his bane up to this point. Whether by the other gladiator's inexperience or Verus becoming far better than even he realised, he dispatched the man with contemptuous ease. This was his seventh victory in the arena, and with the Flavian Amphitheatre nearing completion, Narcissus decided not to squander his prized gladiators in minor spectacles.

Like Priscus, Verus had earned a considerable sum in silver and copper coin since coming to the ludus. After his fifth triumph, he paid Narcissus 600 denarii for his own flat along the north side of the ludus, not far from the lanista's manor house. Priscus lived next door in similar accommodations. The flat was on the ground level with stone steps just inside, leading up to the main living area. There was room for a four-person table, an alcove where Verus kept his statue of Nemesis, and even a clay oven embedded in the back wall.

The sound of running water was constantly heard. The flat also had its own private latrine; albeit this was little more than a single stall. For the privileged living in these 'luxury' flats, the piping of water from the main aqueduct meant that their waste was continuously washed away, alleviating much of the potential wretched smells. There was even a spout and basin near the oven where Verus could access drinking and washing water. It was still very humble and crude, especially when one saw how the patrician-class in Rome lived. However, compared to any place Verus had ever lived, even during his previous life in Dacia, it was an abode fit for a king.

It was now spring. The air was crisp and smelled fresh even within the confines of the claustrophobic city. They were also just two months from the anniversary of Vespasian's passing to the gods and Titus' rise to become Emperor.

"I hear he's going to time the opening games of the new amphitheatre to commemorate both events," Priscus noted.

He and Verus stood atop the roof of their dormitory complex. The hour was late, just after the evening feast. The two spent much time in each other's company, only rarely socialising with the other members of the ludus.

"I overheard Drusus and the doctors mentioning the same thing," Verus recalled.

"The day will soon come when we take part in writing the pages of history," his Caledonian friend said rather philosophically.

"I only wish the games were happening now, as opposed to the middle of summer." Verus had grown to love the time of year in Rome between March and June, when the evenings were still cool and the days pleasantly warm. Come July, the month named in honour of the divine Julius Caesar, it became stiflingly hot and humid in the Eternal City. The risk of heat exhaustion, not to mention constantly getting sweat into one's eyes, were often as much of a threat as any opponent they faced.

"Strange, the things I concern myself with now. It is a far cry from the hellish months I spent in The Pit, and worlds away from my previous life north of the Danube." He paused for a moment and bowed his head slightly. "I have a confession to make, old friend. I look back on my life, my family, and who I was before. It's been not even three years since I was captured and taken from my home, yet I'm not the same person anymore. Verus of the Rhoxolani died in The Pit. Verus the Gladiator was born in the ludus."

"And what will Verus the Gladiator do, should he win his freedom?"

"No idea. Even if I did return to Dacia and found my wife alive, and not re-married, I am no longer the man she married all those years ago. I fear she would not know me, nor I her. I would be a foreigner in my own land." He tried to steer the conversation away from himself. "And what about you? Where will Priscus the Gladiator go, should he win his freedom?"

"I would probably stay here. There is nothing for me in the old country. Besides, it is too cold and wet in Caledonia, and the people are insufferable."

"Including you?" Verus asked with a bemused grin.

"*Especially* me," his friend added.

Their reverie was interrupted by the sounds of chaos and terror in the distance. Both men paused and turned their gazes in the direction of where the Flavian Amphitheatre stood in near completion about two miles to the northeast. The flames of lamp and

179

torchlight were commonplace, especially at night when all the wheeled traffic moved throughout the cramped city. What they saw was not the fire of torches, but a brittle roof being engulfed in flames.

"Nemesis preserve us," Verus whispered under his breath.

Alarms sounded throughout the surrounding districts as the spring winds whipped the flames about, spreading it to all the nearby structures. In just a few short minutes, the fire leapt from a single structure to engulf an entire block of flats, with nothing to stop it from spreading further.

Despite the horrific destruction wrought by the Great Fire sixteen years before, it seemed the Romans had not learned the harsh lesson of building so many combustible buildings, particularly when it came to housing for the poor, so close together. A disaster was unfolding. All the merchant carts and wagons clogging the streets created an even greater scene of pandemonium.

"Claudia!" Verus turned to Priscus, his face etched in horror. "That is where Claudia lives!"

"Damn it all."

Without another word, they raced for the creaky wooden steps down to the lower levels of the structure. They soon found Gulussa. He'd gathered about twenty volunteers near the north gate. The primus palus was organising groups of men to assist the city's firefighters, known as the vigiles. Verus, Priscus, and a few others headed into the growing firestorm, intent on keeping their promise.

The streets leading towards the inferno were clustered with hordes of people trying to escape its fearsome wrath. The smell of smoke assailed their nostrils the closer they came. Vigiles and volunteers were already bringing carts of water, trying to contain the blaze. Their efforts were hampered by the desperate mob attempting to flee. A considerable number of volunteers carried axes and large chains, intent on pulling down structures that could not be saved in an attempt to prevent the flames from spreading. A team of vigiles were forcing their way through the throng. Without hesitation, Priscus seized a coil of rope from their cart before anyone could protest.

The flames had reached a series of flats Verus recognised as being the residence of Severus and Claudia. There was a courtyard in the centre of the complex, and it was through here that many of the residents fled.

"Over there!" Priscus shouted, pointing to the third level of the northeast corner. The fires had already consumed much of the lower floors, and they could see a woman and child trapped.

"Come on!" Verus forced his way past the fleeing denizens.

The stairs leading to the upper floor were burning and impassable. He saw he could readily scale the outside structure, provided the support scaffolding held. These were very crude and unstable. He grimaced as he started to climb, hoping they would support his weight. Priscus was beneath him. He, too, was conscious of not putting too much strain on the cross planks, which were not meant to hold a grown man. The Caledonian had the coil of rope slung over his left shoulder. There were no more cries of help coming from the upper level. Claudia and her young son had collapsed from the heat and smoke.

Verus pulled himself onto the landing, the heat from the burning roof searing into him. He kept low, nearly choking on the gouts of smoke. Without bothering to see if Claudia was alive, he hoisted her onto his back.

"Here," Priscus said, tying the rope to a thick beam. "I'd say we have about two minutes.

Using one hand to hold Claudia's limp arm and leg against him, Verus clutched the rope with his free hand and began to lower himself down. Priscus, meanwhile, took the boy in his arms and started to follow his friend down. The scaffolding planks snapped under the combined weight. Verus' hand cramped trying to keep hold of the rope. He let himself drop the last few feet, twisting his ankle as he landed roughly on the cobblestones. Claudia fell from his back, cracking her head on the ground. She let out a whimper, at least telling Verus she was alive.

"We're not out of this yet," Priscus said, grabbing him by the shoulder. Flames had reached every building in the complex, threatening to trap them in the small courtyard. Verus picked up Claudia once more and hobbled out onto the main street.

The way south, towards the distant ludus, was blocked with people and wagons. The only possible path to safety took them towards the amphitheatre. Screams of horror and pleas from the trapped echoed through the night. Many perished in this holocaust of fire. The inferno had already consumed a residential district nearest the amphitheatre. The arena itself, however, was untouched. There was a vast open space surrounding the colossal structure. Here, with hundreds of other refugees, Verus set Claudia down; more gently this time. Her eyes half-open, she whispered her son's name.

"He's safe," Priscus said reassuringly, setting the boy down next to his mother. He looked his friend in the eye. "We kept our promise."

Verus left Priscus to watch over Claudia and her son, and continued to wander throughout the charred ruins. In a showing of good faith towards their fellow Romans, Narcissus would later order training cancelled for the following week, his gladiators tasked in helping the recovery efforts. He was told that the destruction was not nearly as catastrophic as the Great Fire from sixteen years earlier. This was of little comfort to those who'd lost their homes and loved ones. Many city blocks, mostly residences belonging to the city's poor, were destroyed.

It was with profound surprise that he saw Vipsania near the burning ruins of what was once her apartment flat. The upper floors had collapsed and great torrents of flame shot upward like Vulcan's fury. He barely recognised the woman gladiator. She was covered in ash and soot. Her clothes were torn and burned, eyes bloodshot, and her expression vacant. In her arms, she clutched a charred bundle. When he knelt next to her, Verus saw it was the body of a baby.

"Was this…was this your child?" he asked.

"No." Vipsania slowly shook her head, her gaze still fixed straight ahead at nothing. "But her mother had always treated me kindly. The floor collapsed, taking her into the fire. I sought to repay her kindness by saving her daughter. But I was too late. Too late…"

Verus slowly reached over and pulled the charred remains from her arms. Vipsania did not resist. As he took her by the shoulder and helped her to her feet, she winced in pain. He saw her left arm and shoulder were badly burned. Angry blisters and bloody scorch marks ran from her shoulder down to her forearm.

"Come," Verus said. "Let's leave this place of death."

It took them the better part of the night to make their way back to the ludus. They first crossed the River Tiber at a congested bridge due west of the amphitheatre. They then followed the river south for nearly two miles before reaching a crossing that would take them back to the relative safety of the gladiatorial school. All the while, they could hear the cacophony of chaos in the distance. The northern horizon was red with fire.

It was now two hours past midnight, and while the ludus was alive with activity, the bathhouse was mostly empty. Verus roused a medic whose quarters were just off the bathhouse. The man at first protested, but when Drusus arrived, he quickly relented.

"You live, gods be praised," he said with a relieved sigh at the sight of Vipsania. The woman gladiator nodded tiredly.

Drusus turned to Verus. "Look after her. She is very important to me."

Verus helped Vipsania make her way into the baths, where beneath the floor slaves were stoking the fires to heat up the caldarium. Vipsania forced her way past the medic and unceremoniously stripped out of her filthy, torn garments before gingerly lowering herself into the lukewarm waters. Verus removed his own tunic and submerged himself next to her. The lady gladiator slowly moved her injured arm about. She gritted her teeth as the seared flesh tore when she bent her elbow.

"At least I can still move my arm," she reasoned. "But I won't be fighting for some time."

Verus said nothing. He plunged beneath the waters for a moment, soaking his face and head. Vipsania did the same, eager to wash away the ash and filth.

"Not exactly how I anticipated you seeing me naked," she remarked with a forced smile that looked more like a grimace.

"Believe me, this is about as arousing for me as it is for you," Verus replied with dark humour.

There was little doubt that the fire was a great calamity for Rome. Thousands were likely dead, with many more injured and now homeless. How the Emperor and senate would deal with this was anybody's guess, particularly considering the recent tragedy at Herculaneum and Pompeii. It seemed as if the gods themselves were angry with Rome.

The two washed as much of the grime off their bodies as they were able before making their way to a side room, where a medic awaited them. Vipsania sat naked on one of the massage tables. The medic took a stygil and began to scrape away the charred skin. She clenched her teeth, her face red and eyes wet, yet made not a sound.

No stranger to blood and fearful injuries, Verus felt his stomach twist in knots as he watched, finding himself unable to avert his eyes as layers of blackened skin were scraped away.

A compress of pungent herbs was placed over the wound, which he then loosely wrapped in a bandage.

"Fortuna smiles on you, daughter of the arena," the medic said. "You'll have some nasty scarring, but the muscle and bone are unharmed. Drusus has ordered me to see to you personally. You will need to leave this on for the next few days. It is when we rehabilitate the arm that it will get truly painful."

Vipsania nodded. "Will I be ready to fight in the opening games of the amphitheatre?"

This question baffled the medic. He gave a soft chuckle. "I think the Emperor has more pressing matters at the moment. But, as I said, you will have a very painful recovery when we start strengthening the arm again, which will tear the scar tissue. In a couple months, you should be able to begin training again."

With Vipsania sleeping in the infirmary, Verus returned to his own quarters, emotionally and physically exhausted. He slept well into midmorning, at first thinking the entire harrowing ordeal had been a dream. He found Priscus and inquired after Claudia.

"She's a mess, but she'll live," his friend said candidly. "Her sister lives in the southern districts of the city, and has taken her in. Oh, and Narcissus has suspended training for the week; ordering us to assist in the recovery."

Verus nodded. Like the night before, the day was a complete blur to him. They spent much of their time aiding the vigiles in tearing down the charred ruins of buildings and looking for survivors. This was mostly in vain, as the blistering inferno had engulfed all who failed to escape.

The mood within Rome was very sombre with little said, except for the wailing sobs of those who found the charred and blackened remains of their families. It was a time of hopelessness and sorrow.

That night as Verus was about to retire, there was a pounding on his door. He was mildly surprised to see that it was Vipsania. Her bandaged arm was now in a cloth sling, and she was wearing an ill-fitting borrowed tunic.

"I wanted to thank you for everything," she said awkwardly.

It puzzled Verus that someone so brazen and seemingly unbreakable was now utterly devoid of her usual brashness.

"Of course," he replied.

Before he could say another word, Vipsania grabbed him by the back of the neck with her free arm and kissed him deeply. Caught completely by surprise, he stumbled back against the stone wall. Vipsania ran her lips and tongue against his. She gently bit him on the neck and whispered into his ear, "Don't talk, just let it happen."

Chapter XVIII: An Imperial Summons

Rome
May, 80 A.D.

Emperor Titus

There were mutterings throughout the city that Emperor Titus had brought about disfavour from the gods. No one could say what he had done, but between Vesuvius destroying Pompeii and Herculaneum, and now the horrific blaze which destroyed large sections of Rome, the people could only guess that the Empire was now cursed. Titus knew he needed to act quickly. Rather than relying on the imperial treasury to pay for the rebuilding in Rome, he used his personal funds to aid the survivors. He bought hundreds of carts of food and medicines for the now-homeless. Such generosity drained much of his wealth, yet it also made it clear to the people that their Emperor would personally look after their welfare.

"Providing food and housing for the displaced will not be enough," he said bluntly, when he met with the consuls and imperial council.

As a means of placating his brother and making good on his promise of sharing in the labours of ruling, Titus had named Domitian consul for the entire year, with a series of suffects serving as his colleague.

"People question whether my family is cursed by the gods," the Emperor continued. "In the span of a few months, we've had two cities destroyed by Vulcan's wrath, as well as yet another terrible fire within our beloved city. I, myself, even wonder if such disasters would have befallen us were my father still on the imperial throne."

"While we should honour and respect the gods, Caesar," Senator Nerva spoke up, "we should not give in to childish superstition."

"It does not matter whether *we* give in to superstition," Titus countered. He pointed towards the walls leading out into the city. "It is *they*, the people, whose superstition should trouble us. Barely eleven years have passed since an emperor was slain outside these walls in the Forum."

"To be fair, Caesar," Consul Rufus said, "Galba was a hated tyrant, loathed by both noble and pleb alike. And Vitellius was a pretender who, by your divine father's own words, had overthrown Rome's lawful emperor, Otho."

Titus immediately refuted, "If one were to ask the people, an emperor cursed by the gods is a greater threat than a pretender or a murderous tyrant."

The Emperor paused for a few moments, allowing the senators and councillors to digest his words. No one else spoke, not even Domitian. They waited for him to either proclaim what he thought should be done or ask their advice on the matter.

"While the mob is fickle and potentially violent," Titus at last said, "it can also be easily controlled. The great Flavian Amphitheatre is more than just my father's eternal gift to the people of Rome. It gives us the means of placating the masses; reassuring them that both Emperor and Senate are favoured by the gods. That is why these games *must* be the most spectacular ever seen. The Flavian Amphitheatre is the largest arena ever built for such spectacle, but it will take more than just a massive sand pit surrounded by 65,000 seats. The games honouring the rise of the Flavian Dynasty and Rome's triumph over the Jews will last a hundred days. And I want every day to rival the previous one in spectacle and grandeur. Thankfully, my father was very prudent

187

with the imperial treasury. Even with the building of the amphitheatre, other public works, the reconstruction of Pompeii, Herculaneum, and Rome, there is still ample gold and silver remaining from the captured spoils of Jerusalem. And, of course, I will contribute greatly from my own coffers."

Titus paused once again, allowing the senators time to talk quietly amongst themselves for a few moments. Games were the most obvious and effective means of controlling the humour of the mob. And as disastrous as the recent fire in Rome had been, the Flavian Amphitheatre remained untouched. It was Domitian who pointed this out.

"The fires destroyed the surrounding districts, yet the amphitheatre remains unscathed." He then declared, "It is either a sign that we are favoured by the gods, or that it is stronger than any calamity they wish to inflict on Rome."

For the first time ever, Titus smiled and nodded approvingly towards his brother

"Proclaim to the people," he said, "that it is the will of the gods that the great amphitheatre was spared; a sign of their favour towards the Flavian Dynasty. Starting in July—the month named for the divine Julius Caesar—we will have a hundred days of the greatest gladiatorial contests they will ever see. I want men, women, and beasts alike, from every corner of the Empire. Let them know there will be blood. The gods are demanding a sacrifice, so we shall give it to them in the arena sand."

When the city criers announced the opening games of the Flavian Amphitheatre, there was a renewed sense of energy and purpose amongst the gladiators. If the games were to last a hundred days, every one of them would get a chance to fight; possibly more than once. And if the Emperor himself was sponsoring the contests, the potential for coin, and perhaps even freedom, was as colossal as the new amphitheatre.

For Verus, the concept of 'freedom' had become very abstract. Home now felt as foreign as Rome did when he first arrived. How could he ever face Tamura after all he'd done? And yet, he knew he should not feel guilty for the night of passion spent with Vipsania. In a strange twist, he was ashamed because he *didn't* feel guilty about sleeping with her. In fact, he found himself thinking often about his 'lady of the sand', who he viewed as both lover and kindred spirit. The paradox was, he barely even knew her. They were simply two of 'the damned', who earned their keep by amusing the mob with acts of extreme violence. He assumed they were close to the same age, yet he knew nothing about her family, past life, hopes, dreams, or even her real name.

Verus contemplated this, as he did every morning on his rest days. He decided to head for the baths in hopes of clearing his mind. They were mostly empty during the early hours. This also meant that the caldarium was not sufficiently heated. Still, he appreciated the moments of solitude as he sat in the waters, his arms resting against the edge of the pool.

"Verus," Drusus said. His voice echoed in the chamber, as he walked across the tiled floor. "You are scheduled for a match."

"When?"

"Tonight."

"Tonight?" Verus opened his eyes and sat upright. In every contest he had fought, he was always given weeks, sometimes even a month, to prepare. Not only that, but gladiatorial matches were not known for taking place at night.

"There is a great feast for some important people, and they've asked us to provide a fighter for their 'special entertainment'. It was stressed they wanted one of our best, and Narcissus offered them your name."

"I suppose I should be honoured," Verus replied. He licked his lips nervously and looked up at the trainer who had become more like a mentor, if not quite a friend, over the past two years. "Why do you look distressed, then?"

"Not your concern," Drusus replied abruptly. "My exact instructions were to make certain you are bathed, freshly shaven, and looking your best. You are not to ask questions, just be ready for anything."

"Of course." Verus was perplexed by Drusus' cryptic words.

In all the time he'd known him, the chief instructor was always extremely blunt and deliberate in his speech. That he was being forcibly silenced and hesitant was, in itself, unnerving. Logic told Verus he had little reason to be concerned; outside of the usual

189

hazards of a bout. It must be someone extremely wealthy, to afford to pay for a gladiatorial contest during a dinner party. He figured fighting in a dining hall was pretty much the same as in the arena, albeit the tables, couches, and even the spectators, might create unwanted obstacles. As he continued to lounge in the bath, he began to contemplate strategy, particularly regarding the flooring. If it were a rich man's house, it likely had marble or tile floors, which would be slippery for his hobnailed sandals. He debated if he should fight barefoot or, perhaps, request a pair of slippers devoid of nails.

Verus spent the afternoon attempting to relax. He wandered down to the nearest market and purchased some incense, which he burned at the base of his statue of Nemesis. He ate very little during supper, and he later found himself pacing in his room, growing ever more eager as the sun went down. About an hour after sunset, he saw two rows of torches coming up the lane towards his flat. His door was opened, and one of the school's staff clerks stepped in.

"These men are here to take you to your match," he said.

Verus was surprised to see that his escorts were armoured soldiers from the Praetorian Guard. He opened his mouth to speak, then recalled Drusus' stern warning about not asking any questions. He nodded and rose from his bunk.

"This way," the decanus leading the detail said.

There were twelve of them, with four carrying torches.

As they marched along the road leading out of the ludus, scores of eyes were on them. Curious gladiators and staff members gathered to watch as Verus was led away. There was a lot of talk amongst them. Like Verus, they could not fathom why the Emperor's bodyguards were acting as his escorts.

Verus surmised that the Emperor himself was hosting this party, yet they were not heading in the direction of the imperial palace. He had no idea where he was being taken, only that he was in one of the wealthier neighbourhoods of Rome. Each house, belonging to a single family, was larger than an entire block of flats. All were two to three stories high and home to dozens of servants and personal guards, in addition to the noblemen, their wives, and children. This was where the elite lived. In the encompassing dark of night, Verus could see very little. There was little traffic on the streets, unlike the congested lower quarters of the city.

The detail halted outside a splendid estate belonging to Marius Rufus, the current suffect consul, and one of the most powerful men in Rome. Rumour had it he was one of those tasked by Emperor Titus with finding the best talent for the upcoming games. It seemed he intended to give his sovereign a taste of what was to come.

A section of praetorians stood on either side of the gate, their decanus talking briefly with the man who led Verus' escort. He was led into the outer gardens. Even in the pale, cloudy night he could see a long, raised pool on either side, topped with ornate fountains every twenty feet. Near the steps leading into the main house, he was diverted along a side path that led around to a small entrance flanked by large fruit trees.

The inside was lit with hanging oil lamps, and he could hear music and merriment echoing from elsewhere in the large house. Four guardsmen led him down a narrow corridor and into a side room where he was ordered to strip out of his tunic. Thinking he was changing into his armour, Verus complied. Concerned about his hobnailed sandals slipping on the smooth stone, he removed these as well. Surprisingly, the floor felt warm to his bare feet; no doubt the result of the hypocaust subfloor heating. While common in bathhouses, only the extremely rich could afford to heat their homes this way.

He was puzzled when he was given a shove from behind, into a large foyer. It was very dark. The sky was cloudy and allowed only trace amounts of star and moonlight to shine through the high windows. A porter stood with his hands folded around a long staff near the large double doors across the tiled floor. The praetorian decanus nodded to him, and the porter cracked open the door and slipped inside.

As soon as there was a break in the music, the man beat his staff on the ground three times. "Friends and guests of our noble host, Consul Marius Rufus, and most of all to our noble Emperor, Titus Caesar, it is with great pleasure that our host presents to you the highlight of this evening's entertainment. From the gladiatorial ludus of Marcellus Julianus, with five victories in the arena, I give you the Greek, Pericles!"

There was a notable pause. Verus was astounded by the silence that emanated from within. A hand was placed on his shoulder, and with a push, he stepped through the doors. The occasional oil lamp hanging from a tall stand provided the only light. He was left with the impression it had been much brighter before, but that many of the lights were extinguished to add ambiance and dramatic effect.

There was a large open space in the centre of the floor, encircled by a ring of formal dining couches and tables. In the darkness beyond the circle, he could not tell how many guests were gathered. He reckoned the hall to be large and quite full of the consul's guests. Praetorian Guardsmen stood in a circle between the couches, hands resting on their shields. No doubt they were there to keep the match from spilling over onto the dining nobles. At first, Verus was uncertain which one was the Emperor. He had never seen Titus in person and only gave the occasional passing glance at his statues, which had sprung up rather quickly, following the death of his father. He then saw a group clustered near the edge of the ring, facing him. The man at the centre wore purple robes with gold trim, in a sharp contrast to the colours of the other togas. He had a thick head of curly hair and a full, round face. This was a genetic trait, rather than a sign of being overweight. He was a big, powerful man, whose visible forearms were thick with muscle. Several noblemen were lounging on their couches near him. Verus guessed one of them was the consul who owned the home.

Then he spotted the bare-chested man, standing a few feet to the right of the Emperor. He was roughly the same height and build as Verus. The only notable difference being that he'd elected to leave his sandals on.

"And now," the porter continued. "From the gladiatorial ludus of Marcus Vipsanius Narcissus, with seven victories in the arena, I give you the Dacian, Verus!"

No armour, no shield, Verus thought quietly to himself. *Do I at least get a weapon or do they expect us to beat each other to death?*

His question was answered by the nudge against his arm. He turned to see a guardsman presenting his gladius to him. Verus took the weapon and waved it in short arcs to his front, testing the balance. It was light yet sturdy. With a quick touch, he knew the blade was razor sharp. As it was the praetorian's personal weapon, he knew it was well-crafted and unlikely to break. His opponent was armed in the same manner. With nothing to protect them, Verus ground his teeth. This struggle would be bloody.

192

The porter stepped to the centre of the floor, acting as martial. He held his staff outward in front of him, signalling for the combatants to come forward. Verus' eyes were locked on his opponent. He tried to find something to distinguish him. All he knew was if this Greek had five victories in the sand, then he was clearly a skilled fighter and well versed in the gladiatorial arts. But what style of fighter was he? Was he a provocator like Verus? Or perhaps a murmillo or Samnite? If he was a retiarius, used to fighting with a trident and net, Verus would have the advantage. Unfortunately, there was no way of knowing. Despite a bit of scruff on his face, the man looked young, probably a few years younger than Verus.

There was no time for further assessments, for the porter did not bother with having the men salute their sponsors. Whether this was deliberate or an oversight from never officiating a gladiatorial match before, Verus would never know. His opponent seemed to anticipate this. Before the porter had fully pulled his staff away, he lunged at Verus, attacking with quick stabs and short slashes at his face and torso. Leaping backwards, using his gladius to slap the blows away, Verus ran into the shield of a praetorian who nearly shoved him right into his adversary. Their fighting space was much smaller than he was used to, and the Greek was already attempting to corner him.

Verus had trained in using a sword defensively, but it felt unnatural to him. The gladius was an offensive weapon, and the clanging of blades was something one usually saw done by actors in the theatre, choreographed for dramatic effect. In actual combat, one avoided allowing an opponent's blade to strike their own. With no shield, Verus had little choice. It also rendered his left arm completely useless. His opponent was attacking with such speed and ferocity, he feared if he tried to punch the man, he'd lose his hand in the process.

The Greek was clearly no fool. When his first barrage failed to bring Verus down, he stepped away, catching his breath and allowing Verus to circle towards the centre of the floor. He was grinning, noting that he'd nicked the Dacian several times during the flurry. Verus was unaware of his wounds, thinking it was sweat running down his shoulders and chest rather than blood. The injuries were superficial, yet the streaks of blood brought a few smiles and nods of approval from the noble spectators. Their silence was far more unnerving than the drunken cheers of the mob.

The Greek was standing defensively, allowing Verus to come to him. Knowing the man was studying him, Verus attacked with ferocity, tempering his usual speed and precision, hoping to lull the man into thinking he was slower than he actually was. He also varied his attack, thrusting alternately towards the face and stomach. At one point, he ducked low and swung his blade hard towards the man's shin. This was a risky ploy for Verus. Without a shield, there was nothing to stop his foe from plunging his blade down into his neck. Fortunately, this startled the Greek, and he stumbled out of the way. His sandals lost purchase on the smooth floor, and he nearly fell onto his backside.

Sensing an opportunity, Verus attacked once more, this time with greater speed. In desperation, the Greek took a chance and grabbed a hold of him, their sword arms intertwined. Without thinking, Verus smashed his left fist into the side of the man's face and head. The third blow struck the side of the jaw, and the Greek collapsed to the floor, pulling Verus down on top of him. Now on his knees, Verus wrenched his sword arm free and placed the point on the unconscious fighter's neck.

His breath was coming in gasps, a sign of how frayed his nerves were by this contest; far more than any of his previous matches. The porter did not intervene. He was standing off to the side, watching. Unsure what he was supposed to do, Verus sought out the Emperor, whose couch was off to his right. Titus slowly stood and appeared to be contemplating what he should do. With a wicked sneer, he slowly ran his thumb across his throat. Verus lowered his head, letting out a resigned sigh. It wasn't right. After all, the fallen man, who would never regain consciousness in this life, had fought well. He was a veteran of the arena, and it seemed unjust that his life should end here. Not only that, but Verus had never killed before; not even after seven victories in the arena. His heart leapt into his throat, and he fought to supress the urge to vomit. First pulling himself to his feet, he placed the point of his gladius on the side of the Greek's neck, intent on granting him a quick journey into the afterlife.

"May Nemesis and Apollo guide you on your journey, friend," he whispered, before driving his weapon home. The sharp point plunged easily into the man's throat, severing the jugular.

And while the body gave a few involuntary convulsions, the Greek's eyes never opened, even as the dark crimson of his life's blood gushed onto the marble floor.

With a dismissive wave, the Emperor signalled for Verus to be escorted from the hall. As he reached the doors, a hand grabbed him roughly by the arm. It was the praetorian who loaned him his gladius. Verus was not even aware he still clutched the weapon, and the guardsman had to pry it from his hand. He then shoved the gladiator away, and the porter led Verus back out into the atrium.

"Quite the way to end the evening," Titus said appreciatively, as musicians started to play once more. He raised his cup to Rufus. "My compliments to you, Rufus, on this splendid display of entertainment."

"The honour was mine, Caesar," the consul replied, raising his own chalice.

"And my compliments to Narcissus," Titus added. "Clearly he has fighters worthy of my father's amphitheatre."

"He's been in the business for many years," Rufus noted. "Vile little shit, like most lanistae. But, those are the men who run the best schools. And we will, of course, make certain that Junius is properly recompensed. His man fought well and will not be easily replaced."

"Seems almost a shame really," a voice said behind them. It was the former tribune, Gaius Artorius, whose dining couch was in the row behind the imperial seats.

"What do you mean 'a shame'?" Rufus asked, uncertain if he should take offence.

"That man was a good fighter," Gaius said, sitting upright, watching four servants drug the slain gladiator away. A wide streak of blood followed in their wake. "A pity the people of Rome will not get to see his talents on display in the grand amphitheatre." Not wishing to upset his host, he quickly added, "Of course, it would not be proper to grant lesser men the honour of fighting in a private show for you, Caesar."

This satisfied Rufus, and Titus gave a nod of approval. It was unusual for a member of the equites to be invited to such a prestigious gathering. No doubt there were many senators who felt

195

snubbed that they had not received an invite, yet Gaius Artorius had. As the chief engineer during the Siege of Jerusalem, Titus held him in very high regard. And though Frontinus' term as Governor of Britannia had ended two years prior, his successor, Julius Agricola, invited Gaius to join his entourage to Rome. A venerable soldier in his own right, Agricola had taken part in the violent suppression of Boudicca's rebellion nearly twenty years before. Though their paths had never crossed during their respective military careers, they shared a soldierly bond of mutual respect.

The only other man of the lesser nobility, whose invitation offended members of the senate even more so, was Tiberius Alexander. As former Prefect of the Praetorian Guard, he was not at the banquet as part of his duties, but as the Emperor's honoured guest. Titus' chief-of-staff during the final campaigns of the Great Jewish Revolt, his handling of the immense logistical responsibilities for over 70,000 imperial soldiers was arguably just as important as Titus' conducting of the actual assaults upon the fortress-city that had once been Jerusalem. For many within Rome's nobility, that did not change the repugnant fact that he was a Jew, from Alexandria no less! Titus was aware of the political backlash that came from the honours both he and his father had heaped upon Alexander, which caused him to reconsider his relationship with another Jew from the east.

"I am surprised you have not invited Queen Julia back to Rome," Rufus said, unwittingly raising a painful topic for the Emperor. "I thought for certain she would be one of your honoured guests when you hold the inaugural games."

"Julia Berenice will never return to Rome," Titus replied, ice in his voice.

"Forgive me, Caesar, I meant no offence."

"No, you were bound to find out sooner or later," the Emperor replied, quaffing his entire chalice of wine and demanding more. "You know I loved her."

After an uncomfortable pause, the consul added, "Love can be a fickle mistress."

"A vile cunt, more like," Titus snapped. "I was a fool, Rufus. Julia even told me as much. My father tried to warn me that the people would never accept her as their empress. It wasn't just that she is twelve years older than me. It's that she is a foreign

196

queen…and a Jew at that. It doesn't matter that she and her brother have been faithful allies of Rome or that they supplied us with thousands of troops during the Judean rebellion. They fear another Cleopatra, even though the last of the Egyptian pharaohs was conquered over a hundred years ago."

"The mob is what makes our rule so tenuous," Rufus observed. "We are the noble fathers of Rome. Yet if enough peasants wallowing in shit become incensed, they can undo us."

"Which is why we must keep them distracted," Titus noted. "Give them their bread and circuses, and they will forget their lot in life or, at least, accept it. I need these games to be a triumph, Rufus. I have a feeling the Flavian Dynasty, not to mention my own head, may depend on it."

Verus felt sick to his stomach. In his seven arena victories, he'd never been ordered to kill. During the past two years, he'd witnessed numerous deaths. Most were either gregarii during their pit brawls, or caused by accidents or injuries, like poor Severus. Only twice had a sponsor ordered the death of a combatant, and one of these had been because Narcissus bribed him after Priscus barely defeated the man. To be ordered to kill, not in the arena but at a private party for the rich, felt vulgar and disgusting to him. Still covered in blood, he threw on his tunic and sandals. He was escorted back to the ludus in silence. He could feel the blood of his injuries sticking his tunic to him.

A medic was waiting for him as soon as he reached the ludus. Despite his exhaustion and overwhelming desire for sleep, Narcissus insisted that he bathe and undergo a thorough examination first. After taking a short plunge, Verus winced as the medic prodded at the gashes on his upper arm and chest, as well as the back of his leg. He made Verus sit on a long table while he stitched them up. The gladiator still had an aversion to needles, and he grimaced the entire time as the wounds were sewn shut. They were then rinsed once more and a compress of crushed herbs bandaged around each.

"Now you may go rest," the medic said. "I will inform Master Narcissus that you cannot train or undergo strenuous activity for at least a week."

Verus said nothing but gave a curt nod and left the dimly-lit chamber. There was only one person he wished to speak to, but it was well after midnight. He knew Priscus was either asleep or engaged in carnal activity with one or more of his many admirers.

Priscus was, indeed, enjoying one of the lustful perks of being a famous gladiator; two, in fact. These were noble women of the equites and both divorcees. This was common. Roman society gave women who were divorced an astonishing amount of liberty. They could own businesses and were no longer subject to the whims of their fathers or husbands. And as their previous spouses were required to properly compensate them, those of the equites and senatorial classes were usually left well-off. For these women, with nothing holding back their inhibitions, there was something exotic about satisfying their collective lust with strong, savage men who, at any time, could bleed out in the sand to placate the multitudes.

The loud banging on Priscus' door startled them. He let out a frustrated groan, as it was quickly opened. He was surprised to see Narcissus and a man he'd never seen before standing in the doorway.

"Well, really!" one of the women protested, covering herself with a blanket. "Some people have no manners at all."

"Apologies, ladies," Narcissus said with a bow, before addressing his gladiator. "Priscus, your time with our *gladiatorial familia* has come to an end. This is Junius, your new master. He is here to take you to your new home." He looked to the irritated noblewomen once more. "After you've finished with your guests, of course."

He bowed to the ladies again and closed the door, leaving Priscus and his guests completely dumbfounded. Outside, Narcissus was seething in fury.

Junius grinned broadly. "It's nothing personal. Just business, old friend."

"Just business?" Narcissus retorted.

"Oh, come now, Consul Rufus assures me you will be compensated fairly."

"Compensated fairly?" Narcissus snapped. "Priscus is a fighter you simply cannot put a price on. By Hades' cock, I brought him all the way from Britannia! He's won nine matches for me in the arena and was to be one of my prized gladiators for the opening games!"

"You agreed to the terms," Junius countered. "When the consul requested a pairing for tonight's dinner party, it was contracted that should a fighter die, his lanista would get to choose a replacement from the victor's school. How could either of us have known that the Emperor intended to make this a fight to the death? Had I been aware of this, believe me, I would not have committed one of my best gladiators. I would have sent a tiro or gregarius and still taken your man!"

It was a bitter situation for Narcissus to accept. When a request came from the current consul on behalf of Emperor Titus, a lanista would be a fool to decline. Had he done so, Narcissus would have likely found his entire school banned from the Flavian Amphitheatre before it even opened! He was glad Verus had won. Within less than two years he had become one of Narcissus' best fighters. That still did not lesson the blow of losing Priscus, quite possibly the greatest combatant he had ever seen in his thirty years of dealing in Roman blood sport. The consul had paid him a handsome sum of 10,000 denarii; however, he knew it would be years, if ever, before he found and trained a gladiator of Priscus' calibre.

Chapter XIX: Absent Friends

The Flavian Amphitheatre and Nero Colossus
From an Italian engraving, artist unknown (1831)

The following morning around sunrise, Verus made his way to
Priscus' quarters. He opened the door, calling to his friend, only to
find the rooms empty. All his possessions were gone, to include his
statue of Nemesis. Verus was horrified and quickly sought to find
Drusus or Narcissus. He found the lanista having his breakfast on
the open-air patio of his house.

"Ah, Verus," he said, appearing unconcerned that one of his
gladiators had barged in on his morning reverie. "Splendid
performance last night. I trust you are well?"

"Priscus," Verus said, his voice hard. "Where is he?"

"Priscus?" Narcissus was completely taken aback. He sat upright
and leaned back, folding his hands in his lap. "You surprise me, boy.
You fought quite the savage match last night, in the presence of the
Emperor no less! You've also killed your first man. And judging by
the bandages to your leg and torso, sustained some substantial
injures. And yet you barge in here, uninvited I might add,
demanding to know about another damned gladiator. I'd have you
whipped and placed in confinement for a month were you not one of

my highest earning combatants. Oh, yes, the Emperor was very generous in his remunerations for last night's performance."

He nodded towards a small bag on a nearby table. "I have your share here. It is more than you earned in your last four bouts combined. So tell me why, after what was undoubtedly a life-altering event and one that will likely shape your fortunes in the weeks to come, are the first words out of your mouth about fucking Priscus?"

"Your pardon, my lord," Verus said with a bow. "Please understand…he is my friend."

Narcissus shook his head. "You're in the wrong profession if you're looking to make friends, lad. But as you have enriched me, both in coin and patronage of the Emperor, I'll forget your rather gross transgression, this time. As for Priscus, he's been sold."

"Sold?" Verus asked, his mouth agape.

"Are you fucking deaf, boy?" Narcissus snapped. "Yes, *sold.* Priscus was the greatest fighter to ever come from this school, but for the right price, everyone can be bought. You would do well to remember that. The ludus that bought him has shit for real fighters, and their lanista offered me ten times what any of you lot are worth."

Verus' face clouded with anger. He was startled to feel a hand on his shoulder. He spun about quickly, thinking it was one of Narcissus' bodyguards.

It was Drusus. "Come on." The chief instructor led him away.

"Here, you don't want to forget this," Narcissus called out, tossing the coin pouch to Verus.

"Come, before his good temper changes," Drusus stressed, gently but firmly escorting the gladiator from the home of their master. Once outside, he explained, "You seem to have forgotten that all of you are still property of the lanista, to be disposed of as he sees fit. Until such a day as you either win your freedom or die on the arena sands, you are nothing more than assets used to amuse the mob and enrich men like Narcissus. Whoever he decides to sell to another ludus and why is none of your concern!"

There was both firmness and understanding in Drusus' voice. After all, he too had once been a gladiator. And though he'd been an auctoratus who was freed when his contract expired, he could certainly sympathise with those he now instructed in the art of arena

201

combat. That said, it was naïve for Verus to think Narcissus, or Drusus for that matter, gave a damn about the personal attachments formed between their charges. He was a slave; a piece of property, nothing more.

He returned to his room and tried to console himself with the payment received for the previous night's blood-letting. There were twenty gold coins inside the pouch, freshly minted with the image of Emperor Titus and a scene from the Siege of Jerusalem on the back. The gold aureus was the most valuable coin in the Roman world, not to mention exceptionally rare. Their combined value was five hundred denarii; more than two years' wages for an imperial legionary!

Gold aureus of Titus, circa 80 A.D.

Verus closed the pouch and threw it across the room. For the first time since coming to the ludus, he felt filthy inside. He'd been a gladiator for nearly two years. Including the previous night's bloody exhibition, he now had eight victories to his credit with just two defeats. Of the men who'd bested him, one had been an auctoratus who'd since been granted his freedom. The other died after suffering terrible injuries in the arena.

"At least I've captured the Emperor's interest," he consoled himself as he lay upon his bed, staring blankly up at the ceiling.

His heart told him his time as a gladiator would be coming to an end soon. What that end would be, he was not sure. Rumours abounded that Titus was sparing no expense for the opening games of the Flavian Amphitheatre. The people needed a distraction, after all the recent calamities, and they needed to be reminded of the grandeur that was Rome.

Rumours abounded that Titus and the Flavians had fallen out of favour with the gods. Verus had heard many such conversations on the street. He knew little about the Emperor, and the previous night was the only time he'd so much as laid eyes on him. Despite his feelings of revulsion, he could not hate Titus for ordering him to kill. After all, it was a possibility within every gladiatorial contest. Verus often suspected the reason he'd never been ordered to kill a previous opponent was because the sponsor could not afford to pay for the slain gladiator. But if the Emperor was the sponsor for these upcoming games, how many fallen gladiators could expect to be granted the missio? Verus knew that if Titus wished to make these games memorable, they would need to be both the largest and bloodiest the people of Rome had ever seen.

By late June, the vast network of construction scaffolding was torn down, and the Flavian amphitheatre stood tall in all its brilliance. Its size and scale alone were awe-inspiring. At over fifty meters in height, it towered over all the surrounding buildings and monuments, allowing it to be seen for miles. The paths from the main roads leading to its numerous entrances were paved with cobblestones and lined with various trees and statues. Inside each of the open arches which ran along the second and third levels were even more statues of Roman gods, emperors, and heroes from antiquity. Just outside the amphitheatre's walls stood a gigantic, near-one-hundred-foot-high bronze statue previously known as the *Nero Colossus.*

Nero may have been a madman, despised and feared by the senate and damned by historians, but during his reign he was loved by the people. Rather than removing the statue following the rise of Emperor Vespasian, the head was discretely replaced with that of the god, Apollo. It was enough that the amphitheatre towered over the ostentatious monument to the last emperor of the Julio-Claudian Dynasty.

A rather ingenious addition to the amphitheatre was the retractable roof. Encircling the entire arena were a series of long crane arms and pulley systems attached to massive, brightly-dyed sails. They added a colourful flourish and could be readily extended or retracted based on the time of day or inclement weather. Working this complex system were former sailors from the imperial navy. Indeed, the man who designed the retractable roof was a retired ship's captain who once commanded one of the massive, not to mention extremely rare, octeres-class warships.

On a late June morning, Emperor Titus stood in the centre of the arena, his sandaled feet digging into the sand. He gazed up at the sail-works high above the imperial box, a broad grin spreading across his face. He was joined by a handful of senators including Consul Rufus.

"Magnificent," the consul said, breaking the silence. "Your father would be proud."

Titus gave a slow nod, a trace of regret coming over him at mention of the late emperor. "I wish he could see this," he muttered.

Rufus opened his mouth with the intent of asserting that, as a god, Vespasian had the best view of his colossal amphitheatre from Elysium. However, he wisely refrained from doing so. Titus was not a particularly religious man even though, as Pontifex Maximus, he was head of the Roman state religion. He also felt that any such assertions were both pandering and in poor taste.

Perhaps most surprising of all who accompanied Titus was the Jewish man who'd resided at the imperial palace for the past ten years. Born Yosef ben Matityahu, he now went by the name Titus Flavius Josephus. That he was arguably one of Titus' closest friends was nothing short of profound, given they were mortal enemies during the Great Jewish Revolt, fifteen years before. At the time, Josephus was the rebel Governor-General of Galilee. He brought much grief to the Romans during the bitterly contested Siege of Jotapata.

"I am surprised to see you here," Titus remarked offhand. "Especially since the treasures of your sacred temple paid for all this."

"That is why I had to see it for myself," Josephus replied sombrely. His usually darker complexion seemed pale this day.

While his eyes saw vast numbers of seating, statuary, various décor, and of course the colourful sails ready to spread across the top, his mind was consumed by the utter devastation and loss of life which made it all possible. "Since this is to be a place of violence and death, perhaps it is fitting that its existence is owed to so much pain and suffering."

"Will you be joining us for the games?" Titus asked, suspecting he already knew the answer.

"Though God may have decreed that the Flavians should rule the world, I doubt he will look upon me with much favour should I celebrate men killing each other, especially in the very place that was built by the blood of the Jews."

"A pity," the Emperor said. "I could save you one of the best seats in the imperial box. You know King Agrippa used to attend the games as a young man. As I understand it, he even won a substantial wager from the divine Augustus himself during one particular match."

"Our late king had a habit of flaunting God's laws," the Jewish man retorted with a scowl. "But then, he was raised by Romans."

The accompanying senators, particularly Consul Rufus, glanced at each other, feeling uncomfortable at the tone of this discussion. Despite the perceived awkwardness, for Titus and Josephus this was simply how they conversed with each other. For two men who had once tried to disembowel each other with swords, there was little room for feelings of offence or outage. Josephus often spoke to Titus in terms bolder and more direct than any member of the senate; something the Emperor appreciated rather than scorned.

"And what of your sons? Are they not being raised as Romans?"

"Romanized Jews," Josephus corrected. "But, yes, I suppose they are."

"The Jews of Rome are an...*interesting* lot," Titus observed. "They claim to worship the same god as you, yet they're a lot less observant in many of the nuances."

"Idolatry comes to mind," Josephus said in concurrence. "My wife's neighbour claims to be a rabbi, yet he keeps his hair short, his face shaven, wears Roman-style clothes, and he even has a bust of your late father displayed prominently in the entryway of his house."

The Emperor shook his head at this revelation. "You know, I've never been able to fathom why your wife does not just live with you at the palace."

"She knows I prefer to be left alone," Josephus replied plainly. "Ever since by beloved Judith died in Jerusalem, I knew I would never love again. Even now, eleven years later, her death haunts me. Worse still, I cannot shake the rumour that she took her own life."

The Emperor spoke consolingly, "Given the terrible circumstances she found herself in, with no salvation in sight, can one really blame her? It's not enough that your god so callously abandoned his chosen people. If he also condemns them for taking their own lives after so much suffering, then he truly is without mercy."

Josephus did not reply. What could he say? His entire life was consumed by chronicling the history of his people, as well as the rebellion that brought about their destruction. And yet, everything he was taught to believe from his earliest memories, he now questioned. If the Jews really were God's chosen people, then why would he come to Josephus, leader of the resistance in Galilee, and tell him that his mortal enemy, Vespasian, was destined to rule the world? And how could over a million innocents be allowed to suffer and die within the Holy City itself? The entire enemy garrison at Jerusalem amounted to no more than 30,000 fighters that the populace could have overwhelmed, were they but united. And most of the people died not by Roman blades, but under infinitely more horrifying conditions, wasting away as disease and starvation rotted their bodies. Was this all God's punishment for their failure to stand up to the heretical fanatics who oppressed the people and desecrated the Temple? It was the only answer Josephus had, and all that kept him from being driven completely out of his mind.

But why allow the children to suffer? Was it justice that infants be damned so appallingly, for the sins of their parents? This was the question Josephus could not answer. All he had witnessed during the war flew in the face of everything he'd ever been taught about the love and mercy of God.

Titus was surprised to hear his friend speak so candidly about his first wife. He rarely, if ever, mentioned her. Of Josephus' entire family, only his elder brother, Mathias, survived the Siege of Jerusalem. And while he could only guess as to the level of spiritual torments that afflicted Josephus every day, it was no small wonder that his two marriages in the aftermath of the Jewish Revolt failed almost immediately. The first had been to a former slave, freed by Vespasian and offered to Josephus as his wife. There was no love between them, and Josephus only consented, as he did not wish to offend his patron and Emperor. He was relieved when she left him a few months later. The second was an Alexandrian Jew introduced to him by Tiberius Alexander. They had three sons in rapid succession. The deaths of the younger two destroyed the bonds between them. Prior to their divorce, she took the eldest and fled to Alexandria. It was only when he met Arcadia, a Greek-born Jewish woman living in Rome, that he found some measure of happiness.

"And how goes the writing?" Titus asked, referring to the great histories of the Jews, which to the surprise of many, he was sponsoring Josephus to write.

"There is only one truth that I know," his friend replied. "The legacy of the Jews must be preserved, lest it be relegated to nothing more than stolen treasure which funded this arena of death that you are so in love with."

The population of the Eternal City exploded during the weeks leading up to the Emperor's games. Scouts were sent to various gladiatorial schools around the Empire, searching for talent worthy of the Flavian Amphitheatre. In anticipation, every inn within fifty miles of Rome doubled or tripled their rates. Merchants and farmers from all over Italia and the nearest provinces descended upon the capital to sell their wares, with a substantial mark-up, of course.

This led to a series of camps springing up all around the outskirts of the city. Each ludus invited from around the Empire had its own camp with its fighters on display. The physical specimens were modelled on stages, while competing in mock exhibitions with wooden weapons to give the people a glimpse of what to expect.

For Gaius Artorius, the madness was a far cry from his life in Britannia. While cities were ever-growing, including his home of Portus Magnus, it was still a young province, the rebellious tribes in the westernmost reaches only recently subdued.

"And it's so bloody hot here this time of year," he grumbled, as he and his wife, Aula, strolled along the banks of the Tiber. The imperial palace and Circus Maximus were visible just a few blocks to their left.

"I rather enjoy it," Aula replied with a grin at her husband's sweaty discomfort. "It was kind of Governor Agricola to invite us to join his entourage to Rome. It's been too long since I've visited the Eternal City."

The path was lined with throngs of people. Many were spectators who were unable to find accommodations within the city so they camped along the Tiber like vagrants.

"Too long indeed," Gaius remarked with a trace of sarcasm. They stepped through a series of makeshift camps where swarms of people clustered around, playing dice games, cooking their meals, or just lying about with a rolled-up tunic for a pillow.

"Ah, Artorius!" a voice shouted from near the Bridge of Tiberius. Gaius squinted and was able to make out a young man waving his arms frantically.

"Who is that?" Aula asked, confused.

"I think that's Tacitus." Gaius' assumption was proven true as he forced with way through the mob and over to the young man.

Cornelius Tacitus was in his mid-twenties and recently married to Agricola's daughter, Julia. From an influential family of the equites, he served as a member of the imperial household staff, overseeing the numerous freedmen clerks. Having established himself as an accomplished scholar and historian, despite his lack of years, he freely admitted that he owed his position to Titus' influence.

"I'm surprised to see you out braving the mob," Gaius said, as they reached the young scholar.

He was leaning against the stone railing on the bridge. "They're going to start the ticket lottery in about an hour over by the amphitheatre."

"Don't you already have a guaranteed seat?" Gaius asked.

"Oh, yes, though it's towards the back of the second tier. I may be married to the daughter of a prominent imperial governor and distinguished general, but I'm still just a member of the equites. It does, at least, mean I can get into the games any time I want. I'm

208

only here to watch this mob lose their minds. I think it'll be just as entertaining as the opening games tomorrow!"

Indeed, for the common plebs, there was no guarantee that one could even get into the arena. Tickets were free; however, nearly a third were set aside for the senate, their families, various magistrates, and equites. The rest would be decided by random lottery. With approximately 40,000 tickets available each day, and a hundred days of games, there was no shortage of prospective spectators who would swarm the vendors each night when the lottery was decided for the following morning.

As if it were a single living entity, the massive crowd began to move towards the Flavian Amphitheatre, which lay a few blocks behind the imperial palace just east of the Forum. Gaius and Aula decided to join Tacitus. He was more excited than many of the potential spectators. There were scores of ticket vendors, both in the Forum as well as along the lane that lead to the amphitheatre. As the lottery commenced, Tacitus let out a broad grin.

"And so, the games begin!"

Drusus and the other instructors spent the day briefing their gladiators on which days they would be fighting, and in what style of a matchup. Verus was surprised when not just Drusus, but Narcissus, came to see him in his room that evening. He immediately stood up from his bunk.

"Please, sit," Narcissus said, adding a wave of his hand. He and Drusus occupied the pair of chairs at Verus' small table, and the gladiator sat on his bed.

The lanista smiled and said, "Fortuna has smiled upon us both again. The Emperor has asked for you personally."

"Please tell me I won't have to kill at another dinner party," Verus replied callously.

Narcissus did not reply. He looked to Drusus to explain. "Caesar has asked for you to fight in the main event on the first day of the games. Your skill impressed him greatly, and he believes you will set the stage for the next one hundred days. Give the people, especially Emperor Titus, something to remember you by, and you will be well-rewarded. And I don't just mean in coin."

209

Wide-eyed, Verus looked to Narcissus who concurred. "Though he has not spelled it out exactly, the Emperor heavily implied that those who fight well, particularly in the main event contests of each day, may be given the wooden sword and palm of victory. As a slave, this is your best chance at earning your freedom." He looked around at Verus' sparse room. "And since you've clearly spent so little of the coin you've amassed over the past two years, you could likely retire a wealthy man; perhaps even return home."

"Home," Verus whispered.

Chapter XX: Drowning in Blood

The Flavian Amphitheatre, Rome
July, 80 A.D.

Pollice Verso (with a turned thumb), by Jean-Leon Gerome (1872)

It was the eve of the opening day, and Titus quietly took a walk along the arena floor. The moon shone brightly as Rome's Emperor stood alone in the middle of the sandy pit. He was conflicted by feelings of pride and sadness. The Flavian Amphitheatre was really Vespasian's legacy, and it seemed cruel to Titus that his father had died just a year prior to its completion. At the same time, he felt as if history was coursing through his veins. While memory of even the grandest of arena spectacles faded over time, he knew these would be different. Thousands of years from now, people would still be discussing the games that opened the grandest arena the world had ever seen. It truly was a wonder-of-the-world!

"If only you could see this, Father," he said quietly.

Though all the combatants arrived at the arena well before sunrise, the gladiators themselves would not compete until midday. There was a set schedule of events meant to whet the crowd's appetite. At the start of the morning would be prisoner executions. In Rome, capital sentences were usually carried out within hours, sometimes minutes, of the offender's sentencing. However, as Roman games usually began with massed executions to get up the mob's bloodlust, every death sentence within a hundred miles had been delayed starting about three months prior. Their gaolers had maliciously told them, *'You should feel honoured; for yours will be the first blood to sanctify the amphitheatre.'*

Wishing to make an even greater display of something so mundane as putting murderers and thieves to death, Titus ordered them slaughtered by wild beasts. The day prior to the games, the Emperor had toured the animal pens with the beast master, who promised to douse the sands with blood.

"These creatures are ferocious," Titus said appreciatively, as they walked by the cages of several African lions. These monsters were large with thick muscle, huge claws, and gaping maws full of sharp teeth that could tear a man apart.

"We've done much to build up their appetites, Caesar," the beast master explained. "They have not eaten in a day and will doubtless be ravenous come tomorrow. And as an added measure, we've taught them to enjoy the taste of human flesh."

"Indeed," Titus said.

A lion chewed on a bloody chunk of thigh bone, trying to satisfy its hunger.

"In the provinces, there is no shortage of unclaimed bodies of poor, forgotten wretches," the beast master said.

"And you know the penalty, if they should fail to perform tomorrow," Titus then added coldly.

The beast master raised his hands in resignation. "That I have offered my own life in sacrifice, should be all the reassurance you require, Caesar."

Verus arrived at the arena with the rest of the ludus. They were kept in a large barracks block outside the eastern gate, until it was time for the main contests. This meant they would miss the prisoner executions and gregarii battle, but it also kept hundreds of gladiators from milling about aimlessly, while staff, instructors, and medics tried to keep the event organised. Each ludus was kept separate from all the others, and fighters were prohibited from fraternising with potential enemy combatants.

He was, however, pleasantly surprised to see Vipsania. She was seated by herself on a stool outside the barracks. She was wearing a basic tunic, though her left arm was wrapped in a padded manica. She smiled as Verus approached her.

"I wasn't sure if I would see you here," he said.

"Where else should I be?" she asked, her smile never waning.

"To be honest, I was afraid your arm might have gotten infected."

"It did," Vipsania remarked. "Left me with a terrible fever for about three nights. But, I am still here and ready to make a name for myself before the Emperor."

"You recovered rather quickly," Verus noted.

"I only started regaining my strength about two weeks ago. Haven't been able to train as hard as I would have liked. Whatever bitch they put in front of me today, I'll just have to end her quickly. In another month, maybe two, I'll fight again and demonstrate my true measure as a gladiator."

Verus smiled, but he detected a trace of nervousness in Vipsania's voice. Still wry and supremely confident, there was a noticeable loss of edge in her demeanour. The terrible trauma she'd endured in the great fire had left her diminished. Still, he could see a trace of the spark hidden behind her tired eyes. "I…I had hoped to see you again," he said awkwardly.

Vipsania raised an eyebrow. "Really? I thought we were just having a bit of sport was all."

Verus laughed and shook his head. "The way you talk; it's far different than any woman I have ever known."

"Yes, well, I've never exactly been the 'respectable' type." Her countenance darkened, and she stared off into the void. "There is nothing else for me. I may not be a slave, though one could hardly guess. As a woman, I will always be little more than a novelty, a

213

freak show. I'll never be taken seriously as a gladiator because I fight nothing but ex-prostitutes and dainty little girls. What little coin I make is scarcely enough to keep me out of the gutter. Drusus has allowed me to share a servant's quarters at his house, but for how long? I suspect that once he's found a younger, scrappier wench who doesn't possess a burn-scarred arm, he'll be done with me. I can only hope I face a worthier foe in the arena before then, who mercifully sends me to whatever pathetic realm the gods have for me."

"I thought you didn't believe in the gods?" Verus asked, recalling a conversation they'd had the night they met.

"I question their existence," Vipsania corrected. "I've never outright said they don't exist. None of us really knows what happens after we breathe our last. It's a little terrifying, if one is being honest." She looked up at him, her head slightly cocked to one side, and a smile forming across her face. "I have a feeling this day is going to be savage and bloody. If we manage to survive, will you watch the sunset with me?"

"I would like that very much," Verus said, as strange feelings came over him. It was a simple and somewhat eclectic request. As they faced the brutal unknown, under the constant pall of death, it was somehow fitting.

The crack of whips echoed along the corridors of the arena's prison cells. The condemned were hurried along, sheer terror gripping them. There were twenty in this lot; mostly thieves with a couple of murderers thrown in. They were stripped down to a loincloth or, in some cases, completely naked as they were forcibly shoved out the gate and onto the arena sands. Even in the early hours, the amphitheatre was nearly full. Those fortunate enough to have gained access to the opening day of games did not wish to miss a moment of spectacle.

The group of condemned men clustered together, eyes wide in horror at what might be waiting for them behind the various gates that lined the perimeter. One man screamed as animal pens were flung open, as three tigers and two lions sprung out onto the sand. The crowd let loose a raucous cheer, drowning out any further cries and lamentations from the condemned. Then something went terribly wrong that neither Titus, the prisoners, nor least of the all the beast master could have anticipated.

Lions and tigers were fearsome beasts that could destroy men at will. And these were famished with hunger with an acquired taste for human flesh. Yet none had ever been subjected to the ear-splitting roar of 65,000 people shouting down on them. This was completely foreign and caused the beasts to panic. During all his months of preparations, the beast master had never thought to acquaint them with the deafening thunder of a crowd. Instead of attacking the prisoners, the animals ran gingerly back to their pens or to whatever protection might be offered by the various alcoves lining the floor. The cheers of the masses quickly turned to curses and boos. It was a shameful start to the opening day of the Flavian Amphitheatre.

From his place in the imperial box, Titus glowered at the pathetic sight. He was horrified and enraged in equal measure. Was *this* how the games honouring his father would be remembered? The crowds were either jeering or laughing, and he knew something had to be done.

Turning to his Praetorian Prefect, he said, "Give the people blood."

Guardsmen quickly rushed down the steps, forcing their way past throngs of humanity, until they reached the gate that led to the animal holding pens. The beast master was waiting for them, his head bowed. His moment of triumph, where his name would be sung for years and recorded into the annals of the Flavian Amphitheatre, would now end in ignominy. No one would remember his name, only his failure and that he was the first to die in the arena. Ironically, he'd added the clause to his contract, stating if his beasts failed to perform, he would offer up his own life instead. It was added mostly in jest. Never did he imagine the screaming mob would frighten his lions and tigers, and that he would have to sacrifice his own blood in payment.

Taunts and hisses met the beast master, as he was led out onto the centre of the floor by a pair of guardsmen. His head bowed, he dropped to his knees before the imperial box. A praetorian drew his gladius and looked up at the Emperor, who gave a slow nod. As the point of his weapon was thrust between the hapless victim's neck and shoulder, the crowd gave a loud cheer. Finally, they were given blood. The body was tossed to the animals, where the starving lions and tigers ravenously devoured their former master.

"Well, that could have gone better," Narcissus said, shaking his head. He turned when a voice behind him frantically called out his name. It was one of the organisers of the day's contests. His face was flush from running a great distance.

"Yes?"

"Your gregarii are set to go on at midday."

"That is correct."

The man shook his head. "Not anymore…or at least not all of them. I need five of your fighters, at once. There are some prisoners that still need executing."

As rapidly as they kitted up and armed the five gregarii, it was still half an hour before anything transpired. The condemned remained huddled near the edge of the floor, and the people were starting to grow restless. Titus therefore ordered the first round of prizes to be loosed to keep the mob placated. This was not supposed to happen until just before the main event fights of the late afternoon, but the Emperor knew some improvising was in order.

The prizes in question were inscribed wooden balls. With an announcement from the master of ceremonies, these were flung down from the highest points of the arena by the sailors who were manning the roof sails. There were six hundred in all. Even Titus gave an amused grin, as he watched excited spectators tussle each other to snatch one up.

At the end of the day, these would be taken to a special vender outside the arena where they could be redeemed for the prize engraved upon them. These varied considerably, consisting of coinage, articles of elaborate clothing, as well as slaves or random pieces of treasure taken from the Jewish temple in Jerusalem.

"That's settled them down for a few minutes," Domitian said, with a derisive sneer. He nodded towards the arena floor as some of the crowd let loose another less enthusiastic cheer. "Ah, I see you've sorted out the prisoners."

A small cart bearing broken and rusted weapons was hauled out onto the sand, and the five gregarii marched out in their gladiatorial garb.

The master of ceremonies stood, raising his hands.

"In his infinite mercy, Caesar has declared that the condemned shall have a chance at life! Five gregarii stand between them and a cart of weapons. Should the vicious scum manage to take up arms and defeat these gladiators, they will be allowed to live, given full pardon, and allowed to leave the arena as free men. Combatants! There is to be no quarter given. This contest will end when either the last prisoner or gladiator is slain."

"I think the mob will like this better than feeding them to wild cats," Domitian noted, drawing a smile from his brother. He turned to the seats behind him. "And what does the man who brought down Jerusalem's walls think?"

"A quick and clever solution," Gaius Artorius replied. He was seated next to Tiberius Alexander and the Plebeian Tribunes. His six-year old son, Tiberius, sat next to him, his hand up at his mouth, eagerly awaiting the spectacle to unfold.

"I'm impressed you brought your son to this," the prince remarked.

"Normally, I would say he's a bit young," Gaius said, placing his arm around the boy. "And his mother isn't too happy with me for bringing him. But, she knows this in an historic occasion. I think it would be wrong to deprive him of what will be one of his earliest memories. Years from now, he can tell these stories to his grandchildren."

217

A roar from the crowd and all turned their attention to the arena once more. The gregarii were gladiators in name only, as they were marginally trained and often condemned criminals themselves. The four men and one woman who stood between the convicted and freedom wore leather breastplates and helmets, and each wielded a gladius and circular shield. Women gladiators were supposed to only fight each other. But, it added to the spectacle, not to mention potential humiliation for the prisoners should they be slain by a woman. This particular 'lady of the arena' was a Gaul who stood a few inches taller than most of the damned. Her hair was shorn on one side of her head and pulled tight in the back. Her once attractive face bore several scars, and her very presence was more unnerving than even the bigger and better trained men who fought beside her.

With a blowing of trumpets, the contest commenced. Some of the prisoners ran straight for the cart. Others tried to make their way around. The gladiators quickly formed a circle around the weapons, hacking and stabbing away at those who tried to rush past them. The amphitheatre erupted in cheers as the first victim fell; his guts impaled by a gregarius' blade. Two were rapidly butchered, and a third had his throat slashed open by the female fighter. Their numbers quickly proved to be too much; with nothing left to lose and everything to gain, the survivors clambered onto the cart, grabbing whatever they could to defend themselves. As the first hoisted up a sword, he was stabbed through the lower abdomen, emitting a scream of pain as he tumbled forward, upsetting the cart in the process.

As an added cruel tease to the condemned, most of the weapons were completely useless. Some were rusted and broken, and others were wooden practice swords. There were, perhaps, one or two useable blades in the lot. The prisoners were now brawling with each other, trying to snatch these away before they were killed. For the gladiators, it became a sport. Each soaked in the adulations of the crowd as they slew the hapless prisoners. As gregarii, this was the closest they would ever come to being adored by the people. Within minutes, it was over. Two of the gladiators were slightly wounded. The prisoners were rendered into mutilated, twitching corpses, as their blood soaked into the sand.

From the Zliten Mosaic, depicting numerous gladiatorial contests (circa 2nd century A.D.)

The sun was now shining into the faces of half in the arena, and sailors feverishly worked the sails to extend the colourful roof over their heads. While the hastily conducted 'battle' between the condemned criminals and a handful of gregarii was amusing, it was also amateurish. This was not how Titus wanted the inaugural games to be remembered. After a brief intermission, giving patrons time to visit the numerous latrines and food vendors, the proper matches would commence.

Given the size of the arena, Titus wished to utilise all possible space. This meant numerous pairings battling at the same time. Only the feature bout, taking place in the late afternoon, would involve just two combatants. For the gladiators, this meant having to put on an even greater showing, that they might draw attention to themselves and outshine the others.

Accompanied by musicians' horns and the beating of drums, thirty-six men, two women, and a pair of dwarves marched out onto the vast arena floor. Twenty martials awaited them, and each duo found their place. In addition to their usual task of overseeing their respective bouts, the martials had the added hazard of ensuring that the various pairings did not smash into each other.

All combatants and martials turned to face the imperial box, offering salutes to the Emperor. Titus stood and raised his hand, returning the gesture. And with a swift drop of his arm, the fighting commenced.

219

Unlike most of his previous games, Verus decided to watch the first round of matches from behind a barred window that looked out onto the arena sand. He unwittingly found himself judging those combatants that he could see, analysing their strategies and skill within their chosen art. Was he that much better than they? Had he truly earned his place to fight in the day's feature bout, or had he simply gotten lucky? Judging from the prowess of the nearest pairing, he candidly thought it was perhaps a little of both. As hateful as killing the Greek at the Emperor's dinner party had been, he knew it was the reason Titus asked for him by name. His opponent for this day was still unknown to him, not that it mattered. This would be his finest moment in the arena. If the Emperor was truly serious about offering the rudis and palm to those who performed the best, he would leave the arena with his freedom or not at all. He would not raise a finger in submission; not today.

A change in the cheering of the crowd alerted him, and he saw a murmillo standing over a Samnite who lay on his back, a finger raised. From his place, Verus could not see the imperial box, yet it appeared the crowd was calling for the Samnite's death. This was troubling, though scarcely surprising. It seemed everyone, not just Emperor Titus, wanted these games to be remembered for their violence and bloodshed. A loud ovation from the mob and the murmillo drove his weapon into his opponent's throat. It was clear which way Titus had 'turned his thumb'.

The other fights continued as the murmillo strolled away, his arms raised in triumph. Slaves drug away his fallen adversary. Another pairing was hustled out to replace them. Verus noted two other gladiators had been subdued. He swallowed hard, as he saw both men were killed.

"These games are different," he muttered under his breath.

The two dwarves had ended their match, and once more the loser was ordered slain. Verus could not see the two women combatants from where he sat. He about fell over as one stricken gladiator collapsed right next to the opening, his head banging against the window bars. Within seconds, his body convulsed as the victor, a retiarius, stabbed him through the heart with his trident. Verus stood a few feet away, unable to avert his eyes. Blood from the slaughtered man seeped through the window, trickling down the stone wall. The body was unceremonious dragged away while still twitching. Verus decided he'd seen enough.

Walking towards the medics' chamber, he saw two of their fighters being carried in on stretchers. Both were dead. Four of the ludus' gladiators had emerged victorious, and all carried bloodied weapons. Some relished having killed, while the others were simply grateful to still be alive.

One young victor, an auctoratus who'd sold his body for glory in the arena, was shaking his head in sadness. "It isn't right." He saw Verus and shook his head again. "That secutor fought hard. He nearly had me twice! I thought to buy him a drink when this was finished, yet the Emperor ordered his death."

Despite the volume of slaughter, not every bout ended in death on that bloody afternoon. Titus allowed the crowd to choose whether a fighter lived or died. As the day wore on, their appetite for death seemed to wane a bit. Still, there was no shortage of butchered gladiators who, under most circumstances, would have been given the missio and spared. Verus felt his stomach turning, when he saw three more of their gladiators carried in as bloodied corpses. Proportionally, their ludus was doing well. Five of their defeated gladiators had been killed, with one spared. Twelve had won their matches, with ten required to kill their opponents.

"What is happening?" he asked an ashen-faced Drusus standing solemnly over the body of another auctoratus. With only a month left in his contract, Narcissus had, originally, not placed him on the roster. However, the man was determined to make a fine showing before the Emperor and win some extra coin before leaving the ludus a free man.

"The people want blood," Drusus muttered sadly. "And Caesar is giving it to them." The nearest of the short windows faced the west, and glaring sunlight danced off the trainer's forehead. Regaining his senses, he turned to his prized gladiator. "You'd best start getting ready. It will be your turn soon. And Verus, do not think about what you've seen here. Remember, you are the main attraction today. Fight well, and the Emperor will reward you."

"And if I fail?"

Both men grimaced, as Drusus left the question unanswered. His heart sinking, Verus knew that Titus had already predetermined the outcome of his match. Two men would enter, but only one would leave.

Bout between a secutor and retiarius

Unbeknownst to Verus, his lover, Vipsania, was in one of the replacement pairings. As the fifth butchered combatant was dragged away, she and her adversary sprinted out to meet the martial. She wore her usual metal headband and leather breastplate. She also wore a brass guard on her left shoulder, in addition to the padded manica. The woman she faced was equipped like a retiarius; however, instead of carrying a net, she wielded her trident with both hands. She was helmet-less and wore a similar bronze guard on her left shoulder. Her only armour was a pair of greaves, a wide leather belt around her middle, and a mail manica covering much of her right arm. Vipsania was suddenly regretting wearing the padded manica on her left arm. Not only was it making her scarred arm sweat and itch uncomfortably, it seemed to call attention to the fact that she was injured.

"Ready…fight!"

The retiarius immediately swung the butt spike of her trident in a snapping arc towards Vipsania's arm. She managed to deflect the blow with her shield before her opponent quickly thrust her weapon towards her exposed stomach. It was immediately clear this woman knew how to fight. Vipsania found it unnerving. She was suddenly on the defensive, able to do little except block the flurry of blows. The retiarius was efficient and able to use both ends of her weapon to great effect. Her assault resembled an artistic and rhythmic dance. Several times she clipped Vipsania's shin greaves. Twice she managed to catch her sword arm with the trident, opening a series of hideous gashes.

Vipsania cried out in agony and wrath, as the butt spike slammed into her injured arm. She charged forward, trying to get inside her opponent's superior reach, slamming her shield into the retiarius' chest. She succeeded, but only managed to land a glancing blow. It still knocked her foe off-balance for the briefest of moments, and Vipsania caught her in the side with the blade of her gladius. The retiarius managed to keep her composure, despite crying out in pain. A growing crimson stain spread along the right side of her tunic. She gave a guttural growl, her face red as she kicked Vipsania hard across the thigh. This was not an attack she'd anticipated, and Vipsania fell to her knees as her leg spasmed.

The retiarius attempted to stab her through the throat, but as Vipsania collapsed, the points of the trident embedded themselves in her metal headband. This was subsequently ripped away, and blood streamed down her forehead. Her greatest fear now was being rendered blind, once the blood got into her eyes.

"You'll not take my sunset from me," she snarled.

As her opponent withdrew her trident, the metal band still clinging to it, Vipsania lunged forward, propelling herself with her still-twitching leg. Before the retiarius could back away, she plunged her gladius into the woman's stomach beneath the ribcage. There would be no attempts to surrender in this battle. Vipsania drove her weapon up into her foe's heart as gouts of blood gushed onto her hand and forearm. The woman tried to cry out as she dropped her trident, yet no sound would come. Her eyes scrunched shut, filled with tears of agony as blood erupted from her mouth. Vipsania wrenched her weapon free; her opponent's soul departing even before her violently twitching corpse collapsed onto the sand.

Vipsania found herself sobbing, as she was helped to her feet. She was utterly exhausted and in terrible pain. It seemed every inch of her body was battered or bleeding. Chunks of skin were torn from her sword arm, and she could feel her burn-scarred arm bleeding beneath the manica. The blood streaming into her eyes masked her tears. For a moment, she thought the crowd was cheering for her, though she no longer cared. All that mattered was that despite her terrible pain, both physical and emotional, she would live to see the sunset. Provided Verus survived his battle, it would be enough.

Chapter XXI: The Cruelty of Fate

Provocator with buckler

It was nearly time. Verus tugged on the straps of his armour and gave his gladius a few swings. Everything felt right. His breast plate and greaves fit perfectly, as if they were part of his body. The sword he carried was a fine weapon; one he reckoned was used only for special matches. The blade was etched with intricate scrollwork, and the ivory pommel was accented with bronze fittings. It was razor sharp and well-balanced. Drusus had asked him if he wished to wear a helmet with a grilled mask, but Verus declined. He said he wanted to be able to clearly see the Emperor when he decided his fate.

Narcissus stood silently by the doorway, his hands folded, eyes on the floor. This was perplexing, for Narcissus never mingled with the gladiators during the games.

There was a loud knock, with a voice saying, "It's time."

The lanista finally looked to Verus, giving a slow nod before opening the door.

There was a short flight of steps that bisected the walkway leading into the arena. Across the way, another set of steps led down to the door his opponent would emerge from. The two would march into the arena together. As Verus slowly walked up the steps, he heard the hobnailed sandals of his opponent. His heart stopped and both men halted abruptly when they caught sight of each other.

"Priscus," Verus whispered under his breath.

His old friend, whom he had not seen in months, grimaced and stared down at the ground for a moment. Thousands of gladiators would fight over the next hundred days. And yet, the cruel fates had paired Verus and Priscus against each other. Both men took a deep breath, finding their resolve and accepting what was to come. Each gave a short nod of understanding to the other before marching out onto the sand.

It was only as he stepped into the arena, which was streaked and stained with the blood of the day's fallen, that Verus fully realised the size and grandeur of the Flavian Amphitheatre. There was not an empty seat to be had, and the roar of the crowd—tens-of-thousands of ravenous spectators—filled him with wonder. A lone martial waited for them in the centre of the pit, his staff held across his chest. The mob grew silent as Emperor Titus stood and the combatants turned to face him. Each raised his weapon in salute.

"Hail, Caesar," the martial said. "Your gladiators are ready to fight and die for you."

Titus gave a nod and then outstretched his hand, signalling for them to begin. Verus and Priscus faced each other, the martial's staff separating them. The affection for his friend evaporating from his mind, Verus tried to think of everything he knew about what was easily his most dangerous opponent ever. He knew Priscus was inhumanly strong, and there was a very real chance he could kill Verus before the martial had a chance to intervene. He was also much quicker than he looked. What's more, he had been born to fight in the arena. But Verus knew he was not a god. He had to have a weakness, even if he could not fathom what it was. As the multitude collected its breath in rapt anticipation, none of that mattered now. Freedom or oblivion awaited him.

"Fight!"

At the martial's command, the battle commenced.

The imperial box was filled with senators, dignitaries, and other distinguished guests of Emperor Titus. To his immediate left were the two consuls, including his brother, Domitian. On his right sat the Trajans; father and son. The elder, who'd recently celebrated his fiftieth birthday, was a renowned general and statesman, and one of the few whose reputation flourished during the Jewish Rebellion, when he commanded the venerable Tenth Legion. A loyal supporter of the Flavians during the civil war against Vitellius, he had served as one of Vespasian's most trusted advisors, as well as a mentor to Titus. He returned to Rome just three months earlier, receiving much acclaim from both the Emperor and senate for his mitigating a near-war with Parthia, while serving as Governor of Syria.

As for his son, the younger Trajan was slowly stepping beyond his father's shadow, having already made a name for himself during a series of minor campaigns along the Danube. Given his age of just twenty-six years, there had also been no shortage of controversy when Titus insisted on giving him command of Legio VII, Gemina, following Antonius Primus' final tenure as legate. However, the bickering was quickly silenced when Titus used himself as an example, having also been given his first command of a legion, under Emperor Nero no less, at the same age. Little did anyone in the amphitheatre know, least of all the guests in the imperial box, that one of the men who now stood before them, ready to battle in the day's feature contest, was once a prisoner captured by the younger Trajan nearly three years earlier.

Sword clashed against shield as each combatant sought to feel out the other. It was both a blessing and curse that they were so familiar with each other's fighting styles. For example, Verus was aware of Priscus' tendency to circle left towards his shield arm. Many an opponent viewed this as an amateurish mistake, since it kept them out of reach of Priscus' blade. However, in reality it was a trap meant to lure his prey in, where they would become careless. As deceptively quick as he was on his feet, the Caledonian could change direction and stance, overpowering his opponent with a flurry of strikes before the hapless fellow knew what happened. Priscus was now attempting the same ploy. Verus was having none

227

of it. He aggressively attacked his old comrade's left flank, maintaining a light and fluid stance, ready to evade when Priscus counterattacked.

By the same token, Priscus knew Verus kept his shield straps loose and was willing to sacrifice the protection if it looked like it could throw his opponent off-balance, or otherwise even the odds. He had watched the Dacian employ the tactic against retiarii several times and knew, should they end up grappling, Verus would simply let his shield go if Priscus attempt to wrench it from his grasp. And unless he could finish his old friend immediately, the martial would order him to throw down his own shield, evening the odds once more.

Their in-depth knowledge of each other's fighting styles led both men to be cautious at first. Their attacks were quick, yet the respective counters with shield and gladii were even faster. It almost looked as if the whole spectacle was an elaborately choreographed dance rather than a bitter fight between two old friends-turned-enemies in the arena. After a minute of this, Verus noted a quick and subtle shaking of the head from Priscus. The crowd was cheering voraciously at that moment. Yet both knew, if they did not start attacking each other with greater urgency soon, those cheers would turn to derision. There would be no prize of valour given to the victor in a contest the mob detested.

Giving a quick nod of understanding, Verus launched into a furious storm of thrusts and slashes with his blade. Priscus quickly backpedalled. His teeth gritted, he fought to repel this latest onslaught. A bash to the side of Verus' helm with his shield halted the exchange, bringing a deafening roar of approval from the multitude. Priscus followed this up with a lunging stab towards Verus' throat. His friend, however, was not as dazed as he appeared. Verus managed to quickly side-step, bringing his sword arm down in a hard chop. Priscus was too close, however, and instead of landing a blow from his gladius, Verus' arm became briefly entangled with his adversary. He shoved his foe away, attempting a fierce backhand swing in the process. Priscus' size made him nearly impossible to budge, and Verus could not get enough distance to make his blow count. Instead, his forearm and wrist smashed into the side of Priscus' helm, sending a jarring jolt of pain all the way up to his shoulder. In an unorthodox counter, the large Caledonian kicked him hard in the side, as Verus struggled to maintain his grip on his weapon.

Both men took a moment to catch their breath and assess the situation. In his peripherals, Verus could see throngs of spectators on their feet, clapping their hands and shouting in approval. The debacles of the morning seemed like a decade ago. Even the hours-long bloodbath of the early to mid-afternoon was a distant memory. When those fortunate citizens in attendance recalled the opening day of the games, it would be these two combatants whose names would be remembered.

"Such a splendid display of fighting prowess," Gaius said, shaking his head. "A shame how this will end."

"And why is that, my good Artorius?" Titus asked over his shoulder.

"These are two of the best fighters I've ever seen in any arena..." His voice trailed off for a moment, his eyes growing wide as the name of one of the combatants came back to him. "By Victoria, I even know one of those men!"

"Which one?" the elder Trajan asked, now curious. He kept his gaze fixed on the ongoing battle.

"That big fellow, Priscus. I was there when a lanista from Rome acquired him. It was supposed to be an exhibition for a few guests. Priscus ended up killing the poor bastard before the martial could stop him. He's grown even larger since then!"

"Then you should recall his opponent," the Emperor remarked.

Gaius squinted and leaned over the seat in front of him. "Even with an open-faced helmet, it's difficult to tell. And I missed his name, when the herald announced it."

"Well, he was slightly less armoured then," Titus replied with a sinister laugh. "But you have witnessed his skills before."

"Is that the fellow from the dinner party?" Gaius asked, his mouth agape. He slumped back in his chair. "Forgive me, Caesar, but I think it makes the current circumstances even more regrettable."

"You've said that already," Trajan spoke up. "But why?"

"Because, unless I'm very much mistaken, our good Emperor intends for one of these men to die."

"And what of it?"

The former tribune pondered for a moment. He knew his previous wartime service with Emperor Titus allowed him to speak rather candidly, though he should still choose his words carefully. It would be unwise to offend either the Emperor or one of Rome's most renowned generals.

"Caesar, forgive my being presumptive, but if the day's previous contests have been any indication, it is clear you want blood. The morning was a disaster; let us not fool ourselves. But will one more corpse help sate the mob's bloodlust?"

"By Juno's twat," Trajan interrupted in exacerbation. "Why do you even care?"

"About them? To be honest, general, I don't. What concerns me is Caesar's reputation, not to mention the legacy of these games. Gladiators die, that is nothing new."

"Nothing new…" Titus spoke up, letting his words hang in the air.

Gaius sat back in his seat. The Emperor leaned forward, resting his chin on his steepled fingers.

Not fifty feet away, the two legendary fighters continued their relentless onslaught. Sword clashed against shield; shield smashed into torso or helm, as blades continued to cut and thrust with rapid precision. Having both witnessed, as well as participated in, numerous battles, Titus was very familiar with martial skill and prowess. These men would have made outstanding legionaries! Their speed and fastidiousness were remarkable. Clearly, they had devoted much time to their craft.

The crowd erupted as one combatant—Verus from the look of it—had fallen onto his back. Priscus stomped on his outstretched shield, and made to lay the point of his weapon against his throat, ending the fight. However, Verus was able to rip his shield arm free, rolled out of the way, and was immediately back to his feet. The martial quickly stepped between them and looked to Titus. Knowing the laws of the arena, he nodded his consent before sitting back and running his fingers over his chin once more.

As the official made ready to restart the match, the Emperor glanced over to his right. A scholar and poet named Marcus Valerius Martialis was watching the fight, scribbling furiously on the crumpled scroll that lay across his lap.

"Martial, my good man," Titus called over to him. "I hope you're not missing any of this!"

Verus could feel his heart pounding in his chest, having survived this brush with death. An angry rash had formed on his left forearm where he wrenched himself free from his shield. He was glad to have maintained the same tactic of keeping the holding strap loose; otherwise, Priscus would be sending him to the afterlife.

Observing the law, the martial tapped his staff against Priscus' shield, ordering him to discard it. The burly Caledonian tossed it away, growling through clenched teeth, his eyes red with fury. The odds evened once more, the martial withdrew his staff and ordered the fight to continue.

Despite his intense rage, Priscus refused to allow his wrath to get the best of him. He maintained his composure as he attacked once more, thrusting and slashing in short arcs, utilising his superior reach. Without his shield, Verus struggled to close the distance. Twice he hacked at Priscus' wrist and forearm following a hard thrust, but the big man was simply too quick, and he pulled away just in time. On the second attempt, Verus' blade clashed with his own, nearly knocking his sword away. Instinctively, Verus dropped down to one knee, executing a quick, hard slash towards his opponent's shin. He immediately cursed himself. Both men were wearing greaves, and his blade deflected off with a loud clang. Had he aimed a few inches higher, he could have sliced the Caledonian's thigh open! For his part, Priscus was momentarily off-balance. He kicked Verus hard with his other shin, knocking him back as the metal greave smashed into the cheek guard of his helmet.

His vision clouded momentarily, Verus swung his gladius in a desperate backhand slash and stumbled away. Surprisingly, he felt the blade impact flesh and heard a growl of pain from Priscus. He quickly rubbed his eyes with his free hand, keeping the point of his weapon out in front of him. His sight clearing, he saw Priscus

231

limping backwards, a wide gash on the front of his right thigh streaming blood. Knowing this might be his last chance to end this hateful struggle, Verus lunged towards him, attempting to impale his old friend through the guts. The injury to his leg proving to be mostly superficial, despite how much it was bleeding, Priscus was still quick on the feet. He side-stepped just enough that Verus' blade scarcely missed clipping his side. He then clamped his left arm around Verus' right. The two men tied up like a pair of wrestlers. Priscus tried to get enough space between them in order to drive his weapon home, while Verus desperately attempted to wrench his sword arm free, while keeping Priscus' immobilised. With a hard blow from his left elbow, he jarred his adversary's wrist, causing him to drop his weapon. In his own sense of desperation, Priscus released Verus' sword arm, quickly punching him square between the eyes.

For the second time, Verus' vision became distorted. He stumbled backwards, inadvertently kicking Priscus' gladius away. Squaring off to engage once more, he was halted by the martial, who stepped between them, his staff levelled. Priscus was now disarmed, yet still on his feet. The martial therefore ordered Verus to throw away his weapon. He also tapped each man atop the helmet. Both quickly undid the chin ties and tossed their helmets aside. Each then reached into the small side pouch on their hip belts. Inside was a set of carved stone knuckles, used for bashing an opponent's head in. When the martial halted their fight, he at first thought he was going to allow Priscus to retrieve his gladius. That they would now have to bludgeon each other to death, with rounded stone claws protruding from their fists, was as degrading as it threatened to be painful.

Priscus was hurt, though he struggled against allowing Verus to see it. The few seconds it took for each to toss away his helmet and ready his stone knuckles for the next phase of combat was all it took for their rage to dissipate. Fury was quickly replaced by sorrow. The only way either would survive would be with the splattered brains of the other smeared across his fist. Fighting back his tears, Verus attacked. He first brought his left shin up in a high kick that connected with Priscus' injured leg. The larger man howled, unable to mask his pain anymore. He swung his left fist, which thankfully did not have the stone knuckles, catching Verus on the chin. Propelling himself forward with his bad leg, even as blood

232

continued to stream forth, he grabbed a hold of Verus and beat the stone knuckles into his ribs and side. Verus gasped, his breath taken from him. He tried to keep a grip on his adversary, though both were slippery with sweat. In the struggle, each found himself grabbing onto the other's armour with their left hand, with their knuckled right hand cocked back and ready to smash the other's face in.

"*Hold!*"

The martial's staff quickly came down, and he forced himself between the two combatants. Verus and Priscus released their grip on each other and stepped back, clouded with uncertainty as to what would happen next. The martial signalled for them to turn and face the Emperor, who was now standing. The gigantic crowd, up to this point cheering at a deafening roar, was deathly silent. The martial held his staff across his chest, waiting for Titus' command. With a nod from the Emperor, he threw the staff into the dirt and grabbed each man by the wrist. As Titus raised his hands, so too did the martial raise the hand of both fighters in victory. The subsequent thunderous ovation of the crowd was heard for miles.

"I did not see that coming," Gaius Artorius said, a bemused grin crossing his face.

All sat frozen in the imperial box. Even the poet, Martial, sat with his mouth agape, scroll and quill clutched awkwardly in his lap. Titus' daughter, Julia Flavia, gave a rather wicked grin, and Gaius thought he even saw her lick her lips in lust. It was no secret that Priscus was a favourite of hers. Perhaps she was contemplating giving him a suitable 'reward' later.

The tribune chanced a glance over to Titus, who stood beaming; waving to the adoring crowds on all sides of the amphitheatre, while gesturing once more towards the two combatants, who stood with their hands raised. Whether he had planned this from the beginning or was inspired by what transpired in the arena, he would never say.

Sweat and tears stung Verus' eyes as he slowly tried to catch his breath and comprehend what just happened. Wiping his eyes, he saw a pair of magistrates walking towards them, each carrying a large palm and wooden sword. Verus took the palm and rudis, clutching them close for a moment before raising them high, eliciting further cheers from the crowd. He turned to Priscus, who was also holding his palm and wooden sword in triumph. The Caledonian giant's eyes were also filled with tears, as he at last let his emotions go. He reached for his friend, embracing him hard. Each then held the other's hand up in victory. Both men had triumphed, and both were now free.

Chapter XXII: Glory to the Brave

***

Sweat, sand, and tears blurred Verus' vision as he was taken back to the chamber where he'd prepared for his match. Drusus had rushed back from the barracks block and was waiting for him. The doctor took him by the shoulder, guiding the triumphant gladiator over to a table covered in weapons and armour. Slaves helped him out of his breastplate. He'd left his helmet, gladius, and shield on the arena floor. Drusus ordered a slave to fetch them. Grabbing a semi-clean rag, he handed it to Verus.

"Thank you," the gladiator whispered, his voice harsh. He wiped his face and cleared the grime from his eyes.

"It's been too long since a member of our ludus has won the rudis and palm," Drusus said approvingly. For the first time ever, Verus thought he saw his old instructor smile. "Narcissus told me to congratulate you. He would have done so himself, except he has a few financial matters to sort, particularly after the way your match ended. He asks that you dine with him this evening, that he may personally commend you and give you your final earnings as a gladiator."

Verus gave a tired nod. "Please inform his excellency that I would be honoured to join him. But for now, I need a wash."

"Of course. There is an armed escort waiting to take you back to the ludus." When Verus raised an eyebrow, Drusus was quick to explain. "Don't mistake it to mean you're still a slave. By the Emperor's own hand, you are a free man. But as you can hear, the mob is now spilling forth from the amphitheatre. No doubt there are thousands of fanatical spectators who will wish to see or place their hands on the day's 'hero of the arena'. Such an uncivilised hoard would likely end up trampling you—not to mention each other—to death."

There were, indeed, great throngs of spectators and curious onlookers waiting for him as he emerged from the arena. The guardsmen formed a square around the victorious gladiator. He raised his victory palm and rudis in salute to the crowd, as they

235

chanted his name. He could only assume that Priscus was receiving a similar ovation somewhere amongst the great mass of humanity.

The crowds tapered off the further they walked from the amphitheatre. By the time Verus and his escorts reached the ludus, there was hardly anyone left to assail him or offer any number of carnal delights. He chuckled as he recalled the voices of men and women alike, who would have let him take them right there on the street. For a single day, a gladiator who'd won the rudis and palm was like a god. However, unlike any deities he'd ever heard of, all Verus wanted was to bathe and then sleep for a week.

Sweat and sticky blood stung Vipsania's eyes. She struggled to keep them open as she was helped onto a wooden bench. She bit the inside of her cheek, struggling to supress the pain as the padded manica was unbound from her arm. The inside was soaked in blood. Her injured limb cried out in both agony and relief, as the wrap was removed. Her right arm hung loosely at her side; a mess of cuts and gouges.

"You're a wreck," she heard Drusus' voice say. "I wasn't certain if you still had it in you, but I am glad to see you passed the test."

"What test?" Vipsania asked, while a slave wiped down her face. She winced as a medic examined her injuries. "You knew that woman?"

"Knew her? My dear, I trained her!"

"*What?*" Vipsania's face turned red with anger. Her mouth twisted into a snarl. Rage blotted out the pain, even as the medic rinsed and began to stitch the largest gash on her arm.

"You've slowed, Vipsania," Drusus explained. "And you've never been the same since the fire. I knew I would have to replace you sooner or later. That poor retch was a decent fighter; however, a year ago you would have torn her to pieces."

Feeling indignant, Vipsania gritted her teeth as she held up her burn-scarred arm. "Was this my fault?" she snapped.

"Yes, the fates have been cruel to you," Drusus said, his expression unchanged. "But I am kind." He snapped his fingers, and his manservant handed him a leather pouch. It covered the palm of his hand and looked to be quite heavy. "You served me well,

236

Vipsania. However, we both know that if you try fighting again, it will most certainly mean your death. And trust me, my dear, you are not the only novelty fighter I have at my disposal."

"The test wasn't for me, was it?" she replied, her voice calm, though she felt as if she'd been kicked in the stomach. All the while, the medic continued to work in silence, cleaning and dressing her wounds, stitching the worst of them.

Drusus snorted and gave a half grin of satisfaction. "You're far more astute than I ever gave you credit for. And you are correct; the test was for your proposed successor. Even with a crippled arm, you bested her. Impressive." He hefted the leather pouch.

"Impressive, but also a sign that our little arrangement no longer suits either of us. So, it is good that I am kind. I made a handsome sum off your match today. The Emperor is very generous, and so am I." He tossed the pouch onto the table. "This will be enough to keep you from starving in the gutter for about a year."

Vipsania nodded and hung her head wordlessly. She was exhausted and in a great deal of pain, both physical and emotional.

"You were my fighter, not my lover," Drusus explained. "If it is a lover you want, seek out Verus."

Vipsania's head snapped up as her eyes widened. She was so consumed by her own injuries and new-found plight that she'd forgotten all about him. "Verus," she whispered before asking, "He lives?"

Drusus nodded. "He lives, and he's now a free man."

Verus emerged from the baths. A servant was waiting for him with a fresh tunic, sandals, and a belt covered in bronze plates. "A gift from his excellency," the slave explained with a bow.

The gladiator sighed. He'd forgotten about his dinner with Narcissus. Sleep would have to wait.

The tunic was blue with gold trim. Verus did not know the material it was made from, but it was sturdier and more comfortable than any other garment he'd ever worn. The bronze plates on the belt were highly polished and gleamed in the late afternoon sun as Verus emerged. He was glad he'd shaved that morning, for his face was battered and raw.

A freedman clerk was waiting for him outside the bathhouse, ready to take him to the lanista's manor house. It was now late evening. But as it was the height of summer, the sun would not be setting for a couple more hours. As he walked through the archway leading into the eastern garden, Verus was more than a little surprised to see Priscus seated on a stone bench, apparently waiting for him.

"You look better after a wash," his friend remarked. He stood up stiffly and sniffed. "And you don't smell like sweat and piss anymore."

Verus laughed. "It wasn't me who was pissing his tunic before our match," he replied with a wink before adding with a short laugh, "Alright, it probably was."

"I think we were both a little unnerved," Priscus confessed. He then looked around and smelled the air. The scent of fresh flowers and climbing vines contrasted sharply with the aromas that permeated the city and the ludus. "Still, it was nice of Narcissus to invite us lowly gladiators up to his house."

"To be honest, I'm a bit surprised to see you here," Verus confessed. "I thought your own lanista would offer to feast with you on your first day of freedom."

"Oh, he did, and I told him to piss off. Got all indignant with me, so I held up my rudis and told him to go fuck himself. What's he going to do, have me flogged? I said, *'if you don't like it, you stupid cunt, we can settle this in the arena'*. He didn't much care for that."

"I imagine not. So, what will you do now?"

"Now?" Priscus asked, before letting out a belly laugh. "First thing I will do is make Narcissus regret offering me his hospitality, as I attempt to drown myself in his best wine. After that, I have a few newly-won *friends* who I must show my appreciation to later. Come tomorrow, we'll see if Narcissus still wishes to make good on his most generous offer."

"What offer is that?" Verus was confused.

"Why, to become his new secundus palus, of course! Gulussa is primus palus until he either grows tired of fighting or becomes careless in the arena. I still receive the same benefits as him, as the difference between primus and secundus palus are simply a formality. I fight when I want, who I want, and of course will be negotiating my own fees for future contests."

238

"I don't understand," Verus said, shaking his head. "After all we've been through, you want to continue fighting?"

Priscus let out a low sigh and gave a sad smile. "As I told you when we first met, fighting is all I've ever known or been good at. Why do you think Gulussa came back? He didn't need the coin; he needed a reason to crawl out of bed each morning. I'm no different. If anything, I'm even more addicted to the sport of the arena. But as a free man and a secundus palus, I now fight on my own terms, not somebody else's. Priscus of Caledonia has no master. And what of you? Will Verus of Dacia walk away from all this and return home?"

"Home," Verus said under his breath. He gazed past his friend, his thoughts on the life he'd been taken from in Dacia. Three years had passed, but it felt immeasurably longer. "I don't know if there is a home for me to return to. And even if there is, will I know it? Will they know me?"

"You owe it to yourself to find the answer," a woman's voice said behind him.

Verus was momentarily startled, but smiled as he turned to see Vipsania standing behind him. Her shoulder-length hair hung loosely, though it failed to cover the rather hideous scar on her forehead. She wore a resplendent woman's stola of blue and gold. The folds partially covered her burn-scarred left arm, though it was clear to see that her right was wrapped in bandages. As Verus stood, mouth agape, Priscus grinned and nodded to Vipsania before quietly slipping away.

"It's good to see you too, Verus," Vipsania said, after a moment of awkward silence.

"You...you look beautiful," Verus stammered.

Vipsania laughed. "Beautiful? Please. No amount of that revolting white makeup noblewomen cake on their faces can hide the bruising or this nice gash across my forehead. And even this stola, which Drusus must have spent a fortune on, fails to cover my scars."

"Still, you wear it well," Verus persisted. "It was kind of Drusus to acquire it for you."

"Kind," Vipsania replied with a scowl. Just saying the word tasted bitter in her mouth. She quickly added, "I suppose it was his way of saying goodbye."

239

"You're not fighting for him anymore?"

Vipsania shook her head. "I shouldn't have even fought today. My left arm is not what it once was. But, thank Nemesis, I'm still here, and that bitch's carcass is fed to the beasts."

"Thank Nemesis?" Verus asked with a coy grin. "So you now believe in the gods?"

"I still have my doubts, but am willing to give Nemesis her due, just in case. All I know is that nothing is certain, and nothing promised."

"Except the sunset," Verus replied with a warm smile. "At least now I can keep my promise to share it with you."

With a smile of her own, Vipsania linked her arm in his as they walked over to a waist-high stone wall overlooking the city. To the west, they watched as the red glow of the sun danced off the waters of the Tiber. In the far distance, one could almost see the port of Ostia on the shores of the Mediterranean.

As Vipsania clutched his hand, the setting of the sun held an even greater significance for Verus. No longer a slave, neither was he the same man taken from his home in Dacia, what felt like a lifetime ago. After all he'd been through, could he return to the simple life of a blacksmith in a small village along the Danube?

He then understood; there was no going back. If Tamura lived, she had most certainly taken their son and fled as far as she could from the dominion of the Caesars. And if she'd found another man…well, it did not matter. He owed it to himself to find out what had become of his family. And they deserved to know that he lived.

"I'll help you find them," Vipsania whispered.

Verus smiled and squeezed her hand. What the next chapter of his life held, he could not say. In that moment, with the warm rays of the summer sun casting their final glow in the west, all that mattered was he was alive…and free.

Historical Afterward

The inaugural games of the Flavian Amphitheatre lasted for a hundred days. In addition to gladiatorial contests, there were animal hunts, fights between men and beasts, and more prisoner executions. The people lusted for violence and death, which Emperor Titus eagerly gave them. A tremendous success, they became a massive boon to Titus' popularity with both the senate and people of Rome. Any fear the masses had regarding the Emperor's standing with the gods, died along with the gladiators whose blood saturated the arena sands.

As for Verus and Priscus, theirs was easily the most famous match to ever take place in the Flavian Amphitheatre. Their names are among the only ones that survive in recorded history to this day. One of the only other pairings mentioned by name were in fact two women. Depicted on a marble relief, dating from the 2nd century, we only know that they were called 'Amazon' and 'Achillia', and that they *fought to an honourable draw*.

The poet, Martial, recorded the contest between Verus and Priscus. He praised Titus for his handling of the event, noting that under no other Caesar had such valour and virtue been justly rewarded. The eventual fates of Verus and Priscus are unknown. Following their legendary match, they were each given the victory palm and rudis, signifying their freedom. Afterwards, they disappear from history.

Appendix A: The Reign of Titus

Titus and Domitian

His reputation restored, and without further disasters to contend with, Titus quickly became one of the most popular men to ever become Emperor of Rome. Having ruled jointly with Vespasian for much of his late father's reign, his own policies were very similar, particularly regarding law, justice, and the betterment of Roman society through public works.

Like his father, he abhorred the archaic practice of treason trials, which became notorious during the previous reigns of Tiberius, Caligula, and Nero. He took matters a step further by banning the practice of prosecuting anyone for libel, even against the emperor or gods. In his own words,

'It is impossible for me to be insulted or abused in any way. For I do naught that deserves censure, and I care not for what is reported falsely. As for the emperors who are dead and gone, they will avenge themselves in case anyone does them a wrong, if in very truth they are demigods and possess any power.'

Titus also had a reputation for generosity, and it was his prompt action after the disasters at Pompeii and Herculaneum, as well as the fire in Rome, which led to restoring the people's faith in him. According to Suetonius, on days where no tangible benefit had been achieved for either individuals or the public at large, Titus was known to say, *'Friends, I have lost a day.'* In addition to the Flavian Amphitheatre, the Baths of Titus were also completed early in his reign.

In September of 81 A.D., he departed Rome for a tour of the Sabine provinces, but quickly fell ill with a fever. He was taken to a manor house; according to some it was the same place where his father died. Despite his previously robust health, and the fact that he was only forty-one years of age, Emperor Titus died on 13 September, 81 A.D. His short, albeit rather eventful reign lasted just two years, three months. His final words were reported to be, *'I have made but one mistake.'* The cryptic meaning behind this has been left to speculation.

As Titus' heir, Domitian immediately made for the Praetorian barracks, where he was proclaimed Caesar on 14 September. One of his first acts was to have his brother deified, as well as ordering construction of The Arch of Titus. His controversial reign would eclipse his father and brother's combined tenures, lasting exactly fifteen years, before he was murdered on 18 September, 96 A.D. With his death, the short-lived, yet historically important Flavian Dynasty came to a sudden end.

Improvements would continue on the Flavian Amphitheatre, to include the subterranean hypogeum network, which was dug out and constructed during the reign of Domitian. Though parts are now in ruins, the Flavian Amphitheatre still stands as one of the most famous landmarks in the world. Today we know it as The Colosseum.

The Colosseum, by Giovanni Paolo Panini (1747)

Appendix B: Martial's Account

The contest between Verus and Priscus is recorded thusly by the poet, Martial, from his *Liber de Spectaculis*, XXIX:

As Priscus and Verus each lengthened the contest,
And for a long time the battle was equal on each side,
Repeatedly loud shouts petitioned for the men to be released;
But Titus followed his own law;
It was the law to fight without shield until a finger was raised:
He did what was allowed, often gave dishes and gifts.
But an end was found to the equal division:
Equals to fight, equals to yield.
Titus sent wooden swords to both and palms to both:
Thus skillful courage received its prize.
This took place under no prince except you, Titus:
When two fought, both were the victor.

Appendix C: Glossary of Terms

Auctoratus (plural auctorati) – A free citizen who voluntarily becomes a gladiator. They make up approximately half of all arena combatants.

Damnati – A term used for those condemned. An example is those sentenced to '*Damnatio Gladium*' are sentenced to die in the arena.

Denarius (plural denarii) – A small, silver coin. It is far less commonly seen than the bronze sestertius which it is worth four times the value. Most often, it is used as payment for soldiers in the legions, as a legionary's annual wage of 225 denarii per year is much less bulky and weighty than the equivalent of 900 bronze sestertii.

Doctor – A Gladiatorial instructor

Editor – Organizer of games, most often a senator or member of the equites.

Gladiatrix – A modern term (and therefore one that does not appear in the story) denoting a female gladiator.

Infamis (plural infames) – A person who is considered low-life scum and a social pariah. They cannot vote, hold office, or enjoy numerous benefits of more 'civilised' members of society. Both lanistae and former gladiators are considered infames.

Lanista (plural lanistae) – The manager of the gladiatorial school, and sometimes the actual owner.

Libertus – A gladiator who served out his term (if an auctoratus) or was set free (if a slave). Yet even after attaining freedom, a libertus was still an infamis.

Ludus (plural ludi) – The gladiatorial school where combatants live and train.

Magister – The senior instructor of the ludus.

Manica – A protective sleeve of padded cloth, chain mail, or segmented plate, used to protect a fighter's weapon arm.

Missio (plural missiones) – A term used to denote a fighter who lost his match but was spared from death. Very few matches were ever ostensibly 'to the death', and provided he did not thoroughly embarrass himself and shame the ludus or editor, a defeated gladiator could reasonably expect to receive a missio.

Murmillo – A heavily armed gladiator wearing a distinct crested helm, wielding a gladius and large rectangular shield, similar to a legionary.

Palus – Name for the wooden posts used for training.

Parmularius (plural parmularii) – A common type of gladiator who fights with a smaller round shield (called a 'parma') and gladius. Their armour style of helmet varies, though at minimum they will wear a pair of large greaves on their shins, and usually a manica on their sword arm.

Pollice Verso – The Latin term meaning 'with a turn of the thumb', that denotes whether a defeated gladiator lives or dies. Thanks to the film industry, the 'thumbs up / down' as we know it is actually backwards. A thumb up meant 'send him to the gods', while the thumb down meant 'leave him on earth'. In any case, this was rarely used. More common sign for death was for the editor to slash his thumb across his own throat. And if a fighter fought well, he would usually stand and raise his hands, signalling for the defeated to be helped to his feet.

Primus Palus – The senior gladiator at a school. The name is a tongue-in-cheek reference to the senior army rank of Centurion Primus Pilus. A libertus who has served his term, the primus palus is a famous gladiator who's made a name for himself in the arena and continues to fight as a volunteer, for either money or simply love of the game. He often doubles as a senior instructor at the ludus.

Provocator – Meaning 'challenger', this is a heavily armed class of gladiator, very similar to the murmillo. Their armament is meant to reflect that of legionaries, consisting of a protective breast plate, single greave on their lead leg, and partial manica to protect their lower portion of their sword arm. Their helmet usually has a protective visor, and is most often adorned with a feather on each side.

Retiarius (plural retiarii) – A class of gladiator who fights with a net and spear or trident. They are lightly armoured and usually devoid of helmet. At most, they will have a manica and shoulder protection on their net arm, with a waist belt and wraps around the shins.

Rudis – A wooden sword, presented to a gladiator upon either the completion of his contract or winning of his freedom.

Sacramentum Gladiatorum – The Oath of the Gladiator, binding him to the ludus and the will of the lanista. Whether slave or freeborn, all gladiators swear the same oath, and all become the personal property of the lanista, to dispose of as he sees fit.

Samnite – The oldest form of gladiator, named for the Samnite people of Italia, who were conquered by Rome in ancient times. Armed with a gladius and equipped with a curved rectangular shield (scutum), helmet, and single greave on the lead leg, provocators and murmillos are variants of this much older class.

Scutum –A type of curved rectangular shield, most often associated with the army, as it is the type carried by imperial legionaries. Curved, so that it can be held close to the body, a brass strip protects the outer edge. In the centre is a large metal boss used to protect the hand, as well as punch one's opponent.

Secundus Palus – The second highest gladiator at the ludus after the primus palus. He is also a libertus, who continues to fight on a voluntary basis.

Secutor – Meaning 'chaser', this is a common class of gladiator, similarly equipped, yet more heavily armoured than the parmularius. Their shields were often (but not always) rectangular, a smaller version of the scutum.

Sestertius (plural sestertii) – A large brass coin, and one of the most common forms of currency in Rome. Though much larger, it is worth one-quarter of a silver denarius and one-hundredth of the rare gold aureus.

Tiro (plural tirones) – A new gladiator who has yet to fight in the arena.

Venator (plural venatores) – A class of gladiator specifically trained to fight wild animals. Lightly armed, like a retiarius, they most often were helmet-less, with a single manica and leg wrappings for protection.

Veteres – Veteran gladiators who have at least one victory in the arena.

Bibliography

Dio, Cassius. *The Complete Works of Cassius Dio (Delphi Classics).* Hastings: Delphi Publishing, Ltd, 2014.

Martialis, Marcus Valerius. *Epigrams (Oxford World Classics).* Oxford: Oxford University Press, 2015.

Matyszak, Philip. *Gladiator: The Roman Fighter's (Unofficial) Manual.* London: Thames & Hudson, 2011.

Tacitus, Cornelius. *The Annals: The Reigns of Tiberius, Claudius, and Nero.* Oxford: Oxford University Press, 2008.

Made in the USA
Columbia, SC
17 March 2025

55291986R00150